THE
MIDDLE EAST

► Camels cross trackless sand dunes in the United Arab Emirates.

KINGFISHER KNOWLEDGE

THE MIDDLE EAST

Philip Steele

Foreword by
Paul Adams

KINGFISHER
NEW YORK

KINGFISHER
LONDON & NEW YORK

Consultants: Dr. Anthony Gorman and
Dr. Ben Fortna, School of Oriental
and African Studies, University of London

Copyright © 2006 by Kingfisher
Published in the United States by Kingfisher,
175 Fifth Ave., New York, NY 10010
Kingfisher is an imprint of
Macmillan Children's Books, London.
All rights reserved.

Distributed in the U.S. by Macmillan,
175 Fifth Ave., New York, NY 10010
Distributed in Canada by
H.B. Fenn and Company Ltd.,
34 Nixon Road, Bolton, Ontario L7E 1W2

LIBRARY OF CONGRESS CATALOGING-IN-PUBLICATION DATA
has been applied for.

ISBN: 978-0-7534-6313-0

Kingfisher books are available for special
promotions and premiums. For details contact:
Special Markets Department, Macmillan,
175 Fifth Avenue, New York, NY 10010.

For more information, please visit
www.kingfisherbooks.com

First published in hardcover in 2006
First published in paperback in 2009
Printed in China
10 9 8 7 6 5 4 3 2 1
1SCHOL/0510/WKT/140MA/F

GO FURTHER . . .
INFORMATION PANEL KEY:

Web sites and
further reading

career paths

places to visit

Contents

CHAPTER 2
MODERN COUNTRIES 29

NOTE TO READERS

The Web site addresses listed in this book are correct at the time of going to print. However, due to the ever-changing nature of the Internet, Web site addresses and content can change. Web sites can contain links that are unsuitable for children. The publisher cannot be held responsible for changes in Web site addresses or content or for information obtained through third-party Web sites. We strongly advise that Internet searches should be supervised by an adult.

▼ An oil refinery in Shaybah, Saudi Arabia, sits surrounded by a desert. Oil is the most important industry in the Middle East.

Foreword

What is it about the Middle East? It never seems to be out of the news for long. It is a collection of countries that is the focus of more than its fair share of headlines, a region of deserts and rocky hillsides that preoccupies world leaders more than almost anywhere else and that sometimes threatens global stability.

I grew up with the Middle East. I was born in Lebanon, and my father, a journalist like me, devoted most of his adult life to the region and its conflicts. I've found myself going back there again and again. For all of its difficulties, it is a compelling part of the world. At the BBC, we often ask ourselves how we can bring this complicated region to life for our viewers and listeners. This book does a wonderful job.

There are many great cities in the Middle East: Cairo, teeming with life; Damascus and Sanaa, full of oriental color; Istanbul, a rich meeting point of cultures and continents. But it's perhaps Jerusalem that offers the key to the rest of the world's obsession with the Middle East. Sitting in the center of the region, looking west and east, it's a cauldron of history, religion, and politics. Living there, I often used to think that Jerusalem was cursed by being *too* important to too many people. Jews, Christians, and Muslims compete for holy space inside the walls of the old city. Israelis and Palestinians both claim it as their capital. As you walk around, the streets seem to speak of dramatic events throughout the ages: Jewish revolts against Roman rule, battles between Arabs and Crusaders, and, in recent years, a long list of bloody episodes involving Israelis and Palestinians.

Once, trapped between demonstrating Palestinians and Israeli paramilitary police, I ducked behind one of the heavy wooden doors that lead on to the Muslim Noble Sanctuary (known by Jews as the Temple Mount) as a plastic baton round hurtled toward me. But, in doing so, I unwittingly used an entrance barred to foreign visitors and found myself in the confusion and noise of a full-scale riot. Linger in Jerusalem for any length of time, and you'll find yourself caught up in one of this ancient city's many struggles.

Of course, there are those who look for other reasons for our obsession with the Middle East. On page 25, you'll see that more than 60 percent of the world's proven oil reserves lie under the sands of the region. We're using it up fast, but the politics and economics of oil will be with us for decades to come. When foreign troops marched into Iraq in 2003, securing that country's vast and lucrative oil fields was an important task. Some people said that oil—and not Saddam Hussein's "weapons of mass destruction"—was the reason that the United States, Great Britain, and others went to war in the first place, although their governments denied this.

As you can see, it's easy to portray the Middle East as a region of conflict and division. But it's also the cradle of civilization, where farming and writing first developed. It's littered with magnificent remains, including the Nabataean city of Petra, in modern-day Jordan, which fans of Indiana Jones will recognize from *The Last Crusade*.

As the 2003 Iraq War drew to an end, talks about the country's political future took place under the shadow of another monument: the 4,000-year-old ziggurat of Ur. It was a reminder, to all those present, of this troubled region's glorious past.

Whether it's today's world events or the earliest achievements of civilization that capture your imagination, why don't you spend a little time exploring this remarkable part of the world!

Paul Adams, BBC diplomatic correspondent and former Middle East correspondent

CHAPTER 1

People and places

The Middle East is a diverse and fascinating region that is often in the news, and what happens there is important to the whole world. In its broad river valleys, humans first learned how to farm. It was there that people first built cities and created great empires, governed by the rule of law. Out of these deserts, oases, and valleys came religious beliefs that still guide the lives of millions of people around the world. The region's history has always been stormy. In modern times the discovery of oil has brought wealth to some but has also made powerful nations want to gain control over the region. Too often the news from the Middle East has been about war, but it should not be forgotten that the peoples of the Middle East have a rich culture, a tradition of friendship, and a great desire for peace with justice.

Rugs are rolled out for morning prayers in Mecca, Islam's holiest city, in Saudi Arabia.

▲ Olive groves and wheat fields cover the chalky hills of northern Syria, near the Turkish border. In many Middle Eastern countries, the lack of fertile land and insufficient rainfall allow only limited opportunities for farming.

▲ Israeli children celebrate the feast of Purim with gifts of food and parades. Most of the festivals celebrated in the Middle East are rooted in the region's history or religious beliefs. Purim recalls the story of Queen Esther in ancient Persia (modern-day Iran).

Black Sea

Istanbul
Ankara
ANATOLIA
TURKEY
Taurus Mountains

Alepp
CYPRUS
SYRIA
Mediterranean Sea
Palestinian Territories
LEBANON
Beirut
Damascus
ISRAEL
Tel Aviv
Jerusalem
Amman
JORD
Alexandria
Cairo
Petra

Pyramids of Giza

EGYPT

Nile

Red Sea

Mecca

Where in the world?

We often hear reporters or politicians talking about the "Middle East." It is a useful name to describe the lands of southwest Asia and northeast Africa, but it is not a very precise term. Some people might leave out the African countries or Turkey or Afghanistan; others might include more countries in North Africa or central Asia. In the past, many other names have been used to describe parts of the region—such as Asia Minor, Mesopotamia, the Near East, the Holy Land, or the Levant. The Middle East that we explore in this book consists of Turkey, Syria, Lebanon, Israel and the Palestinian territories, Egypt, Jordan, Saudi Arabia, Yemen, Oman, the Gulf states, Iraq, Iran, and Afghanistan.

IRAQ

Tigris

● Baghdad

Ziggurat
of Ur

Bedouin camel train

KUWAIT

● Kuwait City

Persian Gulf

BAHRAIN

● Manama

Doha

QATAR

● Riyadh

Great Mosque of Mecca

SAUDI ARABIA

*Rub' al-Khali
(Empty Quarter)*

Arabian oryx

UNITED ARAB EMIRATES

● Tehran

● Esfahan

Mosque of Esfahan

IRAN

Palace of Persepolis

Zagros Mountains

Oil rig

● Dubai

● Abu Dhabi

Gulf of Oman

● Muscat

OMAN

Arabian Sea

Hindu Kush

● Kabul

AFGHANISTAN

● Kandahar

YEMEN

● Sanaa

● Aden

Socotra (to Yemen)

▲ An oil tanker noses its way through the
shallow waters of the northern Persian Gulf.
The Gulf region is the world's biggest producer
of crude oil, and oil transportation poses a
constant risk to the marine environment.

The Middle East
The Middle East region that we explore
in this book is shown on the map. It is
a region of vast deserts and rugged
mountains, of ancient cities and ruins,
of inspiring religious sites, of oil refineries
and skyscrapers, of arts and crafts and
dance. It is home to a fascinating
variety of peoples and cultures.

Land and climate

The lands of the Middle East cover an area of more than 3.7 million sq. mi. (9.6 million km²). Across this vast region are barren deserts made up of shifting sand dunes, gravel, rocks, and shimmering salt flats. There too are dusty, windswept plains and snowcapped mountains, long rivers and fertile valleys, wetlands, lakeshores, and tropical coasts with coral reefs. Many of these environments are fragile and under threat.

Across the deserts

The Arabian Desert is the third largest in the world. From there, deserts stretch northward to Syria and westward across Egypt to the Sahara Desert. Three important rivers cross these arid lands. The Tigris and Euphrates rise in Turkey and flow southward through Iraq to the Persian Gulf. The Nile flows northward across Egypt into the Mediterranean Sea. Mountains ring Turkey's Anatolian plateau and also rise in western and northern Iran. Beyond the bleak deserts of eastern Iran are Afghanistan's dizzying gorges and rock-scattered river valleys.

◄ Coral reefs form a wondrous underwater world in the Red Sea. This narrow sea is part of a deep crack in Earth's crust known as the Great Rift Valley. The rift continues northward along the low-lying Jordan valley and southward through Africa.

► Two Egyptian boys climb up a date palm tree at an oasis, a desert location where there is a source of water. With tough fronds and slender trunks, date palms survive well in very hot, dry climates. Several Middle Eastern countries are known for their date harvests (see page 24). However, they need plenty of water in order to thrive and bear fruit.

▼ The Arabian oryx is an endangered species. This beautiful desert antelope was hunted to the verge of extinction by the 1970s. However, it was bred in captivity and reintroduced into Jordan, Oman, Saudi Arabia, Bahrain, and Israel.

Temperature extremes

The Mediterranean coasts have mild, moist winters and warm summers. Farther from the sea, the climate is continental, with very hot summers and cold winters, which are especially icy in the mountains. Deserts experience extremes of temperature. In Saudi Arabia's Rub' al-Khali desert (the "Empty Quarter"), a blistering daytime temperature of 140°F (60°C) can drop to the freezing point overnight. There might be no rainfall for years on end.

The natural world

Famous plants of the Middle East include the cedar trees of Lebanon, the wild tulips of Turkey and Jordan, and the walnut trees of Iran and Afghanistan. Native animals include wild goats, desert foxes, and small rodents such as jerboas. The natural environment has been affected by irrigation and draining, overgrazing, deforestation, warfare, and pollution from the oil industry.

People and languages

More than 340 million people live in the countries described in this book. Many of them share similar living conditions, housing, food, and dress. However, there are also many differences in their origins, their languages and dialects, their customs, and their religious beliefs. National borders do not always match these groupings. For example, Kurds can be found living in Turkey, Syria, Iraq, and Iran.

Ways of living

In the Middle East there are both ultramodern cities and regions where people's lives have not changed much since ancient times. There are desert nomads, who live in tents and move from one oasis to the next with their animals. There are farming villages in areas of fertile countryside. Concrete and glass apartment buildings, hotels, and offices tower over more modern cities. Many country people move to the cities in search of work.

▼ A rich patchwork of cultures and peoples extends across the Middle East. Dress may be modern or traditional, often reflecting the history or religious practices of an ethnic group. Some types of dress were first used because they protected people from heat or dust storms in the desert.

Pashtun elder, Afghanistan

young woman, Iraq

Orthodox Jew, Israel

schoolboy, Yemen

صباح الخير

בקר טוב

Günaydın

bayaanii baash

▲ Alphabets were a Middle Eastern invention, and these four alphabets are among those used in the region today. This is the phrase "good morning" in (from top) Arabic, Hebrew, Turkish, and Kurdish. The flowing lines of Arabic make it ideal for calligraphy, a form of decorative writing, which is practiced as a fine art.

Peoples and cultures

People who share a common descent, culture, or language form an ethnic group. They may or may not share the same nationality. Arabs form the largest ethnic group in the Middle East. Their original homeland is the entire Arabian peninsula, and they are also found across Jordan, Iraq, Syria, Lebanon, the Palestinian territories, Israel, and North Africa. Other major ethnic groups in the Middle East include Persians, Kurds, Turks, and Jews.

Language groups

People in the Middle East speak a wide variety of languages. The Semitic language group includes the Arabic language, which has many dialects, as well as Hebrew, one of the main languages of Israel. The Turkic group includes Turkish, Azeri, Turkmen, and Uzbek. The vast Indo-European language group, which extends from western Europe to India, takes in Greek, Kurdish, Persian, Dari, and Pashto.

Iranian woman

Saudi Arabian woman

Arab family, Bahrain

Holy lands

Three of the world's great religions began in the Middle East—Judaism, Christianity, and Islam. Throughout history, there have been periods of both peace and war among the followers of these religions, but the three faiths actually have a lot in common. At the center of them all is a belief in one God. The Middle East is home to many other religions as well. The oldest of these is probably Zoroastrianism.

Judaism

Judaism is the religion of the Jews. They believe that in ancient times they were chosen by God as his favored people and were promised the land of Canaan (later known as Palestine or Israel). Jews believe that God revealed his Torah, or law, to Moses. Jews worship at a synagogue ("meeting place"). Their Sabbath, or holy day, lasts from sunset on Friday to sunset on Saturday. The number of Jews in the Middle East has been estimated at just more than five million.

▲ Jews pray at dawn at Jerusalem's Western Wall. They are commemorating the destruction of their temple, which took place in 586 B.C. and again in A.D. 70. They carry the Torah, the scriptures that they believe contain the law of God as revealed to Moses.

◄ Jesus Christ died in Jerusalem in around A.D. 30. His cross became a symbol of the Christian faith. This spread rapidly to other lands, such as Egypt, where there has been a Christian community for more than 1,900 years. Worldwide, Christians may now number more than 2.1 billion.

Christianity

Christians live in many parts of the Middle East. They follow the ancient Jewish scriptures, which they call the Old Testament. The rest of their holy book, the Bible, is made up of the New Testament. It declares that Jesus Christ, a Jew born more than 2,000 years ago in Bethlehem, was the son of God. Christians believe that after he was crucified (nailed to a cross), he rose from the dead and ascended into heaven. Various branches of the faith developed over the years. The Christian holy day is Sunday, when the faithful gather to pray and worship in churches.

► Egyptian Muslims are called to prayer by this muezzin (proclaimer) at the Blue Mosque in Cairo, Egypt. Islam has spread around the world from Arabia and now has around 1.3 billion followers.

▼ The pilgrimage to Mecca in Saudi Arabia, called the hajj, is a sacred duty for every Muslim who is capable of the journey. Rituals are performed at Islam's holiest sites. The tawaf involves walking around the Kaaba, the black monument seen in the center of this scene.

Islam

Islam means "submission" to the will of God. Its followers, Muslims, make up by far the largest religious group in the Middle East. The Koran is their holy scripture, their place of worship is the mosque, and their holy day is Friday. They believe that Abraham, Moses, and Jesus were prophets but that Muhammad, an Arab from Mecca born in around A.D. 570, was the last and greatest of the prophets and the messenger of God. Muslims must declare their faith, pray five times each day, give to charity, fast during the month of Ramadan, and go on pilgrimages.

Islam has two main branches: Sunni and Shia. Sunnis believe that their religious leaders are simply guardians of the Koran, while Shiites believe that their leaders, called imams, can reinterpret its meaning.

▼ Each year Zoroastrian pilgrims visit the temple of Chakchak, near Yazd, Iran. They light candles because fire is a sacred symbol of their faith. The Zoroastrian religion is based on the teachings of Zoroaster, who may have lived in Persia (Iran) around 3,000 years ago.

Where civilization began

Ancient peoples of the Middle East were probably the first in the world to domesticate animals and grow crops. They were the first to build walled towns and great cities where the first civilizations could flourish, with governments and laws. It was there that hours were first counted as blocks of 60 minutes. It was there too that the wheel was invented, that writing was first used, that bronze and iron were first worked by metalsmiths, and that glass was first made. All of these developments took place over thousands of years.

▲ The region revived as a center of civilization in the Middle Ages. Scholarship, poetry, and architecture thrived. This illustration is from the *Maqamat* ("Assemblies") of al-Hariri and was produced in around A.D. 1100. It shows a library in Basra, Iraq.

▲ This wall painting from around 1300 B.C. shows an Egyptian farmer plowing with oxen on the banks of the Nile River. The soil was fertile, thanks to the layers of mud left behind by the floods each year. The need to calculate the seasons for planting and harvesting led to the development of the first calendars.

Farmers, smiths, and builders

Farming developed from around 8000 B.C. in the Fertile Crescent, a region stretching westward from Mesopotamia (modern-day Iraq), the land between the Tigris and Euphrates rivers. With an assured supply of food, farmers could settle in one place and trade any extra grain for other goods. As a result, towns developed. By the third millennium B.C., huge monuments were being built. The pyramids of Egypt were royal tombs, while the ziggurats of Mesopotamia were huge temple platforms. Urban populations developed new technologies. Bronze was used widely in the region from around 3200 B.C. Ironworking began in Anatolia (Turkey) in around 1300 B.C.

royal procession accompanied by attendants and musicians

▲ The ziggurat of Ur was a huge mountain made out of brick, built in around 2100 B.C. It was dedicated to Nanna, the moon god, who was believed to live on the summit with his wife, Ningal. Religious ceremonies and sacrifices were held in the temple, and royal processions sometimes took place outside it.

Libraries and scholars

The ruins of splendid ancient cities, such as Persepolis, can still be seen in Iran. They date from the first Persian empire, founded in 550 B.C. The Persians were conquered by the Greeks, who brought their own graceful styles of sculpture and architecture into western Asia. The city of Alexandria, founded by Alexander the Great in Egypt, became famous for its fine library, scholars, and geographers.

Medieval civilizations

In the Middle Ages, Greek, Roman, and Asian cultures coexisted in the Byzantine Empire, with its law courts, palaces, and beautiful religious buildings. This period also was a golden age of Islamic civilization. Arabs and Persians were great astronomers, mathematicians, doctors, musicians, and poets. Many words in the English language, such as *algebra* and *lute*, are Arabic in origin.

sailboats on the Euphrates River

religious ceremony taking place in the Temple of Nanna

ziggurat (step-sided pyramid)

sheep at market

wheeled chariot

▶ People brought animals and goods to trade in the city's market. Writing using picture symbols began in Mesopotamia in around 7000 B.C. and was first used as a way of recording sales. By around 400 B.C., wedge-shaped ("cuneiform") marks pressed into clay were used as a script. Alphabets with letters date back to at least 1500 B.C.

The march of empires

The history of the Middle East is characterized by armies on the march and battles. It is a history of proud rulers who built great cities, temples, and palaces. Today their gigantic statues and pillars of stone lie ruined, but they still impress us. The kingdom of ancient Egypt was founded in around 3000 B.C. when Upper and Lower Egypt were united. The world's first empire (a country that rules over the lands that it has conquered) dates from around 2300 B.C. It was created when the Akkadians conquered the Sumerians. Some peoples sought economic power rather than empires. The Phoenicians, seafarers from the eastern Mediterranean, traded as far away as the British Isles.

Peoples of the ancient world

The city of Babylon, in Mesopotamia, was the capital of a powerful empire twice. The first empire saw the world's earliest known legal code inscribed on stone, during the reign of Hammurabi (from 1792 to around 1750 B.C.). In the second Babylonian empire (625–538 B.C.), King Nebuchadrezzar II rebuilt the city with magnificent streets and a fine temple and palace and planted the palace's leafy terraces known as the Hanging Gardens of Babylon. The first Babylonians battled with the Hittites. These warlike people from Anatolia were the first to master the use of iron. The Assyrians governed most of the Middle East in the 9th century B.C. and were also famed as ruthless warriors.

◀ This bronze head was made some time in the third century B.C. It represents an Akkadian ruler, possibly the great Sargon. He founded the world's first important empire, which stretched from the Persian Gulf to the eastern Mediterranean. It may, however, represent a later ruler, Naram-Sin, who conquered the inhabitants of the Zagros Mountains.

▶ The eighth gate of the city of Babylon was dedicated to the goddess Ishtar and faced with glazed blue tiles decorated with bulls and dragons. It was built for Nebuchadrezzar II, who ruled from 605 to 562 B.C.

Marching onward

The first Persian empire (c. 550–330 B.C.) included lands stretching from Egypt to central Asia. When King Xerxes advanced against Greece in 480 B.C., 47 different nationalities marched in his army. Even this great empire was conquered, in 331 B.C., by a Greek force under Alexander the Great. Later, Roman soldiers marched east, reaching Palestine in the 60s B.C.

The last great empires

Medieval armies included the Arabs in the A.D. 600s, holy warriors of Islam, and Christian Crusaders from Europe in the 1000s. Other fierce invaders, such as the Seljuk and Ottoman Turks, rode in from the east. In 1206 a Mongol warlord declared himself "ruler of the world"—Genghis Khan. A new Persian empire reached its peak around 400 years ago, and the Ottoman Empire lasted until 1922, but by then the age of large Middle Eastern empires was drawing to a close.

▲ The Ottoman Empire was founded in 1299 and from 1453 had its capital in Constantinople (now Istanbul). This picture shows its army fighting against the Hungarians in Europe in 1566. Ottoman power was at its height at this time.

▲ The Romans often met fierce resistance during their occupation of the Middle East in the first century B.C. and first and second centuries A.D. They suppressed a major Jewish rebellion in A.D. 70 and sacked Jerusalem. Sacred treasures looted from its temple were paraded through Rome, as shown by this carving.

Art and culture

The Sumerians invented the lyre, a stringed instrument, as early as 3200 B.C. Their craftsmen dazzled with gold, bronze, pearls, shells, and the brilliant blue stone called lapis lazuli. The Sumerians wrote the first literature, telling wonderful tales about Gilgamesh, the legendary king of Uruk. The ancient Egyptians produced lively wall paintings, harps, and jewelry. Beautiful objects were left in tombs for dead rulers to take with them to the next world. The Middle East continued to produce for thousands of years marvelous arts and crafts such as silk and satin textiles, silver, pottery, and Persian and Turkish carpets.

▲ This elaborately decorated casket is a reliquary, designed to hold sacred Christian relics in the A.D. 800s or 900s. It was made during the Byzantine Empire, the capital of which was in Constantinople (Istanbul).

Another type of music
The Arabian musical tradition has had a wide influence across the Middle East. While European classical music has eight notes and five half tones in a scale, the Arabian form has up to 24 notes in a scale, with quarter tones. It is not based on harmony and uses complex rhythms. Traditional Eastern instruments include the oud (the ancestor of the lute), bowed string instruments, wind instruments, and hand drums.

◀ Western views of the Middle East have been shaped by the *Tales from the 1,001 Nights*, a collection of Arabian, Persian, and Indian folk stories. They were first written down in Arabic in around A.D. 850. They feature characters that have become well known worldwide such as Sinbad, Ali Baba, and Aladdin.

▶ Richly patterned carpets are dried on a cliff in Iran. Carpet making has a history of at least 2,500 years and has become an art in its own right.

◄ Middle Eastern artists explore modern themes as well as more traditional ones. This movie examines life in Afghanistan in 2004. It was directed by a young Iranian woman named Samira Makhmalbaf and is called *Panj é Asr* ("Five in the Afternoon").

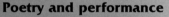

Poetry and performance

Middle Eastern music often involves the recital of stories and verse. Persia (now Iran) has a long history of poetry inspired both by human love and by Sufism, a mystical form of Islam. Sufis seek direct experience with God through music, dance, or meditation. Acting or drama has not traditionally been common in the Middle East, but Turkey has long been famous for its clever shadow puppets, used to act out folktales in popular shows.

Pictures and patterns

The art of the medieval period included the sacred Christian paintings (icons) of the Byzantine Empire, as well as Persian miniature paintings of court life and everyday scenes. Although the human figure does feature in some Islamic art, it is less common than in Western art. Mosques were decorated with elaborate writing (calligraphy) in the Arabic script or intricate patterns of flowers. Beautiful abstract designs can also be seen in oriental carpets, embroidery, intricate woodworking, filigree (fine metal), and tile and enamel work.

Merchants and bazaars

Middle Eastern trade is as old as the first towns. Early potters, weavers, and metalworkers exchanged goods in order to make a living. Later the Phoenicians traded in metal ores, animal hides, and textile dyes. In around 630 B.C., the world's first metal coins were issued in what is now Turkey. Trading routes developed across deserts, mountains, and oceans. As goods traveled along these routes, so did ideas, new religions, crafts, and technologies. Trade funded the great cities and empires of history.

▲ Petra, in Jordan, was a desert city, with its buildings cut out of pink sandstone cliffs. It reached the height of its prosperity in the first century A.D., when it profited from caravans bringing eastern spices. Its rulers were an Arab people known as Nabataeans.

Spices and silk

One center of trade in ancient times was the Red Sea coast. The ancient Egyptians, Axumites, and Edomites all traded in incense, myrrh, gold, and ivory. Spices from India and Southeast Asia passed through Arabian cities such as Petra (Jordan) and Damascus (Syria). Another important trading network from around 200 B.C. was the Silk Road. Goods, including bales of silk, bricks of tea, precious stones, and porcelain, were relayed from China to the Mediterranean through central Asia, Persia, and Syria.

Caravans and caravanserai

Business along the Silk Road peaked in the A.D. 800s. Merchants traveled together in convoys called caravans. Their goods were relayed by strings of camels or packhorses across desolate deserts and mountain passes. The merchandise was sold from one town to the next. In the towns were stopping places called caravanserai, where merchants could sleep, rest, and store their goods.

▲ A camel caravan crosses the desert. The dromedary, or one-humped camel, is native to Arabia. It can carry heavy loads for at least 25 mi. (40km) per day and can travel for six days without water. Desert traders traveled from one oasis to another.

In the market

Common Middle Eastern words for "market" include *souk* and *bazaar*. Markets have always been at the heart of everyday life in the Middle East. Many were covered markets, with small stores and tearooms opening onto a maze of alleys. The tailors would all be on one street, the coppersmiths on another, the carpet sellers on another . . . and so on. Haggling over prices was the way to do business.

▲ An array of delicious dates goes on sale in a covered bazaar in Istanbul. This market dates back to the year A.D. 1461. It includes thousands of stores, cafés, workshops, fountains, and mosques. Business is generally carried out over glasses of black tea.

▲ The Arabs invented the triangular, or lateen, sail, seen here off the coast of Zanzibar on a mashua, or small sailboat. This East African island was ruled by Omani sultans from 1698.

Sailing with the monsoons

Seasonal winds called monsoons, which sweep across the Indian Ocean, took large wooden merchant ships called dhows from the Red Sea and the Persian Gulf to India and Southeast Asia. In the Middle Ages, Arab and Persian merchants settled around the coasts and islands of East Africa, where their culture merged with that of the local peoples to form the Swahili civilization.

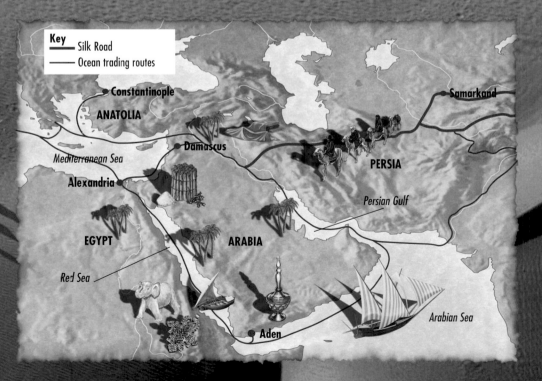

Key
— Silk Road
— Ocean trading routes

Constantinople
ANATOLIA
Samarkand
Mediterranean Sea
Damascus
PERSIA
Alexandria
Persian Gulf
EGYPT
ARABIA
Red Sea
Aden
Arabian Sea

▶ Trade with east, central, and Southeast Asia followed well-established routes by land and sea for more than 1,000 years. Goods were traded from one town or port to the next before reaching the Middle East or continuing westward to Europe.

Resources and work

The two most precious resources in the Middle East are cool fresh water and sticky black oil. In a region of hot deserts, water means survival. It quenches thirst, irrigates crops, and keeps pastures green. In a world desperate for fuel, the Middle East's rich reserves of oil bring wealth and employment to dusty lands with few other natural advantages.

▲ A handful of dates from Saudi Arabia. Other major date growers are Iraq, Iran, and Egypt. Date palms thrive in arid lands and have been cultivated in the Middle East for at least 5,000 years. Fertile areas of the region also produce olives, olive oil, nuts, spices, and Arabica coffee.

Depending on water

Rivers supply many other needs as well as providing the water itself. Boats use waterways to transport goods. Engineers dam rivers to generate hydroelectric power. Water is often too scarce to meet public demand. One way to get more fresh water is to remove the salt from seawater. However, this process, called desalination, is expensive. Water use is a difficult political issue in the region. Turkey, Syria, and Iraq all share the river basin of the Tigris and Euphrates. This has led to disputes among them about dams and irrigation programs.

▼ Palestinians harvest watermelons near Jericho (Ariha). This area of the Jordan River's West Bank (see pages 40–41) is fertile and green, with a mild climate.

▲ Syrian villagers wash their clothes at a well. Water supplies are essential for human health and hygiene. The Middle East and North Africa have 5 percent of the world's population but less than 1 percent of the world's water. In Syria, 94 percent of scarce water resources are used for farming, 4 percent for the home, and 2 percent for industry.

Growing crops

Farming first developed more than 10,000 years ago in the river valleys of the Tigris, Euphrates, and Nile because of the fertile soil left behind by flooding (see page 16). Most of the region is drier now, but crops still need water as well as soil. People depend on irrigation in drier areas and on springs or wells at desert oases. Today Middle Eastern farmers cultivate wheat, barley, beans, and rice. Olives and citrus fruits are grown in Mediterranean lands, while desert oases produce dates, melons, and figs.

Industry—and oil

People in the Middle East make their livings in many different ways. Cotton is a vital crop, and the textile industry is important. An Omani may be a fisherman, while a Turk may work in a car factory. A Jordanian or Egyptian may run a hotel. Gulf citizens may work in banks or at airports.

Oil—"black gold"—is the most important industry. The Middle East has at least 66 percent of the world's known oil reserves. Oil creates great wealth, but this is not shared fairly among the people of the Middle East, and poverty is widespread. Oil is so valuable to the rest of the world—as fuel and raw material for manufacturing—that it has created political problems in the region ever since it was discovered there, leading to invasions and wars.

▼ At a refinery, crude oil is processed and graded for use as fuels, lubricants, chemicals, or plastics. This refinery is in Kuwait, where oil makes up 95 percent of the country's export wealth. However, most of its workers are foreigners.

▶ Delicate jewelry has been produced by Middle Eastern goldsmiths for thousands of years and sold in bazaars. These bracelets and pendants are on sale in Dubai, in the United Arab Emirates, a popular tourist destination.

Hopes and fears

The Middle East is often in the news for many reasons. The price of oil and gas is always important to the rest of the world. There are deep-rooted political problems and ongoing crises. Recently, there have been wars, rebellions, terrorist attacks, and occupations by foreign troops. However, it is easy to forget that the region's peoples have always been great survivors of hardship. Young people there are talented and energetic and full of hope for the future. Theirs is a story that needs to be told.

▲ Two young Iranian women show off their inky forefingers. They have just placed their prints onto ballot papers in the 2005 presidential election. The second round of voting saw a high turnout of 62 percent. The presidency was won by Mahmoud Ahmadinejad, the former mayor of Tehran.

◀ Demonstrators in Beirut, Lebanon, protest against the assassination of former prime minister Rafic Hariri in 2005. Many believed that Syrian agents were responsible for the murder.

Political problems

After the age of empires, the Middle East was in a weakened state. In the 1900s, powerful nations, such as Great Britain, France, the Soviet Union (now Russia), and the U.S., all tried to control the resources of the region. To do this, they often supported governments that were undemocratic or unjust. The ancient homeland of the Kurds was divided up by new national borders. The creation of Israel in 1948 also marked the start of decades of violence across the Middle East.

Rule and misrule

New Middle Eastern countries were created in the 1900s. Few have become democracies. Kings, presidents, or religious leaders often held great personal power and suppressed all opposition. Some governments, including democratic ones, ruled with harshness or even terror. Some rebel organizations have used terror tactics, both within the Middle East and in many other parts of the world.

Peace with justice?

Western countries sometimes demand that Middle Eastern countries adopt Western forms of government. Critics reply that the peoples of the Middle East should be free to devise their own forms of government and laws. Many religious Muslims dislike Western materialism and business methods. They want to see their countries run on strict Islamic principles. However, there are also divisions within Islam.

Some people argue that one way forward for the troubled Middle East is for international laws and human rights to be respected. This should apply not only to terrorist organizations but also to Middle Eastern governments and to foreign governments who intervene in the region. The peoples of the Middle East deserve peace, justice, and prosperity.

▲ A young girl does her classwork at a school for street children in Kabul, Afghanistan. She is a symbol of hope for the future in a country that has seen decades of civil war and the banning, by extreme Islamists, of education for females.

▼ Americans bombed Baghdad at the start of the Iraq War in 2003. The country descended into a period of violence and chaos, from which it may now be slowly emerging.

SUMMARY OF CHAPTER 1: PEOPLE AND PLACES

Land and people

The region known as the Middle East can be defined in various ways. The countries described in this book cover an area of around 3.7 million sq. mi. (9.6 million km²) and are home to more than 340 million people. These people belong to many different ethnic groups, such as Arabs, Jews, Turks, Persians (Iranians), and Kurds, and speak many different languages. Religions, which include Islam, Christianity, Judaism, and Zoroastrianism, play an important part in everyday life and in the politics of the region.

These glass beads were traded by the ancient Phoenicians 2,000 years ago.

A long history

The Middle East includes large deserts, and many places there experience extreme temperatures. However, it was there that farming first developed more than 9,000 years ago in the valleys of major rivers such as the Tigris, Euphrates, and Nile. Villages, towns, and then cities were built. Huge empires developed, ruled by powerful kings. Great civilizations were founded by the Sumerians, Egyptians, Babylonians, Hittites, Assyrians, and Persians. Many inventions that changed the world took place in the Middle East in ancient times. The Islamic states of the Middle Ages have also left a rich cultural legacy, with splendid mosques, fine textiles and metalwork, beautiful poetry, and music. The 1900s saw powerful nations from outside the Middle East, such as Great Britain, France, Russia, and the United States, attempting to control the region, which holds the world's biggest known oil reserves. It also saw the creation of new, independent countries, including Israel in 1948. The Middle East has experienced rapid modernization, religious and political unrest, and terrible warfare in the past 50 years. Its peoples need peace and hope for the future.

Go further . . .

 Read about the history of the Ottoman Empire: http://www.bbc.co.uk/religion/religions/islam/history/ottomanempire_1.shtml

Mosque by David Macaulay (Houghton Mifflin, 2003)

Life in Ancient Mesopotamia by Lynn Peppas (Crabtree Publishing Company, 2004)

World Faiths: Islam by Trevor Barnes (Kingfisher, 2005)

The Arabian Nights edited by Fiona Waters and illustrated by Christopher Corr (Pavilion Children's Books, 2003)

 Archaeologist
Studies ancient ruins and physical remains in a scientific way in order to find out about the past.

Ecologist
Studies the relationship between living things and the environment.

Egyptologist
Studies all aspects of life and death in ancient Egypt.

Historian
Studies past events by looking at written or visual records.

Linguist
Studies ancient or modern languages and may work as an interpreter.

 See a fantastic collection of treasures from ancient Egypt and Mesopotamia: The Metropolitan Museum of Art, 1000 Fifth Avenue, New York, NY 10028-0198 Phone: (212) 535-7710 www.metmuseum.org

Find excellent museums on Mesopotamia and Islamic art: The Pergamon Museum complex, Staatliche Museen zu Berlin, Genthiner Str. 38D - 10785 Berlin, Germany www.smb.spk-berlin.de

Explore the world's greatest collection of ancient Egyptian remains: Egyptian Museum, Midan El Thairir, Cairo, Egypt 11557

CHAPTER 2

Modern countries

Sixteen independent Middle Eastern countries are featured in this chapter. They are Turkey, Syria, Lebanon, Israel, Egypt, Jordan, Saudi Arabia, Yemen, Oman, Kuwait, Bahrain, Qatar, the United Arab Emirates, Iraq, Iran, and Afghanistan. The Palestinian territories, conquered by Israel in 1967, are not a country in their own right, but they have a degree of self-government and aim to gain statehood soon. Some of the borders of the Middle Eastern countries follow natural features such as rivers. Many more borders are the result of historical treaties or conquests. The Middle Eastern countries have many different types of governments. Some are democracies, with a choice of political parties. Others are governed by all-powerful royal families or by dictators.

A modern clock tower arches over central Dubai, in the United Arab Emirates.

International cooperation

No countries exist in isolation. The countries of the Middle East have, over the years, shared much of their history and culture. Many have similar advantages, such as oil resources, and disadvantages, such as water shortages. However, shared experiences have not always led to greater peace or understanding within the region, and wars have been all too common. The Iran-Iraq war of 1980 to 1988, a bitter dispute about the border between the two countries, may have killed close to two million people—with no lasting gains for either side.

Political and economic ties

There are many political, economic, and military groupings in the Middle East. The Arab League includes all of the Arab countries in the region and beyond. It is focused on defense, economics, communication, culture, labor, agriculture, and the environment. International trading groups, such as the Organization of Petrol Exporting Countries (OPEC), also influence the region's economics.

▼ An Iranian relief worker directs a Danish search-and-rescue team to a collapsed house after the terrible earthquake in Bam, Iran, in December 2003. Iran and its neighbors all lie in earthquake danger zones. Expert teams from many countries helped with the rescue effort following this disaster. The cooperation goes both ways, as aid workers from the Middle East play a role in disaster relief elsewhere in the world.

▲ United Nations troops have served as peacekeepers in many Middle Eastern trouble spots. These soldiers are shown working in Nicosia, Cyprus, in 1996. Their job was to guard the line that divided the Republic of Cyprus from the unrecognized Republic of Northern Cyprus, founded after a Turkish invasion in 1974.

The international arena

All of the countries of the Middle East are members of the United Nations (UN). UN agencies work for health, human rights, refugee support, education, science, culture, children's rights, and industrial development all over the world. The UN has also been involved in major political decisions such as the founding of Israel in 1948 and economic sanctions against Iraq from 1990 to 2003. Voluntary organizations are also active in the Middle East, undertaking work in disaster relief or human rights.

Building bridges

Shared sports or cultural interests can bring countries together. The Asian Football Confederation calls soccer "Asia's unifying passion." Music may also serve as a route to international understanding. Asian folk music and Western rock music may blend and feed into each other. Moviegoers in the U.S. or Europe may watch a movie from Iran or Turkey.

▲ The flags of the Red Cross and the Red Crescent are symbols of international assistance in times of war, conflict, and disaster. This nonpolitical international federation provides medical assistance and also monitors conditions for prisoners of war. The cross is a Christian symbol and the crescent a Muslim one, so a new, nonreligious symbol of a crystal shape is now sometimes used.

▲ The Iranian women's soccer team (in red) takes on the Palestinians (in white and blue) during a game in Jordan in 2005. Sports often help further international relations and are also helping provide a less traditional role for women.

Turkey

Turkey is the westernmost nation in the Middle East. It lies on the border of Europe and has coasts on the Black and Mediterranean seas. The summers are hot and dry, but the winters can be snowy and bitterly cold. Most of its area is taken up by the broad peninsula of Anatolia, a plateau ringed by mountain ranges and lakes. The population numbers almost 70 million and is made up mostly of Turks, with a large Kurdish minority. Large cities include Istanbul and Ankara, the capital. People may be employed in car manufacture, tourism, or growing fruits, olives, and cereal crops.

▶ Members of a Turkish family gather for an open-air meal. Grilled lamb, chicken, or fish are popular choices. Meat may be cooked on skewers as kebabs. These women are wearing head scarves, which is common in the countryside, but Turkish women who have government jobs and girls at school are not allowed to wear this traditional headgear.

▶ Robes swirl as the Mevlevi, or "whirling dervishes," spin around in Konya, in Anatolia, Turkey. This form of dancing is part of the mystical Sufi tradition of Islam and is a form of meditation. The Mevlevi revere as their founder the great poet and teacher Celaleddin Rumi (1207–1273).

Turkey's past

In prehistoric times, Anatolia played a pioneering role in the development of agriculture, towns, and metalworking. Çatal Hüyük was already a major town around 8,000 years ago. The region was later ruled by the Hittites, Persians, Greeks, and Romans and was the center of the Byzantine Empire. In the Middle Ages, it was settled by waves of Turkish peoples such as the Seljuks and Ottomans. Istanbul was the capital of the Ottoman Empire from 1453 until 1923, when Turkey became a republic.

▲ Turkish schoolchildren hold up paper masks in memory of Mustafa Kemal (1881–1938), known as "Atatürk" (meaning "Father of Turks"), who founded the Turkish republic. He created a modern state that reduced the role of religion in public life. He is still greatly admired today.

Turkey and Cyprus

The Mediterranean island of Cyprus was once part of the Ottoman Empire and then was ruled by the British from 1878 to 1960. Today, it is an independent republic. Geographically part of Asia, Cyprus is home to ethnic Greeks and ethnic Turks. Following years of conflict between these groups, the northern part of the island was invaded by Turkish troops in 1974, dividing the country. Today, the leaders of both sides have committed to trying to find a solution to the island's problems.

Modern Turkey

Turkey modernized rapidly in the 1900s. Many of the country's Kurds have been unhappy with Turkish rule. This has often led to violence, and the government has been accused of human-rights abuses. Today, Turkey is applying to join the European Union (EU), but some members oppose the inclusion of a large Muslim country.

▶ A family harvests lemons in Lapithos in the north of Cyprus, an area invaded by Turkish forces in 1974. The economy of the island as a whole depends on its sunny climate, which produces grapes, citrus fruits, olives, wheat, and tobacco and attracts many tourists.

▲ The massive stone castle of Krak des Chevaliers is a reminder of the stormy history of Syria in the Middle Ages. Its walls still tower over the valley between Homs and Tripoli. Krak served as a fortress of the Kurds in the A.D. 1000s. In the 1200s, it was rebuilt by Christian Crusaders, knights from Europe who fought against the Muslims for control of the region.

Syria

To the south of Turkey, Syria stretches all the way from the Mediterranean coast to the borders of Jordan and Iraq. Syria has a rich history of trade, crafts, and religion dating back thousands of years. Its capital, Damascus, is the oldest continuously inhabited city in the world. Syria's main geographical regions are the fertile coastal plain, which supports olive groves and other farmland, mountain ranges running parallel to the coast, and, to the east and south, the arid wilderness of the Syrian Desert, crossed by the Euphrates, or Al-Furat, River.

Syria's place in history

Syria was part of the great empires that governed the Middle East in ancient times. In around 1750 B.C., the Babylonians ruled the land. They were followed by invading armies of Hittites, Assyrians, Persians, Greeks, and Romans. Syria was an early center of Christianity, and this continued throughout the period of Byzantine rule, ending with the Arab conquest of A.D. 634. The country was ruled by Ottoman Turks from 1516 to 1918. Full independence did not come until 1946. Today Syria is a republic.

Modern Syria

Most Syrians live in the west of the country. Nine out of ten are Arabs, and Arabic is the most common language. There are also Armenian and Kurdish communities. Six million people live in the ancient city of Damascus. Many Syrians work in the oil industry, in clothing manufacture, and in food processing. Farmers grow cotton, olives, and lentils and raise sheep or goats.

◀ Cloth is block printed by hand in the northern city of Aleppo (Halab in Arabic). Syria has long been famous for its textiles, producing wool, linen, cotton, and silk. One patterned weave became known as damask, named after the city of Damascus.

Political tensions

Syrian politics have been controlled by the Ba'th Party since 1963. Israel has occupied the Golan Heights region since 1967. Syria and Israel were at war in 1973 and have not yet made peace. Syria sees itself as leading the Arab opposition to Israel's occupation of Arab land. Relations with Lebanon are also tense.

◀ Syrian troops withdraw from eastern Lebanon in 2005, after almost 30 years of intervention in that country's affairs. Syria plays a key role in Middle Eastern politics, and its support is essential for any general peace agreement in the region.

▼ Religious buildings have occupied this site in Damascus for at least 3,000 years. This is the Umayyad mosque, founded in A.D. 706 when the city was at the height of its power in the Muslim world. It has been rebuilt several times.

Lebanon

Lebanon is a small country on the eastern shores of the Mediterranean Sea, a region once known as the Levant. A coastal strip rises to mountains that run parallel to the coast. Eastward lies the fertile Bekaa Valley and the Litani River. The summers in Lebanon are hot, but the short winters are mild and rainy. Farmers grow wheat, citrus fruits, grapes, and olives. Today Lebanon is rebuilding after a civil war in the 1970s and 1980s.

The land of cedars

In ancient times, Lebanon's coast was the home of Phoenician seafarers. From ports such as Tyre and Sidon, they traded in cedar wood from the country's forests, which were then very large, and in an expensive purple dye. Romans came to the region in the first century B.C. and Arabs in the A.D. 600s. Lebanon became part of the Ottoman Empire in 1516. It was governed by France from 1920 to 1941 and became independent in 1943. Lebanon fought its neighbor Israel in 1948, and in the years that followed many Palestinian refugees settled there.

◀ A sea of Lebanese flags marks a large demonstration in Beirut in 2005. Protestors hold up portraits of former prime minister Rafic Hariri, who was assassinated. The protestors blamed Syrian agents for his death and called, successfully, for Syrian troops to be withdrawn from Lebanon.

◄ Worshipers light candles at a Greek Orthodox church in Beirut. Lebanon is also home to Armenian and Syrian Orthodox churches and to Maronite, Melkite, Catholic, and Coptic churches.

► Grapes ripen in the sun at a vineyard in Mansoura in the Bekaa Valley. Wine has been produced in Lebanon for more than 5,000 years.

Peoples and faiths

The main cities of Lebanon, Tripoli and Beirut, are on the coast. Islam is the most common religion, and Arabic is the main language. The Druze faith, a breakaway sect of Islam, has many followers, too. There is a large Armenian community. Christians make up around 40 percent of the population and belong to many different sects such as the Maronites.

A time of conflict

A civil war raged in Lebanon from 1975 to 1990. Christians and Muslims fought each other, and Israel invaded from the south. Syrian troops also intervened. Israel withdrew from most of Lebanon in 2000. However, in 2006, the Lebanese Shiite group Hezbollah captured two Israeli soldiers in a raid, and Israeli troops reentered Lebanon. They were met by fierce resistance from Hezbollah and eventually forced to retreat, but the cost to Lebanon was high. More than 1,000 people, mainly civilians, died, and Hezbollah's popularity soared.

◄ Beirut was devastated in the civil war years, but reconstruction began in the 1990s, and life returned to normal along the city's palm-lined seafront, the Corniche. Peace was shattered once again in the war of 2006.

Israel

Israel, on the southeastern coast of the Mediterranean Sea, extends from Lebanon in the north to a short stretch of the Red Sea coast in the south. Its landscape includes highlands, deserts, and limited areas of fertile farmland. Israel exports oranges, vegetables, and industrial products such as textiles and cut diamonds. Israel occupies most of the region sometimes known as Palestine or the Holy Land, an area that is important to Jews, Christians, and Muslims. Many of the political tensions in the Middle East today are concerned with the national status of Israel or the location of its borders.

▲ A traditional ram's horn, or shofar, is blown to mark Rosh Hashanah, the Jewish New Year. Meals served at this time include apples and honey, symbols of sweetness in the year to come. Jews believe that the land of Israel was promised to them by God in ancient times.

An ancient history

The Hebrews, the ancient Jewish people, founded kingdoms called Israel and Judah in Palestine in the 11th and 10th centuries B.C. Babylonians, Persians, Greeks, and Romans later invaded the region. In A.D. 70 a Jewish revolt against Roman rule was crushed, and many Jews were forced into exile. Their descendants went to live in other parts of Asia and in North Africa, Europe, and the Americas. Among many later conquerors of Palestine were Muslim Arabs, who increasingly settled in the region from the A.D. 600s.

▲ In 1967 young Palestinians who fled from fighting in the Six-Day War between Israel and its Arab neighbors, Egypt, Jordan, and Syria, gather in a refugee camp in Al-Mafraq, Jordan. The fate of the Palestinian people—and the borders and status of any future Palestinian state—remains uncertain today.

The state of Israel

In the late 1800s, Jewish nationalists in Europe, called Zionists, decided to recolonize their ancient homeland. Ottoman rule ended in 1918, and from 1920 the British governed Palestine on behalf of the international League of Nations. Jewish settlers arrived from all over the world, especially after the terrible persecution and murder of Jews in Europe in the 1930s and 1940s. After a period of violence and then all-out war, the British withdrew and Israel declared independence in 1948.

Years of crisis

Large numbers of Palestinian Arabs were forced to flee from their homes during the fighting that established the state of Israel. Arab states declared war on the new state. Then, in 1967, Israel captured East Jerusalem, the West Bank region, the Gaza Strip, the Sinai Peninsula, and Syria's Golan Heights (see page 41). Israel's occupation and settlement of the West Bank, East Jerusalem (and Gaza until 2005) was opposed by Palestinians and many in the international community. Palestinian frustration has resulted in demonstrations and eventually terrorist attacks. Attempts to secure peace for the region have so far failed.

▲ Israeli conductor and pianist Daniel Barenboim is a campaigner for peace. Here he performs in Ramallah, in the West Bank, in 2005. His West-Eastern Divan Orchestra is made up of young people from both Israel and Arab countries. He aims to increase understanding, friendship, and cooperation across the political, ethnic, and religious divisions of the Middle East.

▲ An Orthodox Jew in Jerusalem wears the dress of the mystical Hasidic tradition, which originated in central Europe. He is pointing out the Western Wall, one of Judaism's holiest sites, and the Dome of the Rock, which is sacred to Muslims. Both Israelis and Palestinians claim Jerusalem (also known as Yerushalayim or Al-Quds) as their capital.

▲ An Arab sells fruits and vegetables at a market in the old city of Jerusalem. Produce of the region includes tomatoes, eggplants, peppers, green beans, melons, figs, and olives. Foods popular with both Jews and Arabs include falafel (chickpea balls) and kebabs (grilled meat on skewers). Both Jews and Muslims have strict rules about the preparation of food, and neither group will eat pork.

Palestinian territories

The Palestinian National Authority was set up in 1994–1995. It governs around 15 percent of the land that made up Palestine before 1948. At the moment, these territories are not recognized as an independent state, but most peace plans propose that the area should be the basis of a Palestinian state. It is currently made up of two territories. Gaza is a narrow strip of arid land bordering Egypt and the Mediterranean Sea. The West Bank borders the Jordan River and the Dead Sea.

▲ Palestinians wait at an Israeli army checkpoint in 2002. This was at the height of the second uprising, or intifada (meaning "shaking off"). At this time of tension, Israeli troops made many incursions into (sudden attacks on) the Palestinian territories.

Jerusalem

The city of Jerusalem is sacred to three religions: Judaism, Christianity, and Islam. It is claimed as a capital by both Israelis and Palestinians. Does it have a shared future, or could it possibly be designated as an international "holy city"? The question of Jerusalem arouses very strong emotions. No solution that is acceptable to both sides has yet been proposed.

▼ In 2002 Israel began the construction of a long barrier of fences and high concrete walls. Israelis claimed that this was to provide security against Palestinian terrorist attacks. However, sections of the wall passed through Palestinian territory. Palestinians claimed that the real goal of the Israelis was to annex, or take possession of, more land from the West Bank.

Jerusalem

Muslim Quarter

Christian Quarter

TEMPLE MOUNT

Church of the Holy Sepulchre

Western (Wailing) Wall

Dome of the Rock

al-Aqsa Mosque

Jewish Quarter

Armenian Quarter

▲ The old city shown on this map is only one small part of the big modern city of Jerusalem. It lies within East Jerusalem and was ruled by Jordan before 1967. It is now governed by Israel, but citizens of East Jerusalem were allowed to vote in the Palestinian elections of 2006.

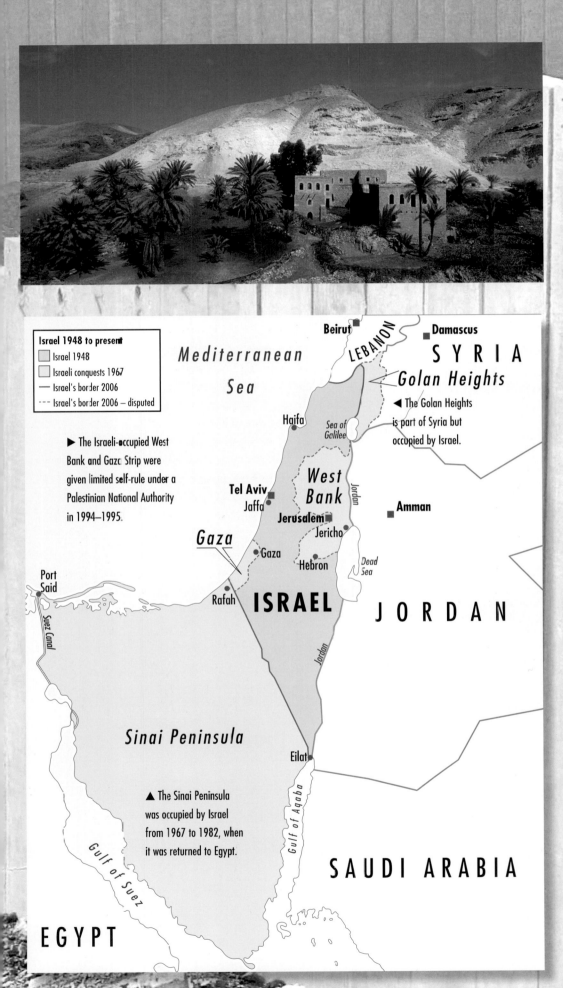

◀ Wadi al-Qelt is a fertile oasis on the West Bank. Since ancient times its natural springs have been used for irrigation or have been carried along aqueducts (water channels) to the city of Jericho.

Israel 1948 to present
- ▨ Israel 1948
- ▨ Israeli conquests 1967
- — Israel's border 2006
- --- Israel's border 2006 – disputed

► The Israeli-occupied West Bank and Gaza Strip were given limited self-rule under a Palestinian National Authority in 1994–1995.

◀ The Golan Heights is part of Syria but occupied by Israel.

▲ The Sinai Peninsula was occupied by Israel from 1967 to 1982, when it was returned to Egypt.

Mediterranean Sea

LEBANON
Beirut
Damascus
SYRIA
Golan Heights
Haifa
Sea of Galilee
West Bank
Tel Aviv
Jaffa
Jordan
Amman
Jerusalem
Jericho
Gaza
Dead Sea
Gaza
Hebron
Port Said
Rafah
ISRAEL
JORDAN
Suez Canal
Sinai Peninsula
Eilat
Gulf of Aqaba
Gulf of Suez
SAUDI ARABIA
EGYPT
Jordan

Troubled years

After the new Israeli state was set up in 1948, Gaza was administered by Egypt, while the West Bank and East Jerusalem became part of Jordan. Israel's defeat of these countries in the Six-Day War of 1967 led to Israeli occupation of these and other territories. Jewish settlers began to build towns in the conquered lands, which was against international law. Some groups within the Palestinian Liberation Organization waged terrorism campaigns against Israel. There began a long cycle of violence and retaliation on both sides.

In 2005, Israel withdrew its settlers from Gaza, but the borders remained closed. There were continued rocket attacks on Israel, as well as Israeli army incursions into Gaza. In 2008, a ceasefire was announced, but both sides broke the conditions. In 2009, an Israeli siege killed more than 1,300 Palestinians, including more than 400 children. The Israelis claimed the siege was an attempt to stop Palestinian rocket attacks (which were in fact mostly harmless). It failed to stop them but destroyed many schools, houses, and other buildings.

The Palestinians

Palestinian Arabs make up the majority of the population of the Palestinian territories, with Jewish settlers now accounting for 17 percent of the West Bank population. The Palestinians are mostly Muslim, although around 6 percent are Christian. Farmers produce olives for oil, dates, and citrus fruits. Industries process foods and produce soap, cement, and textiles.

Egypt

Egypt is an African country, but it has had close links with southwest Asia for thousands of years, and so it is also generally considered to be part of the Middle East. This is a land of hot, shimmering, sandy deserts and palm-fringed oases. Flowing through it all is the Nile River on its 4,151-mi. (6,695-km)-long journey from central Africa to the Mediterranean coast, where it forms a lush delta region. To the east is the Red Sea, linked to the Mediterranean Sea by the Suez Canal. Egypt's major cities include Cairo, the capital, and the ancient city of Alexandria.

▲ Crowds jostle in the streets of the Egyptian capital, Cairo (Al-Qahira). This is the biggest urban center in Africa. It has a population of around eight million living in the city itself and possibly a further eight million in the greater Cairo area. Cairo is a city of hotels and embassies, honking traffic, mosques, minarets, and street markets. It has a huge bazaar called Khan al-Khalili.

◄ An Egyptian wall painting illustrates the link between Egypt and the rest of the Middle East. It features Arabic writing and depicts the hajj, the annual pilgrimage of faithful Muslims to Mecca in Saudi Arabia. The painting shows that the people who live here have made the hajj.

▶ Wooden boats called feluccas sail downstream near the southern town of Aswan. Sailboats may have been used on the Nile River for around 6,000 years. The river's flow is now controlled by the massive Aswan High Dam, completed in 1970.

Land of the pyramids

The civilization that thrived from around 3000 B.C. for over 2,000 years still impresses the world today. It was followed by Persian, Ptolemaic, Roman, and Byzantine rule. The Arab conquest of A.D. 641 introduced Islam to the land. Egypt became part of the Ottoman Empire in 1517, France invaded in 1798, and in 1882 Great Britain occupied the country. Great Britain withdrew from Egypt after the disaster of the Suez Crisis in which Great Britain, France, and Israel attacked Egypt in response to Egypt's leader's decision to nationalize the canal.

Modern Egypt

Various attempts to unite Egypt with Libya and Syria failed. Most of Egypt's history since 1948 has been dominated by military conflict with its neighbor Israel, but a peace treaty was signed in 1979. This triggered unrest among many groups, including Islamists, who assassinated President Anwar Sadat in 1981. His successor, Hosni Mubarak, has been criticized for suppressing opposition. Egypt is one of the key countries in the politics of the Arab world and of the Middle East as a whole.

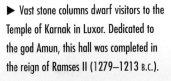

▶ Vast stone columns dwarf visitors to the Temple of Karnak in Luxor. Dedicated to the god Amun, this hall was completed in the reign of Ramses II (1279–1213 B.C.).

People of the Nile

Egypt has a population of almost 80 million. Its language is Arabic, and 99 percent of the people are descended from the original inhabitants, as well as Arabs, Berbers, and Nubians. Islam is the religion of most Egyptians, but at least one in 20 is a Christian of the ancient Coptic church. Despite its modern cities and industries, life in the peaceful riverside villages along the Nile River has not changed much in thousands of years.

Jordan

Three fourths of the kingdom of Jordan consists of parched, sandy deserts, and the country suffers from a severe shortage of water. The Jordan River and the Dead Sea lie on its borders with Israel and the Palestinian West Bank. Jordan has a short coastline on the Red Sea, with a port in Aqaba. The country has few natural resources other than phosphates and potash. Farmland is also scarce and depends on irrigation to produce citrus fruits, olives, tomatoes, melons, wheat, and barley. Many tourists come to visit the country's ancient sites.

▲ Jordan's famous Desert Patrol was founded in 1931 to police the bedouin tribes of remote desert regions. Today its role is changing, because many bedouin people have moved to the cities.

Historical Jordan

In ancient times, parts of Jordan came under the rule of peoples such as the Ammonites, Moabites, Edomites, and Israelites. Many Jordanian sites feature in Hebrew, Christian, and Muslim scriptures and traditions. For example, Mount Nebo is believed by many to be where Moses died. The Nabataeans, an Arabian people who occupied southern Jordan in the fourth century B.C., profited from the spice trade. Their desert city of Petra still astounds visitors today.

Muslim Arabs ruled the area from A.D. 636, and Christian Crusaders ruled from 1098 to 1187. From the 1500s, Jordan was part of the Turkish Ottoman Empire. After World War I, Palestine and Jordan together were placed under British rule by the League of Nations.

An independent kingdom

Jordan won its independence in 1946. After Israel was founded in 1948, Palestinian Arab refugees poured into Jordan. Jordan controlled the West Bank territory from 1948 until 1967, when it was seized by Israel. A peace treaty with Israel was signed in 1994.

Desert and city

Modern Jordan has had a difficult path to follow. It has generally supported its Arab neighbors and, at the same time, attempted to keep the confidence and friendship of the world's most powerful nations. It has also struggled economically.

Jordan has a population of more than five million. It is 98 percent Arab and includes Palestinian refugees, desert-dwelling bedouin, and also city people. More than 1.5 million people live in the capital, Amman. The large majority of Jordanians are Muslims, mostly of the mainstream Sunni tradition. Jordan's population has been swollen by refugees from the violence in Iraq, and the city of Amman has grown tremendously.

▼ Jordan was part of the Roman Empire from 63 B.C. onward. The ancient site of Gerasa, now known as Jerash, lies to the north of the capital. It was a center of trade, and the remains of its streets, columns, temples, market, and theater may still be seen. The city reached the height of its prosperity in the first and second centuries A.D.

▲ A tourist floats in the Dead Sea (known in Arabic as Al-Bahr Al-Mayyit), held up by the extreme saltiness of the water. This lake, fed by the Jordan River, is the lowest place on Earth, descending to 1,370 ft. (417.5m) below sea level. It is divided among Jordan, Israel, and the Palestinian territories.

▼ A young bedouin shepherd, in traditional headgear, shows off one of his sheep. Sheep and goats are important to the economy of Jordan, but overgrazing can turn pastures into dust.

Saudi Arabia

The desert kingdom of Saudi Arabia fills most of the Arabian peninsula, which lies between the Red Sea and the Persian Gulf. It is a land of rocks and dunes, a wilderness that includes the Rub' al-Khali, or "Empty Quarter," one of the most inhospitable places on Earth. By day, temperatures may climb to 140°F (60°C) in the desert, yet nights may be frosty. Saudi Arabia has no rivers and little rainfall. Fresh water is made by removing salt from seawater in an expensive process called desalination. Saudi Arabia has immense wealth because it owns the world's biggest reserves of oil and natural gas.

▲ Students work in the student lounge of the King Saud University in Riyadh. Like many of the city's institutions, the university is named after a member of the royal family. In Saudi Arabia, the royal family is large, very rich, and holds great political power. No political parties are allowed in the country, and alcohol is strictly banned. Punishments are severe, even for minor offenses.

Out of the desert

For thousands of years, the deserts of Arabia were home to nomadic herders. Trade in south Asian spices thrived in Arabia's Red Sea ports in ancient times, while camel caravans braved sandstorms to cross the deserts. In A.D. 622 the prophet Muhammad began to preach the message of Islam from Mecca. Soon Arab armies were spreading this religion from India to Spain. Arabia later came under the rule of Egypt and Turkey, but, by 1932, the royal dynasty of Saud had secured rule over the country and established the Saudi state.

◀ Embroidering this cloth is a sacred task—it is the kiswah, the cloth that is draped around the Kaaba, the central sanctuary in Mecca (known in Arabic as Makka). Mecca, Islam's holiest city, is in western Saudi Arabia. As guardians of the holy sites, the Saudi royal family has special responsibilities in the Islamic world.

▲ Traditional pastimes, such as falconry (hunting with birds of prey), are still very popular across the Arabian peninsula. Although wealthy Saudis own expensive cars and luxurious palaces, many still admire the way of life of the desert nomads. Traditions such as loyalty and lavish hospitality are important.

◀ An oil pipeline snakes throughout the desert near the Iraqi border, in the northeast of Saudi Arabia. Ninety percent of Saudi Arabia's export earnings come from oil and natural gas. Most Saudi oil is shipped out in supertankers through the Persian Gulf.

Saudi life

Oil riches have transformed Saudi Arabia. There are now gleaming modern cities and airports, although many ordinary people remain poor.

Saudi Arabia has remained a conservative country. Traditional dress, ideal for hot, dusty deserts, is common. Men wear an ankle-length tunic (thobe) and a head scarf (ghutra) secured by a cord. Women wear a thobe over pants and a black cloak (abaya) and cover their faces with a veil or mask. Western dress can also be seen in the cities.

Political issues

The Saudi government has come under criticism from some Muslims for allowing non-Muslim troops on Saudi soil. It has also been criticized internationally for its failure to support human rights and democracy.

Saudi Arabia is also the birthplace of Osama bin Laden. A zealous Muslim, he was funded by the Saudi and U.S. governments to fight the Soviets in Afghanistan from 1979. However, he became a violent opponent of Saudi and U.S. policies and organized an international terrorist alliance called al-Qaeda ("the base"). This alliance is believed to have been responsible for terrorist campaigns around the world, including the attacks on the U.S. on September 11, 2001.

Yemen and Oman

The southern coast of the Arabian peninsula consists of two small states, Yemen and Oman. Yemen borders the Red Sea and the Gulf of Aden. Only a narrow strait, the Bab el Mandeb, separates it from Africa. Yemen is a land of deserts and dusty plains, rising to mountains in the south and west. The southwest has the highest rainfall, and most of the country's people live there. Oman is another land of deserts, with mountain ranges in the north. Its coastline runs along the Gulf of Oman. A further patch of Omani territory occupies the Musandam peninsula, at the entrance to the Persian Gulf.

▲ Yemeni territory includes the beautiful tropical island of Socotra, 217 mi. (350km) to the south of the mainland in the Indian Ocean. The island has many unique plant and animal species. This blossom belongs to a form of desert rose that is found only on this island. Its thick, bottle-shaped trunk acts as a storehouse for water.

▼ A herder waters his cattle at a communal pool in the town of Hababa, to the northwest of Sanaa, Yemen's capital. The classic Yemeni houses, multistoried and flat-roofed with decorative windows, are much better suited to the climate and geology of the region than modern concrete buildings are.

The land of Sheba

Yemen's position at the entrance to the Red Sea made it an early center of Asian and African trade. Yemen was part of several ancient kingdoms, including Saba (or Sheba) in the 10th century B.C. Islam arrived in A.D. 628 and continued to thrive over the years under the rule of Egyptians, Ottoman Turks, and tribal leaders. In 1839 Great Britain took over the city of Aden, and this became an important port of call for ships when the Suez Canal opened 30 years later. The 1900s were marked by warfare against the British and by a bitter civil war between royalists and republicans. Out of the chaos there emerged two rival, independent states in the north and south, which finally united in 1990.

Khat and coffee

Most Yemenis are farmers or herders. The green southwest of the country produces wheat and millet, fruits, and tomatoes. Cotton is grown, and so is khat, a shrub whose chewed leaves are used as a mild drug. Coffee was probably discovered in Ethiopia, but early in its long history the coffee from the Arabian peninsula became the finest known. "Mocha" coffee takes its name from the port of Al-Mukha. Yemen also produces and refines oil.

▲ Smiling Omani children peek out of a latticed window. Oman has fewer resources than some of its neighbors, but its oil wealth has helped build more schools in the towns and greatly increase the number of people who can read and write. Children's health care has also greatly improved since the 1970s.

▲ Green fields are a rare sight in Oman. These terraced slopes were built by farmers on the edge of a canyon in Sayq, to the northeast of Nazwa. There, in the northern mountain range of Jabal al Akhdar, the climate is cooler, and water is carefully conserved.

Muscat and Oman

Merchants may have been sailing along the Omani coast for 5,000 years. Arabs settled the region in the ninth century B.C., and for many years Persia (Iran) ruled the north of Oman. Islam became the principal religion from A.D. 630. Muscat, Oman's capital, and part of the coast were controlled by the Portuguese from 1507 to 1650. The Omani sultans (rulers) were at the height of their power in the early 1800s. Muscat and Oman came under British control in the late 1800s, and independence was not won back until 1951. Oil was discovered in 1964, and the wealth it created transformed this desert land into a modern state.

The sultanate today

Omanis are still a seafaring people, and many coastal villagers make their living by fishing. On land, the produce includes limes, melons, and dates, but farmers depend on very limited irrigation. Oil and gas are the major industries. The sultans of Oman have great power, and there are no official political parties in the country. Traditions are highly valued. The national emblem is the khanjar, an ornate curved dagger worn with traditional male clothing.

The Gulf states

Four very small states are grouped around the western and southern shores of the Persian Gulf along the Saudi Arabian border. They are Kuwait, Bahrain, Qatar, and the United Arab Emirates (U.A.E.). All are desert countries where oil and natural gas have funded the development of modern cities, businesses, and airports. The Persian Gulf has been an important trading route since ancient times. The Gulf states have Muslim Arab populations but also many foreign residents. All are kingdoms or emirates (countries ruled by princes called emirs) in which political parties play no part in the government.

Kuwait

Beneath Kuwait's barren, featureless land lie enormous oil reserves. Kuwait has an estimated 10 percent of the world's known reserves of crude oil. It is still recovering from the effects of the 1990 invasion by its neighbor Iraq. This invasion, led by the Iraqi dictator Saddam Hussein, and the war that followed proved to be an economic and ecological disaster for Kuwait. In 2003 the country became a base for large numbers of U.S.-led international forces that invaded Iraq.

▲ The luxury Burj Al Arab hotel towers over Jumeirah Beach in Dubai, U.A.E. It is shaped like the sail of a dhow, the traditional trading ship of the Arab seafarers. Dubai's rapid development as a big city is remarkable, but the construction of tourist attractions places a strain on fragile coastal and desert environments. The man-made islands off the coast of Dubai are advertised as being so big that they can be seen from space.

▼ Bahrain is a wealthy state, and its ruling classes enjoy sports such as motor racing. Here, Shaikh Fawaz Bin Mohammad Al Khalifa greets Formula One world champion Michael Schumacher before the desert Formula One Grand Prix outside Manama in 2004.

Bahrain

Bahrain is a sweltering island of rock surrounded by the turquoise waters of the Persian Gulf, linked by roads to the mainland. Over the years, it was ruled by the Persians, Arabs, Portuguese, and British. In 1968 it became part of a regional federation but firally became a state in its own right in 1971. The oil reserves that created Bahrain's wealth are running low, so new businesses and industries are now being developed.

▲ Workers at one of Kuwait's many modern oil rigs sink new pipes. Kuwait owns 10 percent of the world's oil reserves, and these are expected to last for around 100 years. Kuwait's oil industry employs thousands of foreign workers, mostly from southern Asia and other Arab nations.

▲ Aljazeera television journalists work from the station's newsroom in Doha, Qatar. This satellite news network began broadcasting in Arabic in 1996 and launched an English-language service in 2005. It is the only Arab-language news channel that is not state owned and has been hugely successful, despite attracting criticism from the United States and some Arab governments and Muslim organizations.

Qatar

Qatar is a peninsula lying between Bahrain and the U.A.E. It did not join a federation with its neighbors and gained full independence from Great Britain on its own in 1971. It is flat, dry, desert land with high reserves of oil and 5 percent of the world's reserves of natural gas. Most of its wealth comes from these reserves, and the people of Qatar enjoy a high standard of living. Desalination converts seawater to fresh water. There are fisheries, but little farming is possible in this arid land.

United Arab Emirates

These desert emirates used to be known as the Trucial States, because they signed a peace treaty, or "truce," with Great Britain in the 1800s. They tried to form a federation with neighboring states in 1968, but Bahrain and Qatar withdrew in 1971. The seven remaining emirates formed an independent country, made up of Abu Dhabi, Dubai, Sharjah, Ajman, Umm al-Qaiwan, Ras al-Khaimah, and Fujairah. The land is parched but produces desert fruits such as dates, and the coast provides fishing. The U.A.E.'s great wealth derives from huge reserves of oil and gas. This wealth has been used to develop business, commerce, and tourism.

Iraq

Iraq consists of the lands around the Tigris and Euphrates rivers that were known in ancient times as Mesopotamia. The rivers and the agricultural plains between them dominate central and southeastern Iraq. Northeastern Iraq is mountainous, while hot, sandy deserts cover most of the sparsely populated western and southern regions. The capital, Baghdad, lies in the middle of the country and has a population of almost six million. Iraq is a land of date palms, oil wells, and oil pipelines, but its prosperity has been destroyed in recent years by dictatorship, sanctions, wars, and violence.

◀ Kurdish farmers gather hay near the city of Arbil, in the mountainous northwest of Iraq. Iraq's Kurdish community has long campaigned for independence. It was persecuted under Saddam Hussein and so benefited greatly from his downfall in 2003. The Kurds now have a degree of autonomy, or self-government.

The Iraqi people

More than three fourths of Iraqis are Arabs—and Arabic is the official language—but there is a large minority of Kurds living in the north. Ninety-seven percent of all Iraqis are Muslim, and there are both Shia and Sunni groups in Iraq (see pages 14–15). Kurdish Iraqis mostly belong to the Sunni Muslim minority, while most Arab Iraqis follow the Shia tradition of Islam. Unity of the new Iraq depends on the healing of old wounds between different groups.

The cradle of civilization

From around 3400 B.C., Mesopotamia saw many advances in civilization with the growth of great cities and empires (see pages 16–17). The Sumerians, Assyrians, and Babylonians ruled these lands, and they were followed by the Persians, Greeks, and Romans. Arab armies brought Islam in A.D. 637 and founded an Islamic state, or caliphate. In A.D. 750, with the rise of the Abbasid Empire, Baghdad became a center of Islamic culture and learning, and Iraq began a golden age of trade and prosperity. However, in later years it was weakened by Mongol invasions, and in 1534 it became a backwater of the Ottoman Empire, ruled from Constantinople.

▶ Sunni and Shia Muslims join together in prayer at the Imam Musa Kazim mosque in Baghdad. If Iraq is to remain a single, united country, then ethnic and religious differences must be put aside and the increasing violence between the various communities halted.

Kings and dictators

After World War I brought an end to the Ottoman Empire, Iraq was under British control for a short time and then achieved independence, as a monarchy, in 1932. The king was overthrown in 1958, and in 1963 a military coup brought the Ba'th party to power. From 1979, this party was led by Saddam Hussein, a dictator who crushed all political opposition and persecuted both Kurds and Shia Muslims. In 1980 a long and disastrous war began between Iraq and its neighbor Iran. Soon after this war came the Iraqi invasion of Kuwait in 1990. Iraqi troops were pushed back from Kuwait by an international U.S.-led coalition in 1991.

▲ This map shows the invasion route taken by the U.S.-led coalition in 2003 and the centers of conflict during the occupation that followed. For example, Fallujah saw one half of its homes destroyed and many people killed during a U.S. operation in November 2004.

The Gulf wars

After 1991, there was a long period of international sanctions against Iraq, restricting the trade of goods. This brought disease, poverty, and even death to many Iraqi people. In 2003, U.S. and British troops invaded Iraq, accusing Saddam Hussein of illegally developing weapons of mass destruction. The dictator was overthrown, but no such weapons were ever found. There was growing violence, and life was wretched. Elections were held in 2005, but in 2006, Iraq was on the brink of civil war. Since then, the violence has lessened, and plans are in place for foreign troops to leave the country.

◀ A U.S. soldier uses a metal detector to check women in Baghdad for weapons. In 2006, politicians disagreed on when foreign troops should withdraw. Some said they should stay until the country was stable, but others saw them as the problem, not the solution.

Iran

Iran is the second-largest country in the Middle East after Saudi Arabia. Before 1935, it was known as Persia, and its history goes back thousands of years. Modern Iran stretches from Turkey to Pakistan, from the Caspian Sea to the Persian Gulf coast. Its snowy mountains include the Elburz range to the north of the capital, Tehran, and the Zagros Mountains. Iran's landscapes vary from rolling grasslands to expanses of deserts, salt flats, and seashores. Ethnic Iranians (or Persians) make up the largest part of the population.

◀ Young women walk past the Sheikh Lotfollah mosque in Esfahan. This beautiful building was completed in 1619 during the reign of Shah Abbas I. It is covered in colored tiles and intricate patterns made up of flowers and peacock tails.

▲ Mullahs (Muslim clerics) sit in the Esfahan sunshine. Most Iranians follow the Shia tradition of Islam, which differs from the mainstream Sunni tradition in its belief about the role of religious leaders (see page 15). The 1979 revolution handed over the government of Iran to religious leaders.

Ancient and medieval Persia

From 550 to 330 B.C., the vast Persian Empire was the wonder of the ancient world, with its powerful armies and royal palaces. It was overthrown by the Greeks, but splendid new Persian empires arose in the A.D. 200s–600s and again in the 1500s–1700s. Persia produced great poets, musicians, artists, and craft workers. In the 1800s, European powers began to seek control of the region, which lay between the rival empires of British India, Russia, and Turkey.

Shahs and religion

In 1925 an army colonel, Reza Khan, seized power and had himself crowned shah (king) with British consent. He was replaced by his son, Reza Shah Pahlavi, in 1941. In 1979 the monarchy was ended by the Islamists, who created a fiercely religious state. Eight years of war with Iraq had a staggering cost of close to two million lives. Political reforms took place in Iran in the late 1990s, but great tension remains between Iran and the United States.

▲ A fashionable young woman from Tehran puts on makeup while a friend looks on. Strict religious rules about clothes and cosmetics were introduced by religious authorities in the 1980s but are increasingly challenged by young people in the cities.

Iranian life

Iran is rich in oil and gas reserves, and most of the country's economy is controlled by the government. Farming varies greatly from region to region, producing cereal crops, such as wheat and barley, in some parts and rice and sugarcane in others. Sheep and goats are raised by herders, and common ingredients in Iranian cooking include lamb, rice, fruits, and nuts. Some men wear robes and turbans, while others wear Western clothing. Women are expected to remain veiled in public.

▶ Most Iranian houses are built out of concrete or mud bricks, but in the village of Kandovan, to the southeast of Tabriz, people have carved dwellings from cones of volcanic rocks. These have been occupied for 800 years.

Afghanistan

Afghanistan lies at the crossroad of Asia, east of Iran, on the edge of the Middle East. Afghanistan's geographical position has resulted in a long history of military conflicts, as powerful countries have tried to gain control of the region. The land is beautiful but bleak, with barren deserts, enormous mountain ranges, and white-water rivers rushing through ravines and gorges. These harsh landscapes have hindered farming, trade, and communication, and the country remains very poor.

▲ Water is taken from a well outside the Friday mosque, or Masjid-i-Jami, in the western city of Herat. Afghanistan remains in desperate need of reconstruction, development, health care, and education.

Empires and warriors

In the sixth century B.C., Afghanistan was part of the first Persian empire. The region later came under the rule of the Greeks, Indians, and Persians. In the 1800s, the British and Russians competed to gain control over these lands, which lay between their two empires. In 1979 the Soviet Union (now Russia) invaded to support Afghanistan's communist government. It came under attack from Islamist guerrillas, many of them from countries such as Pakistan and Saudi Arabia and funded by the U.S. and Western powers.

◄ Women and girls line up at a health clinic. Many women in Afghanistan wear a burka, a tentlike robe and veil with a face panel made out of mesh. Women suffered greatly during the period of rule by the Taliban, but women's rights have improved since 2001.

The ancient city of Herat saw fighting from 1979 during the Soviet occupation. The city was captured by the Taliban in 1995 and by the Northern Alliance in 2001.

The southern city of Kandahar was a Soviet center of command in the 1980s and in the 1990s was the birthplace of the Taliban movement. The Kandahar region remains a flash point of troubles and fighting.

The mountainous border between Pakistan and Afghanistan is a center of resistance to the government in Kabul.

Kabul is the capital of Afghanistan. It was occupied by Soviet troops from 1979 to 1989 and was bitterly fought over by Islamist groups from 1992 to 1996. It was captured by the Northern Alliance in 2001 and is the center of the government headed by Hamid Karzai.

Modern times

In 1989 the Russians withdrew amid civil war. From 1996, one Islamist group known as the Taliban ("seekers of knowledge") controlled most of the country. They supported a strict interpretation of Islamic law. They carried out public executions, banned women's education, and even made music illegal. Because Afghanistan was a base for the international terrorist group al-Qaeda, believed to have carried out the attacks on New York City and the Pentagon in September 2001, the country was invaded by U.S. troops and their allies in 2001. The Taliban were overthrown with the help of the Northern Alliance, an anti-Taliban federation. Democratic government was introduced, but the Taliban have been able to regroup, and violent resistance continues, especially outside of the cities.

Afghan life

Afghanistan is home to many different ethnic groups, including Pashtun, Tajiks, Turkmen, Hazara, and Baluchis, as well as speakers of Dari, the eastern form of Persian. About 80 percent of Afghanis are Sunni Muslims, and about 19 percent are Shia. Barley, maize, and rice are grown in valleys, though opium is the most valuable export crop. Sheep, goats, and camels are raised in most regions. The country's nearness to Central Asia, Iran, and China gives it an important position in the routing of fuel pipelines.

▲ A tank of the Northern Alliance enters Kabul in 2001. The capture of the Afghan capital marked the end of Taliban rule. However, supporters of the Taliban were still fighting foreign troops in parts of the country in 2010.

SUMMARY OF CHAPTER 2: MODERN COUNTRIES

Resources and economics

The 16 Middle Eastern countries and the territories covered in this book share many problems but also many advantages. Farming is often difficult in regions where there is a water shortage, and irrigation is generally necessary. Common crops include citrus fruits, olives, cotton, melons, and dates. The riches of the region come mostly from huge reserves of oil and natural gas. However, in many of the countries there is considerable poverty alongside the pockets of wealth. Trading has always been at the core of Middle Eastern life, and today this may take place in traditional souks and bazaars or in the air-conditioned banks and airport lounges of the Gulf states.

A camel race gets off to a flying start in Saudi Arabia.

Political issues

Traditional and modern styles exist side by side in many aspects of Middle Eastern life, from clothing to architecture and transportation. There is also often a deeper clash, between "Western" and traditional Islamic values. These may be questions of everyday customs such as diet, the use of alcohol, methods of banking, the way in which people dress, or the role of women. There may be questions about government and laws. Should countries be founded on religious principles, as in Iran, or should the state and religion be separated, as in Turkey? Religion itself is often a cause of division and violence. International disputes are centered on Israel and the Palestinian territories, Syria and Lebanon, Iraq, Iran, and Afghanistan. Human rights are threatened in many parts of the region, from Egypt to Saudi Arabia. As elsewhere in the world, areas of concern include the treatment of prisoners, torture, capital punishment, freedom to vote, women's rights, censorship, and corruption in public life. These types of problems cannot be solved quickly. The future of the Middle East depends on peace, justice, and genuine international understanding of the region with its marvelous history and potential for the future.

Go further . . .

 Find out about the latest news from the Middle East and read children's own reports from the region at the BBC's children's news site: http://news.bbc.co.uk/cbbcnews/hi/specials/iraq/default.stm

Mud City by Deborah Ellis (Groundwood Books, 2004)

A Little Piece of Ground by Elizabeth Laird (Haymarket Books, 2006)

Eyewitness Islam by Philip Wilkinson (Dorling Kindersley, 2005)

Israel and Palestine by John King (Raintree, 2005)

 Economist
Studies work, money, resources, and production.

Interpreter
Translates "live" from one language to another so that people who speak different languages can communicate face to face. Languages of the Middle East include Arabic, Hebrew, Turkish, Kurdish, and Farsi (Persian).

Journalist
Reports on news or covers other stories for newspapers or broadcasters.

Production engineer
Is responsible for extracting oil or natural gas from land or the seabed.

 Visit the Topkapi Palace Museum in Istanbul, Turkey, formerly the home of Ottoman sultans:
Topkapi Sarayi, Sultanahmet, Eminonu, Istanbul, Turkey
Phone: +90 212 512 04 80
www.ee.bilkent.edu.tr/~history/topkapi.html

Discover more about Jordan's history:
Jordan Archaeological Museum, Citadel Hill, Amman, Jordan
Phone: +962 (0) 6 463 8795

Find more information on places to visit if you travel to the Middle East:
www.worldtravelguide.net/country/countries.ehtml?o=9

Glossary

administer
To govern, manage, or organize.

assassination
A murder for political reasons.

bazaar
A Middle Eastern market, open-air or covered.

calligraphy
Fine handwriting as a form of art.

caravan
A group of merchants and their pack animals who travel together for safety.

caravanserai
A building where members of a caravan can rest, feed, store their goods, and stable their animals.

Christianity
A religion based on the teachings of Jesus Christ, who was born in Bethlehem in around 6 B.C. Christians believe that Jesus is the son of God.

civil war
A war fought between groups of people in the same country.

civilization
An advanced society with laws, government, art, and technologies.

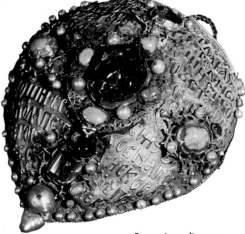

Byzantine reliquary

cuneiform
"Wedge-shaped"; a style of writing on clay tablets that was first developed in ancient Mesopotamia.

democracy
A system of government by elected representatives of the people.

desalination
Removing salt from seawater so that it can be used for drinking.

dialect
A form of language other than the standard version, spoken regionally or by a particular group of people.

domesticate
To tame a wild animal, such as a sheep or goat, so that it is of use to people.

Druze
A group of people who broke away from mainstream Islam more than 1,000 years ago. Most live in Lebanon, Syria, and Israel.

economics
Matters of money, resources, and work.

emirate
A state ruled by an emir, a traditional leader in the Arab world.

empire
A number of different countries or peoples brought together under a single ruler.

ethnic group
A group of people, sometimes of shared descent, who share characteristics such as social customs, language, or religion.

federation
A group of different organizations that have joined together in a league. For example, the United Arab Emirates is a federation of countries.

Persian carpet

fertile
Productive or rich (of soil); good for growing crops.

filigree
Delicate ornamental metalwork.

guerrilla
An irregular fighter who wears down the enemy with raids and surprise attacks rather than pitched battles.

hydroelectric power
Electrical power generated by water-driven turbines.

irrigation
Bringing water to crops by pipes or channels.

Islam
A religion based on submission to the will of God (Allah). It was founded by the prophet Muhammad, who was born in Mecca, Saudi Arabia, in around A.D. 570.

Judaism
The religion of the Jewish people. It is based on laws that are believed to have been revealed by God to Moses in around the 14th century B.C.

millennium
A period of 1,000 years.

Reference

Facts and figures

Which is the biggest country in the Middle East and which is the smallest? How are these nations governed? What are their ethnic and religious differences? What are their resources and what goods do they produce? Statistics help us understand the background for many issues.

AFGHANISTAN

Area: 250,001 sq. mi. (647,800km²)
Population: 29,928,987
Capital: Kabul
Main languages: Pashto, Dari (Persian), Uzbek
Main religions: Sunni Islam, Shia Islam
Type of government: republic; government control not effective over the whole country
Main exports: opium (illegally exported), dried fruits and nuts, carpets and rugs, wool and hides, cotton, precious and semiprecious stones

BAHRAIN

Area: 257 sq. mi. (694km²)
Population: 688,345
Capital: Manama
Main languages: Arabic, Urdu, Malayalam
Main religions: Shia Islam, Sunni Islam
Type of government: kingdom; constitutional monarchy
Main exports: petroleum, aluminum, textiles, basic manufactures

EGYPT

Area: 386,662 sq. mi. (1,001,450km²)
Population: 77,505,756
Capital: Cairo
Main language: Arabic
Main religions: Sunni Islam, Coptic Christianity
Type of government: republic; dictatorship
Main exports: petroleum and petroleum products, cotton yarn, textiles, clothing, basic manufactures, metal products, chemicals

IRAN

Area: 636,296 sq. mi. (1,648,000km²)
Population: 68,017,860
Capital: Tehran
Main languages: Farsi (Persian), Azeri, Kurdish
Main religions: Shia Islam, Sunni Islam, Baha'i
Type of government: Islamic republic
Main exports: petroleum and natural gas, chemicals, carpets, fruits, pistachios, iron and steel

IRAQ

Area: 168,754 sq. mi. (437,072km²)
Population: 26,074,906
Capital: Baghdad
Main languages: Arabic, Kurdish
Main religions: Shia Islam, Sunni Islam
Type of government: republic; government control not effective over the country
Main exports: petroleum and petroleum products

ISRAEL

Area: 7,922 sq. mi. (20,517km²) (this area includes East Jerusalem and the Golan Heights)
Population: 6,864,000 (including East Jerusalem and the Golan Heights; 2004 official estimate)
Capital: Jerusalem
(Jerusalem is not recognized by the international community as Israel's capital. Almost all countries treat another city, Tel Aviv, as Israel's capital)
Main languages: Hebrew, Arabic
Main religions: Judaism, Sunni Islam, Christianity
Type of government: republic; democracy
Main exports: machinery and transportation equipment, software, cut diamonds, chemicals, clothing, food (particularly fruits) and drinks

JORDAN

Area: 35,637 sq. mi. (92,300km²)
Population: 5,759,732
Capital: Amman
Main language: Arabic
Main religion: Sunni Islam
Type of government: kingdom; partial democracy
Main exports: clothing, phosphates, fertilizer, potash, fruits, vegetables, nuts, manufactures, pharmaceuticals

KUWAIT

Area: 6,880 sq. mi. (17,820km²)
Population: 2,335,648
Capital: Kuwait City
Main language: Arabic
Main religions: Sunni Islam, Shia Islam

Type of government: emirate; partial democracy
Main exports: petroleum and petroleum products, fertilizers

LEBANON

Area: 4,015 sq. mi. (10,400km²)
Population: 3,826,018
Capital: Beirut
Main language: Arabic
Main religions: Shia Islam, Sunni Islam, Druze, Greek Orthodox, Maronite Christianity
Type of government: republic; democracy
Main exports: precious stones and jewelry, chemicals, consumer goods re-exports, foodstuffs, tobacco, construction materials, textiles, paper products

OMAN

Area: 82,031 sq. mi. (212,460km²)
Population: 3,001,583
Capital: Muscat
Main languages: Arabic, Baluchi
Main religions: Ibadiyah Islam, Sunni Islam, Shia Islam
Type of government: sultanate; absolute monarchy
Main exports: petroleum, re-exports, fish, metals, textiles

QATAR

Area: 4,416 sq. mi. (11,437km²)
Population: 863,051
Capital: Doha
Main languages: Arabic, Urdu, Malayam
Main religion: Sunni Islam
Type of government: emirate; dictatorship
Main exports: petroleum, fertilizers, steel, chemicals

SAUDI ARABIA

Area: 756,985 sq. mi. (1,960,582km²)
Population: 26,417,599
Capital: Riyadh
Main language: Arabic
Main religion: Sunni Islam
Type of government: kingdom; absolute monarchy
Main exports: petroleum, petrochemicals

SYRIA

Area: 71,498 sq. mi. (185,180km²) (this area includes areas of the Golan Heights occupied by Israel)
Population: 18,448,752
Capital: Damascus

Main languages: Arabic, Kurdish
Main religions: Sunni Islam, Shia Islam, Christianity
Type of government: republic; dictatorship
Main exports: crude petroleum and petroleum products, fruits and vegetables, textiles and fabrics (including cotton fiber), meat

TURKEY

Area: 301,384 sq. mi. (780,5805km²)
Population: 69,660,559
Capital: Ankara
Main languages: Turkish, Kurdish
Main religion: Sunni Islam
Type of government: republic; democracy
Main exports: textiles and clothing, foodstuffs, iron and steel, transportation equipment

UNITED ARAB EMIRATES

Area: 32,000 sq. mi. (82,880km²)
Population: 2,563,212
Capital: Abu Dhabi
Main languages: Arabic, Hindi, Urdu, English
Main religions: Sunni Islam, Shia Islam, Hinduism
Type of government: federation of sovereign emirates
Main exports: crude and refined petroleum, natural gas, re-exports, dried fish, dates

YEMEN

Area: 203,850 sq. mi. (527,970km²)
Population: 20,727,063
Capital: Sanaa
Main language: Arabic
Main religion: Sunni Islam
Type of government: republic; partial democracy
Main exports: petroleum, coffee, dried fish

WEST BANK AND GAZA STRIP (PALESTINIAN TERRITORIES)

Area: 2,324 sq. mi. (6,020km²)
Population: 3,762,000 (2004 census provisional figure)
Capital: the Palestinian Authority claims East Jerusalem as its capital; the center of administration is Ramallah
Main language: Arabic
Main religions: Sunni Islam, various Christian churches
Type of government: republic; democracy
Main exports: olives, fruits, vegetables, flowers, limestone

monsoon
A seasonal wind that blows across the Indian Ocean, bringing rain to the dry lands of southern Asia.

mosque
A place of worship for Muslims.

mullah
An Iranian cleric who is an expert in the sacred laws of Islam. The word means "teacher" or "scholar."

Muslim
A follower of Islam.

nomad
Someone who does not lead a settled existence but travels with their herds from one pasture to another.

oasis
A spot in the desert where there is enough water for drinking, growing crops, or feeding animals.

pilgrim
Someone who undertakes a journey for religious reasons, traveling to a sacred place or shrine.

raw material
A basic substance that can be processed in order to manufacture goods.

refugee
Someone who is forced to flee from home because of war, hunger, or poverty.

republic
A country that has no king or queen but is ruled by representatives of the people.

resource
A natural substance that is of use to a country such as water, timber, oil, or coal.

sanctions
Restrictions placed on one country by others in order to limit its ability to trade, move freely, or engage in other activities.

Shia
A branch of Islam that believes that the prophet Muhammad's cousin Ali was his true successor and that Shia leaders, called imams, are the messengers of God.

shofar
A ram's horn trumpet that is traditionally used in Jewish religious festivals.

souk
A Middle Eastern market; a bazaar.

Sufism
A mystic tradition in Islam associated with meditation, dance, chanting, and poetry.

sultan
The king or ruler of an Islamic country.

Sunni
The mainstream branch of Islam. Sunnis honor four caliphs (leaders) as the true successors of Muhammad and believe that religious laws should be made within the Islamic community.

synagogue
A Jewish place of worship.

terrorism
Using acts of extreme violence to create a climate of fear and thus bring about political change. Terrorism may be a policy of governments, of illegal armed groups and organizations, or of individuals.

United Nations (UN)
The world's largest international treaty organization, of which most nations are members. The UN, founded in 1945, promotes peace and cooperation. UN agencies act in areas including health, economic development, and human rights.

ziggurat
A type of massive monument first built by the Sumerians and later by the Assyrians and Babylonians. Ziggurats were pyramids with terraced sides.

Zionist
A supporter of Jewish nationalism.

Zoroastrianism
A religion based on the teachings of Zoroaster, who lived in ancient Persia (Iran). Zoroastrians believe in one God, and their sacred symbol is fire.

Assyrian carving showing a chariot

Index

YOUR KIDS
ARE
YOUR
OWN FAULT

WHAT LARRY WINGET'S FANS ARE SAYING:

"He's overwrought with righteous awesomesauce."
—Michael Wilson

"Thank you, Larry, for being bold, bald and truthful!"
—Ken DeWitt

"Larry, you are the MAN! Keep telling it like it is and thank you for waking ME up! Things are getting better because I'm getting better. I live and die by the Winget!"   —Dean Gutierrez

"There should be school courses—Winget 101—starting in grade school. The USA would start getting back to what it used to be."   —Steve Watson

"He strips you naked, beats the hell out of you, and gives you tools to put yourself back together, idiot-proof!" —Dan Surface

"You Rock, Larry . . . there is nothing else to say. You Rock!!!!!!!!!!!"   —Daphne Alexander-Christ

"Great stuff, Larry. You tell it like it is . . . what people need to hear instead of what they would like to hear."   —Paul Barker

"Every time you write and/or speak, it always 'fires me up' to keep being the best I can be. Thanks, Larry."   —Jeff Scanlan

"Like a bucket of cold water, I needed that."   —James Nimon

"You freaking rock, Larry!! Thanks for inspiring so many of us."
—Patrick Haley

"I love your books! I always refer back to them when I start to drift off my path to accomplishing my goals. You are the best because you know how to keep it real and tell it like it is . . . a no-nonsense kind of guy . . . really cool!"   —Melehola Tagaga

PRAISE FOR *YOUR KIDS ARE YOUR OWN FAULT*

"Larry challenges us as parents to complete the job and embrace the journey of responsible parenting. This book is a great reminder and road map, full of good, tough love for parents!"
—MC Hammer

"Larry is no stranger to confrontation, and in his book *Your Kids Are Your Own Fault* he sets the stage for your success as a parent, and your child's success as a productive member of our society—that is, if you are ready for the cold, hard facts. His in-your-face approach is fresh and relevant to raising a generation of youth who will make us all proud to call them our own. A coach has a playbook, and as a pastor, I use my bible for daily instruction. *Your Kids Are Your Own Fault* is a playbook for parenting for generations to come."
—Dick Bernal, pastor and founder
of the Jubilee Christian Center in San Jose, California

"First, this book scared the hell out of me. Then it gave me hope. It scared me because Larry is brutally honest about the challenges and dangers facing kids today. The hope came from Larry's message that our kids will probably be just fine if we take full responsibility as parents. This book will make you squirm, make you mad, sometimes make you laugh out loud, and mostly make you think very carefully about how you're raising your kids."
—Joe Calloway, Cate and Jessica's dad,
author of *Becoming a Category of One*

"One of the lessons it's important to teach kids is not so much about how much money you have but how you use the money you have. Sadly, that lesson is rarely taught. Brilliant, bold, and true! Larry says it all in these few words. Thank you, Larry!"
—Sharon L. Lechter, coauthor of *Think and Grow Rich*,
Three Feet from Gold, and *Rich Dad, Poor Dad*

continued . . .

"In the Hispanic/Latino family there is always a lot of love and appreciation. However, there is not a lot of training or education, especially about money. I have been a radio and television host for twenty-three years and did not know how to manage my finances until I was thirty. I wish I knew in my teen years what Larry's book teaches. He provides the tools and tips for every parent to train a successful generation of great and productive citizens. I recommend this book wholeheartedly."

—Marco Antonio Regil, international TV host
of *Family Feud*, *The Price Is Right*, and
Are You Smarter Than a Fifth Grader?

"Larry Winget's book on taking responsibility for what kind of adults your kids become is outstanding. I have seven children, and laying the foundation for the next generation and what kind of adults they become starts from day one. My oldest son, Romeo, attending USC is no accident. Read this book. No more excuses."

—Percy "Master P" Miller,
CEO, BBTV, and recording artist

YOUR KIDS
ARE
YOUR
OWN FAULT

*A Guide for Raising
Responsible, Productive Adults*

LARRY WINGET

GOTHAM
BOOKS

GOTHAM BOOKS
Published by Penguin Group (USA) Inc.
375 Hudson Street, New York, New York 10014, U.S.A.
Penguin Group (Canada), 90 Eglinton Avenue East, Suite 700, Toronto, Ontario
M4P 2Y3, Canada (a division of Pearson Penguin Canada Inc.); Penguin Books Ltd,
80 Strand, London WC2R 0RL, England; Penguin Ireland, 25 St Stephen's Green,
Dublin 2, Ireland (a division of Penguin Books Ltd); Penguin Group (Australia),
250 Camberwell Road, Camberwell, Victoria 3124, Australia (a division of Pearson
Australia Group Pty Ltd); Penguin Books India Pvt Ltd, 11 Community Centre,
Panchsheel Park, New Delhi—110 017, India; Penguin Group (NZ), 67 Apollo
Drive, Rosedale, North Shore 0632, New Zealand (a division of Pearson New
Zealand Ltd); Penguin Books (South Africa) (Pty) Ltd, 24 Sturdee Avenue,
Rosebank, Johannesburg 2196, South Africa

Penguin Books Ltd, Registered Offices: 80 Strand, London WC2R 0RL, England

Published by Gotham Books, a member of Penguin Group (USA) Inc.

First printing, January 2010
10 9 8 7 6 5 4 3 2 1

Copyright © 2010 by Larry Winget
All rights reserved

Gotham Books and the skyscraper logo are trademarks of Penguin Group (USA) Inc.

LIBRARY OF CONGRESS CATALOGING-IN-PUBLICATION DATA

Winget, Larry.
    Your kids are your own fault : a guide for raising responsible, productive adults /
by Larry Winget.
        p. cm.
    ISBN 978–1–592–40495–7 (hardcover)
    1. Child rearing.   2. Parenting.   I. Title.
    HQ769.W788 2010
    649'.1—dc22   2009036015

Printed in the United States of America

Set in Janson Text
Designed by Spring Hoteling

While the author has made every effort to provide accurate telephone numbers and
Internet addresses at the time of publication, neither the publisher nor the author
assumes any responsibility for errors, or for changes that occur after publication.
Further, the publisher does not have any control over and does not assume any
responsibility for author or third-party Web sites or their content.

For my parents, Dorothy and Henry Winget,
who taught me the principles I live by and teach others.

For my boys, Tyler and Patrick.
I taught them what I knew and they continue
to teach me things I need to know.

CONTENTS

PREFACE

Why am I writing this book? Look around. Our kids are a mess! They are overmedicated, overindulged, overweight, overentertained, undereducated, underachieving, underdisciplined, disrespectful, illiterate brats with a sense of entitlement that is crippling our society. And it has to change!

Don't agree? Then you aren't paying attention.

"Not my kid," you say? Then you aren't paying attention.

If you were paying attention, then you would know that our society is full of kids who can't read, can't write (except with their thumbs when texting on their cell phones) and think that their teachers, their employers, their government and their parents owe them a living.

Yeah, yeah, there are exceptions. If you know of one, count your lucky stars. If you have actually raised one of those exceptions, then bless you. And thank you. We all owe you a debt of gratitude for raising a productive, contributing, responsible member of society. I'd hug your neck if I could.

For the rest of you, wake up. Your kids are a disaster.

How do I know that young people are such a mess? Take a quick trip to the mall. You'll see insolent teens smoking cigarettes outside the front doors, skateboarding punks who dominate the sidewalks and the young, professional "$30,000 millionaires" buying crap they can't afford to feel good about themselves and impress people who don't give a crap about them.

While you are there, I want you to buy a cup of coffee. You will be lucky to get a young person working in the coffee shop to look you in the eye, say "thank you" or do much more than grunt at you. Yet they are ticked off if you don't drop money in the tip jar.

Then walk into any retail store. You will be lucky if you can get the employees to stop talking to one another long enough to notice you are in the store or put down their cell phones long enough to speak to you.

When you leave the mall, go home and turn on your television and watch the news for a while. You will see that it's full of stories of people who bought houses they can't afford and want to blame the predatory lenders for giving them the money, even though they lied on their credit application to get it. You might also hear stories about how, on average, American students are ranked below two-thirds of other countries.

Then I want you to flip the channel to any of the entertainment news shows. Check out *Entertainment Tonight*, *Access Hollywood* or *TMZ*. Look at how the young Hollywood elite behave. See them drunk, without their underwear, crashing their cars, filming their sex lives. Then know that these are the role models for your kids.

Then turn the channel to ESPN or any of the other sports news shows and see how our athletes are being busted for drug abuse, rape, dogfighting and any number of other felonies and know again that these are the role models for today's youth.

"Hold it, Larry; I thought this was a parenting book." It is. And all of these issues are parenting problems.

PAY ATTENTION HERE.

Financial problems? Bad parenting.

Poor customer service? Bad parenting.

Illiteracy? Bad parenting.

Lousy educational system? Bad parenting.

Bad grammar? Bad parenting.

Crime? Bad parenting.

Teenage pregnancy? Bad parenting.

Bad driving? Bad parenting.

Entitlement issues? Bad parenting.

Corruption? Bad parenting.

Racism? Bad parenting.

Sexism? Bad parenting.

Childhood obesity? Bad parenting.

Got it? Have I been clear or should I keep adding to the list, because, believe me, I could. Here is what it comes down to: All societal problems could pretty much be prevented through better parenting. Are there exceptions? Of course there are. There are always exceptions, so don't bother raising any with me. I know about them already. My point is that for the most part, the problems in our society exist because of lousy training from Mama and Daddy.

And don't bring up the whole "a lot of people don't have a mama and daddy to teach them, Larry." I am aware. For now, I'll give all of those people a pass. Not for long. No one gets a pass for long. Even the people who didn't have parents, had lousy parents or were raised by wolves sooner or later have to learn and demonstrate personal responsibility. But it still goes back to the fact that kids learn or don't learn their values and what is and isn't acceptable behavior from their parents. Those kids grow into adults and practice that behavior in their personal and professional lives, creating a society that reflects the cumulative result of parental training.

Meaning: Messed-up society? Messed-up parenting.

Want to fix the world? Fix the parents.

The only reason we have stupid kids is because we have such stupid parents. The goal of this book is to fix stupid kids by fixing their stupid parents!

And that means: Don't expect to change your kid's behavior unless you are willing to change your own.

> "Children might or might not be a blessing, but to create them and then fail them was surely damnation."
>
> —Lois McMaster Bujold, *Barrayar*

YOUR KIDS ARE YOUR OWN FAULT

INTRODUCTION

For those of you who are familiar with my work and have read my other books, you know by now that I am a one-trick pony. This means that there is one central theme in all that I do. That central theme is personal responsibility. In my first book, *Shut Up, Stop Whining & Get a Life: A Kick-Butt Approach to a Better Life*, I emphasized my theme in terms of personal development. In *It's Called Work for a Reason! Your Success Is Your Own Damn Fault*, I exploited my message of personal responsibility in the area of business. Then I used it again in *You're Broke Because You Want to Be: How to Stop Getting By and Start Getting Ahead* in the area of personal finance. I followed that up with *The Idiot Factor: The 10 Ways We Sabotage Our Life, Money, and Business*. In that book, I once more pound home the idea that you must take control of every area of your life, stop blaming others for your problems and be willing to do whatever it takes to create the life you want. Four books with the central theme of personal responsibility. I am back again to harp on that theme, this time in the area of parenting. Our society is a mess today and will only get worse because parents are not taking responsibility for teaching their kids the principles of how to lead successful, productive lives. That trend has to stop and stop now! My intention is to turn that cycle of destruction around in this book.

"I HAVE GREAT KIDS, LARRY. I DON'T NEED THIS BOOK."

I know you have great kids. All kids are great. And if you don't believe it, just ask their parents. Rather than argue that point, I am going to give in and just say all kids, in the beginning, are great kids. Kids come into this world as blank slates that you, the parent, get to write on. Whatever you write on that slate will determine whether your great kid will turn into a great adult or whether he will become a leech on society. So while your kid is a "great kid," that isn't really the point, is it? The real point is to teach your kids to become the best adult version of themselves they can be.

IS THIS BOOK FOR YOU?

This book is for the parents who love their kids, want the best for them, and are willing to do whatever it takes to turn that kid into a great adult. Maybe they just need a reminder of what's really important and that it's time to get back to basics. Or maybe they need a wake-up call so they can turn a bad situation around. Or maybe they need a kick in the pants to tell them they have been messing up and they need to get back in control of their family.

This book is for the millions of hardworking parents with normal situations and regular kids who want to raise these kids to be responsible adults who will make a good living, be good people who do the right thing and grow up to raise their own good kids. It is for the single mom and the weekend dad and for the parents who have solid marriages. It is for parents like those who are serious about raising responsible children.

WHAT YOU CAN EXPECT FROM THE BOOK:

In this book I am going to cover exactly what has gone wrong with parenting and the lack of it and why kids end up the way they are and act the way they do. I am going to give you many examples of what I consider to be bad parenting and point out the long-term effects that kind of parenting is having on our society. I am going to talk about what I believe we should teach our kids so they will grow to be responsible adults. That is my one goal for every parent: creating responsible, productive adults.

WHAT YOU CAN'T EXPECT FROM THE BOOK:

I am not going to deal with the people who should never have had kids to begin with. We all know those folks are everywhere! They are on television being arrested for abuse and abandonment. They are running to the sperm bank or getting fertility treatments so they can have another eight kids when they can't afford to take care of the six they already have. Some people should not be allowed to reproduce. I am talking about people who take no interest in their kids and who have no values worthy of passing on. That's all I am going to say about these worthless wastes of skin. Kids are both a privilege and a responsibility. If you aren't ready for the responsibility, you shouldn't get to experience the privilege of having them. And if you aren't ready for the responsibility, try birth control or learn to keep it in your pants.

I am also not going to deal with any of the extreme issues that many parents face, like raising children with mental or physical challenges, though most of the parenting principles I am addressing here would apply to those kids as well. I know that many kids have very special needs that require special attention. I am also not addressing child abuse, whether it is sexual, physical or mental. I don't have the expertise, the credentials or the inclination to write about that.

In fact, this isn't much of a how-to book at all. I am not going to talk about how to change diapers or how to get little Jimmy to drink his milk or brush his teeth. I am not going to tell you how to get little Sally to clean up her room. I am not going to hold your hand and pass out basic information about every parenting issue you have already faced or will eventually face. I simply cannot address every situation you are ever going to come up against, so don't expect me to. Besides, there are plenty of books out there that will teach you all of that basic stuff better than I ever could.

Ultimately, how you teach your kids is always going to be up to you, because every kid is different and requires a unique, personalized approach. Plus, most parenting lessons can't be planned in advance. Most lessons are taught on the fly as the situation occurs. No true how-to can work in those circumstances.

This is actually more of a what-to book. I am going to show you what to teach your kids more than how to teach your kids. In the long run, it's what they know that is important. The method you use to get that information into their brains is up to you.

"WHAT GIVES YOU THE RIGHT TO TEACH PARENTING, LARRY?"

That is a fair question since I am known as either a business consultant or a personal development guru or a financial coach. Yet that is exactly what gives me the right to talk about parenting. Besides, I am not really teaching parenting and we need to get that straight from the outset. I am teaching fiscal responsibility, discipline, consequences, goal setting, education, love, charity, ethics, how to work and how to have fun along with many other principles of a productive life. These are the principles that I have taught in every one of my books thus far. These are the principles every person must learn and adhere to in order to lead a successful, happy, financially secure life. These are the "what-to"s I just referred to. All I am doing in this book is offering the lessons I am best known for on a level where they can be taught to children. I am not teaching parenting, I am teaching life.

In every book I have written, I point to my personal experience as my right to teach others what to do. I clearly point out what I have done wrong in my personal life, my business life, with my money, what consequences I experienced and what I did to overcome the mess I made. I teach the lessons that I learned the hard way. I also teach what I have learned from my reading and study on the subject.

This book is no different. I am going to cover what I did wrong as a parent and what I learned from my mistakes. And I am going to cover what I did right as a parent and the influence it had on my now adult sons. You will also get the benefit of the research I have done by studying the works of many of the world's leading parenting experts.

But what most gives me the right to talk about parenting comes down to just two reasons: Aaron Tyler Winget and Patrick Mason Winget. Two responsible men who tell the truth, take responsibility, work hard, pay their bills and contribute to society. Anyone who can raise two good kids when there are so many idiots roaming the streets has a thing or two to teach others.

I CAN'T FIX YOUR KID.

You may have purchased this book thinking I am going to teach you the keys to fixing your kid. Sorry. This book is not about fixing your kid. First, I don't really believe your kid is broken; therefore he or she doesn't need to be fixed.

"What? But I want my kid fixed!" Too bad. That's not what I'm here to do. I know your kid may be a mess, but it's not your kid's fault that he is a mess. And believe me, I know there are a lot of messed-up kids out there. But again, it's not their fault. The fault lies with the parents.

Therefore, this is not a fix-your-kid book. This is a fix-the-way-you-parent-your-kid book. When you fix the way you parent, your kid will get fixed. That's the sequence. I want to be very clear so you won't be surprised: It's not about them; it's about you! Like I said a few pages back, if you want to fix your kid's behavior, change your own behavior.

That is going to be your biggest obstacle in this whole

process of raising responsible, productive kids: becoming a responsible, productive parent. And don't tell me you are a responsible parent who has done everything right and you still have kids who are a mess. That's not how it works. Let me repeat a basic premise from all of my books:

Business gets better right after the people in the business get better.

Sales get better right after salespeople get better.

Customer service improves right after the people who deliver the customer service improve.

Employees get better right after their managers get better.

Wives get better right after their husbands get better.

Husbands get better right after their wives get better.

AND . . .

Kids get better right after their parents get better.

MEANING . . .

Everything in your life gets better right after YOU get better and nothing in your life is ever going to get better until you get better.

This isn't going to be an easy process because it requires that you get better by taking a long, hard look at the way you are raising your kids. And you have to get better long before your kids are ever going to get any better. If your kids are a mess, it's time to take responsibility for it. Consider what you have done wrong as a parent and tell yourself that you are ready to do whatever it takes to improve your skills so you will end up with a responsible, productive adult. Remember, your kids are your own fault.

So let's get started. There is no time to waste!

A FEW WORDS OF WARNING:

Warning #1.

I hate it when people tell me how great their kids are. Nothing makes me want to puke quicker than someone who goes on and on about how cute their kid is or bores me with all of their kid's accomplishments. Yuck! I bet you feel the same way. Here is my problem: I can't explain how I believe you should parent your kids without telling you how I parented my kids. I can't talk about what to teach your kids unless I tell you what I taught my own kids. Therefore, you are going to hear quite a bit about my boys. Sorry. I am not going to go on and on about how great they were though, I promise. Because the fact is, they weren't all that great. They were just kids. Some days, they were pretty good. Some days, I wanted to choke them out. Most days, they were just kids. They are both men now and I'm proud of the kind of men they turned out to be. But trust me when I say they were idiots a good part of the time growing up. I will do my best to keep a good balance between describing the idiot kids they were and the responsible adults they became so you won't want to puke. But remember the most important thing to take away when I talk about my sons is the lesson involved in the story. And I promise, there won't be a story unless there is a lesson.

Warning #2.

I take a hard line on discipline. I believe lines should be drawn in the sand in terms of acceptable behavior and unacceptable behavior. When those lines are crossed, consequences must be imposed. Those consequences must be carried out whether you are busy or preoccupied with other things, whether it is convenient, whether you feel good, and even when your heart isn't in it. You drew the line; it was agreed upon with your child and a deal is a deal. If you have a problem imposing consequences for unacceptable behavior then you are going to hate this book.

Warning #3.

I speak in generalizations. I make blanket statements that apply to *most* people in *most* situations. There are exceptions. I recognize that. I am fully aware that there are few situations that there are no exceptions for. So don't bother pointing the exceptions out to me. I don't discount the fact that there are exceptions to every point I make in this book. I just don't intend to deal with them.

Warning #4.

I quote a lot of statistics in this book. I don't footnote every statistic I use. That's not my style and it doesn't seem to be the style of those who read my writings. I don't make stuff up. The statistics quoted all came from reliable sources. If you want to find out where they came from, then I encourage you to do a little research: Google them. You can find verification for every statistic in the book by investing just a few minutes of your time in a Google search.

MY PERSONAL REQUEST TO YOU.

You are not going to agree with everything I say in this book. In fact, I hope you don't agree with everything. If you did, you wouldn't be thinking on your own. I don't want blind followers, I want fully aware, engaged people to read my words and agree where they feel they should and disagree where something opposes their own personal belief system. A good healthy disagreement means you are involved and thinking. Being involved and thinking critically is always a good thing whether you agree or not.

My request to you is this: If you find something I say that you vehemently disagree with, move on. Go ahead and disagree with me on that one idea and keep reading. Don't throw out everything else that you might be okay with and be able to use simply because I lose you on one point.

I once received a letter in response to something I said in my book *The Idiot Factor: The 10 Ways We Sabotage Our Life, Money, and Business.* The guy told me he had to discount the contents of the entire book, even though he saw applications for a good bit of it in his own life, simply because he disagreed with a statement I made about bottled water. All I could think of was how sad that is. One line that had almost nothing to do with the overall message of the book caused this guy to abandon things he openly admitted he needed to do.

Please don't do that with this book. Parenting is a touchy subject. Talking to people about their kids and pointing an accusatory finger in the faces of the parents causes people's hackles to rise! All I ask is that you be open enough to find one thing in this book you can use to raise a better kid. One good idea is my goal for you. One idea so that at the end of the book, you can close it and have the resolve to take action to improve the life of the person you brought into this world and are in charge of. Deal? I hope so.

Okay, that's it. Are you ready to get started raising better kids? If so, get your pencil and keep reading.

BEFORE YOU BEGIN:

I am a huge believer in making books interactive. My books all include worksheets to fill out and this one is no exception. I want you to get out a pencil right now and go to work on the next few pages before you even begin to read my suggestions on raising good kids. Please don't skip the exercises, as these will form the basis for your entire approach to parenting.

BEGIN WITH THE END IN MIND.

If you want to build a house, you begin with the end in mind. You visualize the finished product and then create the plans to make your vision come to fruition. You hire an architect, find a builder and go to work. Your general contractor keeps close watch on all the subcontractors to make sure they are doing their job and that the project stays on track. You put your time and your energy and your money into the project to make sure what you picture in your mind is what you actually end up with.

That is exactly what parenting is about, too. You begin with the end in mind. Only, in parenting, you are the architect, the builder and the general contractor. There are some subcontractors in there, too. Those subcontractors are grandparents, family, friends, babysitters, teachers, coaches and others who will have periodic and temporary responsibility for your child's development throughout her life. As the general contractor you are in charge of those subcontractors to make sure they do their job and help you keep the overall project on track.

Imagine this: You decide you want to build a beautiful new house, so you go to the lumberyard and order a bunch of lumber, some pipes and wires, a cabinet and some doors, then throw in a toilet bowl, a sink and some lawn seed. Then you have all of that stuff delivered, piled up at your building site, and you sit looking at it with no plan at all. Would you do that? Of course not. That would be stupid. But that is how most people parent. They parent without a plan. They have all this fun creating the baby and then nine months later when the baby gets delivered they've got the diapers, the nursery, the bottles and the formula, but they don't have a plan to create the end product. They don't know what kind of adult they want to raise. Sure, they may say things like, "He's going to be a doctor!" Or, "She could be president of the United States!" But do they have a plan to get them there? Rarely.

Parents may spend a lot of time looking into the future and

picturing the end product, but most haven't put a lot of time into figuring out what has to be done every single day to make sure it happens. It's not enough to just picture the end product; you also have to focus on the daily effort it takes to get there.

That is my approach in this section. I want you to begin with the end in mind. I want you to think about what kind of adult you would like to create. That is what parenting really is: creating adults. I may have hooked you with the title, but I want to make one thing clear to you right now: This book is not about how to stop raising irresponsible kids; it is about how to create a plan for raising smart adults. Few parents think far enough through the process of parenting to understand that concept.

The subtitle of this book is *A Guide for Raising Responsible, Productive Adults*. I know some will say, "Didn't you mean to say *Kids* instead of *Adults*?" No, I meant adults. I don't believe you raise kids as much as you raise adults. If your children stayed kids forever I would have written about raising kids. But they don't. Kids grow up and become adults.

You create the adults the rest of us will have to put up with. You typically have your children under your roof for eighteen years and then they begin to make their own decisions and the rest of us end up living with the consequences of those decisions. You have them for eighteen years as children, but the rest of the world has them for about another sixty years as adults. Your few years at the beginning are what create the person they become after you get them out of the house.

In order to figure out what those first eighteen years are going to entail for you as the parent, you must begin by looking at the adult you want to create.

LET'S VISIT THE TIME MACHINE.

Stop thinking of your kid as he is today. Forget that he is a drooling ten-month-old in his high chair throwing Cheerios. Instead, picture your kid at the ripe old age of thirty-five. What do you want him to look like? What habits do you want him to have?

What lifestyle do you want him to embrace? How much money would you like for him to be earning? Do you want your kid dependent on you? Unable to make decisions? In debt? Still living at home? Still going to school? Out of work? In a series of bad relationships? Those are the questions you must ask yourself before you even enter into the whole raising-a-child mode. Picture your kid at thirty-five and work backward.

Why do I want you to do this? I have seen way too many parents looking at their thirty-five-year-old kid wishing they had done things differently when their kid was little. Their thirty-five-year-old "child" is broke, unhappy, can't figure out how to be in a relationship, may still live at home or is still dependent on them. And those thirty-five-year-olds will go out there and pass on the same faults when they have kids of their own.

If you are looking at a thirty-five-year-old disaster, face it, folks: It is too late. You have failed as a parent. You have failed yourself, your child and your child's children. You have failed society. And all of us will end up bearing the burden of your failure. Thanks! Think of that the next time you bump into a thirty-five-year-old idiot; you should send his parents a thank-you note because it's their fault.

HINDSIGHT IS 20/20.

You've heard that old saying. Twenty-twenty hindsight is fine when you are thinking on Monday about how you shouldn't have washed your car on Sunday because you heard it would rain and sure enough, it did. It's fine when you are looking back at how some investment didn't turn out to be your finest decision. While the consequences may be serious, a bad investment normally isn't a life-destroying issue. However, looking at your thirty-five-year-old disaster of a human being and wishing you had done things differently is not okay. Twenty-twenty hindsight doesn't matter at that point. It's too late. You can't go back and re-raise your child. You have to have *foresight* when raising your kid. That's what I am trying to help you develop with this exercise: foresight. I want you to have the foresight to actually design the thirty-five-year-old adult you want your child to eventually become.

Take the time right now, yes, right now, to fill out these pages.

WHAT KIND OF ADULT DO YOU WANT YOUR CHILD TO GROW UP TO BECOME?

_____
_____
_____
_____
_____
_____
_____
_____
_____
_____

WHAT INFORMATION WILL YOUR CHILD NEED TO KNOW TO BECOME THAT KIND OF AN ADULT?

_____
_____
_____
_____
_____
_____
_____
_____
_____
_____

WHAT HAVE YOU ALREADY TAUGHT YOUR CHILD THAT WOULD LEAD HIM OR HER TOWARD BECOMING THAT KIND OF AN ADULT?

WHAT DO YOU STILL NEED TO TEACH YOUR CHILD?

Congratulations! You have just written your own book on how to raise a productive, caring, smart, loving, responsible, well-adjusted adult. Now that you have written yours, read mine.

SECTION ONE

WHAT HAPPENED?

CHAPTER 1

HOW DID WE GET INTO THIS MESS?

I get this question in response to just about every problem I address, whether I am talking about why employees don't work harder, why our economy is a mess or why people make stupid decisions. People always want to know *why*. I guess that "Why?" is a fair question when I step back and consider it. So let's examine why we are in this mess.

At this point in my life, I am a bit amazed when people ask why our society is such a mess. Because regardless of the area we are discussing, the answer is always the same. The mess happened because we either didn't care enough to keep it from happening or we weren't involved enough to know it was happening. Either way, we allowed it to happen. We sat back on our fat butts and allowed it to happen without doing much except griping, whining and complaining.

We watched the mess happen first in our own lives. Then it spread to our families, where we watched the mess start to slowly grow. Then the mess spilled over into our work and business. Then we watched the mess get bigger and bigger and bigger until all of society was dealing with the mess. When that happened, we began seeing the mess pop up on various television news programs and we started reading about it in the newspapers. Then we watched some YouTube video of people dealing with the mess and even spoofing the mess. The mess became the topic of blogs and was covered in depth on various Internet sites. No matter where we turned, there it was. At that point, we became so used to being surrounded by the mess that we became desensitized to it. Eventually, we built up such an immunity to the mess that the mess wasn't a mess at all, it was just the way things were. We no longer even recognized it as a mess because we had reached the point where we accepted it as a way of life. And that is when it stabbed us in the back. Yep, the back. Not the front. We turned our back on the mess and walked away from it. We were probably walking into the mall or to the refrigerator but regardless of where we were headed, it nailed us.

We have all seen this process happen many times. The mess comes in many forms. It happened in our society when it comes to obesity. We weren't always the fattest people on the planet. We are now. It happened again when the mess stabbed us in the back in terms of education. We used to be at the top of the educational charts worldwide. We aren't now. It happened in our businesses, too. We used to be number one in manufacturing products. Now we aren't. It happened in our economy as well. It happened in nearly every area of our society from our health to our economy to our government. And it happened with our children, too.

That is why our kids are a mess today. We allowed it to happen. Our kids didn't become a mess overnight. The crisis sneaked up on us because we turned a blind eye to it and ignored it and pretended it wasn't true. Because admitting it was true would mean we would have to actually deal with it and sadly, people don't ever really want to deal with their problems. That is, until it is damn near too late.

When do people finally decide that it's time to lose weight? When they get diagnosed with diabetes or have a heart attack. When do they finally think it is time to quit smoking? When they are diagnosed with emphysema or lung cancer. When do they finally realize that they need to go to work and actually do the job they were hired to do and are paid to do? When they are about to lose their job. In other words, we tend to get concerned about fixing something when it is damn near too late to fix.

That's how it is with our kids, too. Maybe that is especially true when it comes to dealing with the problem of our kids. Why especially? Because about the last thing anyone wants to admit is that their own kids are a mess. Oh, we are each great at saying *your* kids are a mess or *their* kids are a mess, but *my* kids? That simply can't be true. After all, these are *my* kids we're talking about!

News flash! Your kids *are* a mess. And if they aren't now, chances are they are headed in that direction. I am not going to argue that point. I am just going to say it and let you figure out whether I am right or not as you read the pages of this book and work through the exercises.

Now let's return to the original question: How did we get into this mess? I am not just going to take the easy way out and leave my answer at "we stopped paying attention." I actually want to address the question with some solid answers you can use to evaluate how you are doing as a parent and determine which road you are headed down.

WHY DO KIDS DO WHAT THEY DO?

That seems to be the big question when people talk about why kids do the wrong thing . . . WHY? I have come up with eight reasons for why kids do what they do.

1. You let them.

Kids do what they do because their parents allow it. Kids become what they become because that is what their parents allow them to become. It's that simple.

If you are a parent with a kid who has made a mess of his life, you aren't going to like that answer. You are going to come back at me with a ton of excuses. You are going to talk about movies, music and sex and violence on television as the influencing factors for why your kid turned out the way he is. You are going to blame the educational system. You are going to talk about peer pressure and how we live in a society that promotes irresponsible behavior. Trust me, I have heard it all before. I have watched parents say it all on television as they moan and groan and whimper and cry over what their child has become. Their sweet little baby! I have even used some of these same excuses a time or two myself. But none of it holds water. So shake off your indignation and realize this basic truth: Your kids are a product of your parenting. Period. Deal with it. The faster you get a grasp on that, the more progress you can begin to make.

ARE YOU GUILTY OF ALLOWING YOUR KID TO ACT IN WAYS THAT CONFLICT WITH YOUR GOALS FOR THEIR BEHAVIOR? HOW? EXPLAIN IT TO YOURSELF.

_____

_____

_____

_____

_____

_____

_____

---

2. There are no consequences for bad behavior.

Parents let their kids do what they do with little direction or training or communication of what is acceptable and unacceptable behavior. Then when things go wrong, there are no consequences for the unacceptable behavior. A basic principle of human behavior is that people will always pretty much do what they can get by with.

I am going to spend a lot of time talking about consequences, discipline and punishment later on in the book. Just know this now: Part of the reason we got into this mess to begin with is because we failed to enforce the consequences of unacceptable behavior with our children. We warn them by saying, "If you do *that* then *this* will happen." And, "If you don't do *this*, then you can expect *that*." Then they don't do *this* and *that* never happens. They don't perform as we expect and tell them to, and we let it slide. We don't enforce the consequences we have promised. Know what that makes the parent who says they will do something and doesn't do it? A liar. Yep, we teach our kids to behave badly because we are liars. We are just too lazy to keep our word and impose consequences for bad behavior—consequences that we gave our word would happen.

ARE YOU GUILTY OF NOT COMMUNICATING THE BEHAVIOR YOU EXPECT FROM YOUR KIDS? ARE YOU GUILTY OF NOT IMPOSING CONSEQUENCES? HOW? EXPLAIN IT TO YOURSELF.

_____

_____

_____

_____

_____

_____

_____

---

3. You tell your kids they are special.

They aren't. Lost a few of you loving parents just now, didn't I? For those of you who actually believe your little angel is special, please hear the truth once and for all about your baby: Your kid is *not* special. If you tell her she is, you do her a huge disservice. Your kid is special to you and only to you. Your kid is not special to anyone else.

Your kid didn't do one thing to deserve your love and shouldn't have to. Your kid was born with all of your love and it's a wonderful thing when she knows that. However, when your kid walks out your front door and gets to school, she is just one more little kid in the third row and there is nothing special about her. At school your daughter is no one's little princess. In the real world your kid isn't the apple of anyone's eye. She is just one more kid. She needs to understand that and learn how to deal with it. When she goes into the workforce, she certainly isn't special to anyone. She needs to grow up knowing that the instant she leaves your loving arms and enters the real world, no one loves her for the fact that she exists. In the real world, success, love and happiness are not her birthrights. It's performance that counts.

ARE YOU GUILTY OF TELLING YOUR KIDS THEY ARE SPECIAL INSTEAD OF COMMUNICATING THAT THEY ARE GOING TO BE JUDGED AND REWARDED BASED ON THEIR ACCOMPLISHMENTS? HOW? EXPLAIN IT TO YOURSELF.

Let me throw another shocker out to you:

4. You made your kids the most important thing in your life.

They aren't. "What? Blasphemy!!"

I know that you think they are, but again you are wrong. If

you let your kids think they are the most important things in your life, they will learn how to manipulate that emotion and you will end up being under their thumb. And more important, kids who believe they are the most important thing to their mama or daddy learn to use that little piece of information to play one parent against the other and to play their parents against every other adult who interferes with their wants. As the parent you will find yourself involved in squabbles with teachers and coaches and other adults in a supervisory role because little Jimmy knows that he is number one in your eyes.

Your kids are important, don't get me wrong. Your children should be loved unconditionally, for sure. But parents who put their kids' happiness above all else sacrifice their own life and sanity, and sometimes they sacrifice their marriage, too.

If you have done your job as a parent, your kids will grow up and leave you in order to lead healthy, happy lives on their own. When that glorious day arrives, you are stuck with just your spouse. If all of your time and energy have been spent only on your children, when they leave, you won't even know that person you are left with. That is why so many relationships fall apart after the kids are gone. That's why people are "fine" for twenty-five years and then get a divorce. The only common ground these couples had was their kids. Then the "common ground" grew up and disappeared and the couple is left with nothing in common.

It even happens in single-parent homes. The single parent spends so much time and energy on his kids that he sacrifices his own life in the process. He thinks that he is serving his kids well by putting his own life "on hold" while he raises them. Then the kids leave and he is left alone with few friends and no special person to grow old with. The single parent becomes that spooky old person who dotes on his fifty-year-old baby like he's four years old.

You don't serve your kids well by making them the center of your life. And you certainly don't serve yourself, your spouse or your other relationships well either.

> *"A mother only does her children harm if she makes them the only concern of her life."*
> —W. Somerset Maugham, *The Razor's Edge*

ARE YOU GUILTY OF MAKING YOUR KIDS THE CENTER OF YOUR LIFE TO THE ABANDONMENT OF YOUR OWN LIFE? HOW? EXPLAIN IT TO YOURSELF.

_____

_____

_____

_____

_____

_____

_____

_____

_____

_____

_____

5. There is a sense of entitlement that has become pervasive throughout our culture.

People of all ages seem to think that success, wealth and happiness are owed them. We see grown men and women who are looking to the government and saying, "Where is my bailout?" when our plight is clearly our own fault. Yet, we want the government to send us a check to cover the expenses of our own stupidity. We have fifth-generation welfare recipients who have never seen anyone in their family do more work than walking to their mailbox for their government check. We see unwed welfare mothers having eight babies and getting multimillion-dollar book contracts. We see CEOs getting millions of dollars in bonuses, and for what? Ripping off their stockholders and cheating the American public.

Our children watched when Mama and Daddy fudged their loan application in order to buy a house that was bigger than they needed and cost more than they could afford and then ended up losing it to foreclosure. And they heard their parents complain about how they were victims of predatory lending. They watched their parents go to the mall and charge up their credit cards and even take out every store credit card they could get their hands on, then max them all out because the family "deserved" to have nice things.

I got an e-mail recently from a woman who told me that she and her husband filed for bankruptcy eight years ago. Now, eight years later, their debt is right where it was back then. Bankruptcy gave her a second chance and she blew that, too!!!

She went on to say that she and her husband don't buy anything for themselves but do have three daughters who, in her words, "don't want for anything." Her question was how to explain to her daughters that they have financial problems and need to "cut back" without "failing" them? You can imagine how nice my reply to her was. First, her statement about how her daughters "don't want for anything" is a lie. They want for responsible parents who are smart enough to learn from their mistakes—who know how to provide for their family's future—who have put money away for college for their three kids—who have their priorities straight—who can teach them about financial planning and budgeting—who know how to live a lifestyle they can afford—who aren't idiots! As for her worry about how to cut back on her expenses without "failing her daughters": Are you kidding me? Too late for that one, because she and her husband have already failed their daughters. She said that her three daughters have cell phones that run more than two hundred dollars a month, but that they are barely scraping by as a family. She told me that she doesn't think it is fair that her daughters should have to "suffer" because of her mistakes. Holy crap!!!!! Since when is a teenager doing without a cell phone called suffering?

Is it any wonder that our children think that they are "owed" a new car when they turn sixteen? Of course, television shows like *My Super Sweet 16* don't help. And why are we surprised when our kids think that they deserve a cell phone? We have failed to set proper examples for our children. We have failed to teach them the difference between rights and privileges.

I recently watched an interview with psychiatrist Dr. Keith Ablow, host of *The Dr. Keith Ablow Show,* talking about how kids have reached the point where they feel entitled to receive an A for just showing up to class. He said that kids no longer relate grades to performance but feel entitled to them just for the minimal effort of showing up.

**ARE YOU GUILTY OF FOSTERING A SENSE OF
ENTITLEMENT IN YOUR KIDS? HOW? EXPLAIN IT
TO YOURSELF.**

---

6. You work so hard at giving your kids a healthy self-esteem.

You can't give your kids their self-esteem, so give up trying. "What? My job is to build up my kid's self-esteem," you say. Which bozo told you that? Look at the word, *self-esteem. To esteem* means "to regard highly or favorably with respect or admiration."

Precede esteem with the word *self* and it means that you have to "regard *yourself* highly or favorably with respect or admiration." Based on the definition alone, you can't give someone else self-esteem. Self-esteem comes from within. The same applies to *self-worth* and *self-confidence*. If it begins with the word *self*, then no one else can do it for you. It's too bad more self-help gurus don't understand this idea. With them, their approach is focused way too often on "help" and not nearly enough on "self"!

Sadly, we want to give our kids a healthy self-esteem because we have been led to believe that high self-esteem is the key to doing great things. That's backward. High self-esteem is *not* the key to doing great things. Doing great things (or pretty much anything) is the key to attaining high self-esteem. Being able to regard yourself favorably is the natural result of accomplishing something. Accomplishing something is not the result of regarding yourself favorably.

Self-esteem is an earned condition that comes from having accomplished something. Since that idea is not reinforced by society, it has to be reinforced at home. Society will reward you with status for being rich. Or for being pretty. Or for being born to celebrity parents. Or for being rich, pretty, born to celebrity parents and forgetting to wear your underwear. But in the real world, most people have to earn their status. Any kind of status. In fact all status, good or bad, is earned. Status can also be called esteem. How you are esteemed is based on what you accomplish.

Isn't that how it is where you work? You are esteemed based on your contribution. I earn my money: How much I get, how often I get it is based on how good I am at my job. It works that way with you, too. Your accomplishments contribute to your self-esteem. Even when I try to do something and don't do it well, I feel better about myself for having tried.

As parents we have made the grave error of trying to bestow self-esteem on our children instead of teaching them how to esteem themselves. The role of the parent is not to give their children a high self-esteem but to help the child try different things and teach them to feel good about taking the action. It is the action—the trying, the succeeding, even the failing—that will bring the esteem of accomplishment. Offering praise when deserved, encouragement to continue to do better, training when necessary, even criticism when something is done poorly, is the job of the parent. In that way, the parent can help the child learn to hold himself in high esteem.

ARE YOU GUILTY OF TRYING TO BESTOW A HEALTHY SELF-ESTEEM ON YOUR CHILDREN INSTEAD TEACHING THEM HOW TO ESTEEM THEMSELVES? HOW? EXPLAIN IT TO YOURSELF.

_____

_____

_____

_____

_____

_____

_____

_____

_____

---

7. You turn to medicine to fix what you are too lazy to deal with.

ADD—ADHD. I am going to take a lot of flack for this one but that's okay. When I was a kid, we didn't have attention deficit anything. We simply weren't paying attention.

We didn't have so many depressed people walking around either. And if you were depressed, you didn't tell others about it or use it as an excuse. You had good days and you had bad days and you learned to live with them. I still have good days and bad days and I just deal with them. Yep, even Larry Winget gets down in the dumps. What do I do to get over it? I get busy. I occupy myself in other ways so I don't expend any energy on the "downer" feelings. I have never met anyone in my life who didn't have bad days and downer feelings. But I don't take drugs and neither do most of the people I know. Instead, we learn to cope.

"But, Larry, you don't understand! Some people can't just get busy and get over it." Yes, I do understand. And some people, including children, do have to be medicated. However, medication is always a last resort in my book, not a first resort. In our society, we have gotten lazy and are quicker to throw a drug at a problem than we are to put in the time and work to correct it.

You have to teach your kids that good days and bad days are normal. You have to teach them coping skills. You have to teach them that bad moods come and go. And you shouldn't run to the doctor with every little thing that goes wrong in the life of your kid. Remember, doctors make their money through office visits. Many even get paid to pass out pharmaceuticals. They want you to become dependent on them and their expert advice. (Okay, doctors, you have just received one of my generalizations. Deal with it. Not all doctors are on the take. Not all are in it for the money. Some are amazing people who genuinely care about the welfare of their patients. To them I say thank you. To the others, you should be ashamed of yourselves.)

In terms of your child's health, try a little good old-fashioned common sense first. Give the problem a chance to work itself out and then go to the doctor if it doesn't. I am betting that in most cases, the commonsense approach will work. It is amazing how effective common sense, time and work are when fixing any problem.

As a little boy, I was moody and I had a short attention span. (By the way, if your kid doesn't have a short attention span, I would have her examined by a doctor. What normal kid doesn't have a short attention span?)

When I entered the fourth grade, my teacher, Mrs. Bow-man, separated me from my three buddies and put us each in a corner of the room facing the wall. She made it clear on day one that we had a reputation for being disruptive and for talking too much and she wanted to nip it in the bud. Was she wrong for doing this? Nope. Did I hate it at the time? Yep. But our reputation preceded us and she took the necessary steps to make sure her class would run smoothly. My mother didn't like it because after all, I was her little angel, but my dad understood it and went along with the judgment of the teacher.

The lesson from this little tale is that kids are moody, disruptive and have short attention spans and that is normal. A little training and discipline go a long way in correcting these issues. But the easy thing to do is to trot the child off to the doctor and get him a prescription to level him out so you don't have to discipline him. It's easier to say that Tommy isn't doing well in school and has ADD than it is to stick Tommy's butt in a chair and force him to sit there until his homework is done. It's easier to drug him into submission than to take your own precious time away from *Dancing with the Stars* to make sure he learns his multiplication tables.

Medication is easier to administer than discipline. It takes ten seconds to get your kid to swallow a pill. It takes constant 24/7/365 effort to discipline your child. Many parents numb their kids with drugs because they are too lazy to discipline them or claim they don't have the time to become fully involved as parents.

Teachers are just as bad—maybe worse! Teachers have twenty-five little monsters who aren't paying attention and are looking out the window, picking their noses and eating their boogers instead of learning their lessons. When one or two in the class need some extra attention in order to behave, rather than messing with the fragile psyche of a child by putting him in the corner like Mrs. Bowman did to me, some teachers call the parents of the kid and suggest Ritalin.

The government is even worse about this. At one point, the

Massachusetts Behavioral Health Partnership reported that almost two-thirds of children under state care were being treated with drugs for behavioral disorders. In a 2004 report, *Forgotten Children*, Carole Keeton Strayhorn, the Texas comptroller, uncovered evidence that 60 percent of children in the Texas foster care system were being treated with powerful psychotropic drugs. An investigative series in Ohio found that forty thousand children ages six through eighteen who were covered by Medicaid had been prescribed psychotropic drugs. I found dozens of other examples like this but I believe you get my point. When time is limited, the easiest way to get the behavior you desire is to drug the kid.

As I conducted my research, the one question I found repeated most was this: Are we choosing to medicate because it is cheaper and easier than taking the time to properly evaluate or administer non-drug-based therapy? I would assume that the answer is *yes*. Another question that also requires consideration: What are the long-term side effects of prescription psychotropic drugs on children? I don't know the answer to that one. But I do know that there are no negative long-term side effects of using love and discipline to improve your child's behavior.

At this point I know that some of you are screaming and throwing this book across the room. Your argument is going to be that your child needs the medication to survive in school and to function normally. Okay, it's your kid and not mine. I am just expressing my opinion here. But tell me how the baby boomers, the most productive generation in the history of our nation, were able to accomplish so much without childhood drugs? How did all of us deal with our hyperactivity without medication? The answer: Our parents and teachers busted our skinny little butts and told us to shut up, sit still and pay attention! That's how.

Further proof.
Sixteen percent of Americans are on three medications and 14 percent are on five medications or more. We are overmedicated as adults and we turn right around and overmedicate our kids.

The model we offer our kids is that you need medication to live normally and comfortably. That has become our belief system. My dad always believed that if you got a cold, you would get over it in about a week, so he didn't take any cold medicine because he knew in about seven days, the cold would be gone. Ask a doctor how long it takes to get over a cold when you take cold medicine. The answer is about a week. The only difference in attaining the same result is the drug. Many people in our society have made drugs their best friends. They wake up to them, count on them to make them happy and to never feel pain of any sort and then they go to sleep with them at night. It even seems to me that the pharmaceutical companies must be making up illnesses just so they can create drugs to cure them. Think restless leg syndrome.

We have to give up our constant reliance on drugs and begin again to rely on our own ability to control our emotions.

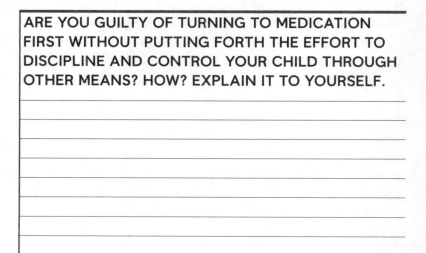

ARE YOU GUILTY OF TURNING TO MEDICATION FIRST WITHOUT PUTTING FORTH THE EFFORT TO DISCIPLINE AND CONTROL YOUR CHILD THROUGH OTHER MEANS? HOW? EXPLAIN IT TO YOURSELF.

8. You set a bad example and your kids followed it.

Do you ever wonder why kids dip their toast in their eggs when they eat breakfast? Because they saw their parents do it. You have never heard of dipping your toast in your eggs? Want to know why? Because your parents didn't do it. That wasn't your role model.

Why do some kids like football and others like baseball? Often it's because their parents liked one more than the other. Or why do some kids love video games while some would rather go outside and play? Same reason: Their parents either play video games or enjoy being outdoors. The kids follow the model that has been set for them.

I recently watched a discussion with elementary school teachers who talked about how young children sometimes act out the scenes from porn movies. How does that happen? Because porn movies are playing on the television at home and the kids see that as acceptable behavior. With them it isn't about right or wrong, they are just modeling the behavior they see on a regular basis.

Adults cheat on their taxes and brag about it. Kids cheat on their spelling tests and brag about it. An adult gets back a dollar too much when the clerk gives him his change and he laughs about how he cheated the store out of a buck. His kid then sees another kid's money lying on her desk and takes it and laughs about it.

Years ago there was a commercial in which a teenager got caught by his dad with marijuana. The father confronts the teenager and screams, "Where did you learn this?" The kid calmly looks back at his father and says, "From you, Dad." The dad looks like he has just been kicked in the gut. But that is the way it works. Kids model the behavior they are shown to be acceptable by their parents.

Remember the song "Cat's in the Cradle" by Harry Chapin? It is the story of a man who has a son and just can't seem to find the time to spend time with his growing boy even though the son begs him to. As the man grows older, the roles reverse and the father wants to spend time with his son. The son offers his father the same excuses that he received growing up. This line says it all:

And as I hung up the phone it occurred to me, he'd grown up just like me; my boy was just like me.

ARE YOU GUILTY OF THE "DO AS I SAY, NOT AS I DO" STYLE OF PARENTING? HOW? EXPLAIN IT TO YOURSELF.

_____

_____

_____

_____

_____

_____

_____

_____

_____

_____

The eight reasons kids do what they do:

1. Parents let them.
2. There are no consequences for bad behavior.
3. Their parents tell them they are special.
4. Parents make their kids the most important thing in their lives.
5. Kids have a sense of entitlement.
6. Kids don't develop a sense of self-worth through accomplishment.
7. Kids are overmedicated.
8. Parents set bad examples for their kids.

WHO IS TO BLAME?

You are. I am. We all are.

You saw that coming, didn't you? By now I hope I have made

that point clear: Your kids are your own fault! But you know me: Let's kick this ball around a bit more before we move on.

When the elementary school kids in Idaho were chanting "Assassinate Obama" on their school bus, where do you think those kids heard that? Their parents. They had heard their parents say that so they thought it was acceptable.

When you see the little three-year-old running around the restaurant screaming and bothering the other people dining, it's easy to get upset with the kid. I know I usually want to grab the kid and have a little talk with him for sure! But is it really the kid's fault? No. The fault lies with the parents. The kid is small and can be controlled and it is the parents' responsibility to do it.

When you watched Britney Spears on television acting like an idiot with her childish, immature, dangerous, irresponsible antics, it was easy to trash her and blame her. I was certainly quick to say, "What an idiot!" But when you look a little deeper at Britney and her antics, whose fault is it really? The fault lies with her mama and daddy.

Paris Hilton runs around getting her picture taken without her panties on. She even goes to jail for drunk driving and, during a radio interview about her DUI, said that "it was nothing." It's easy to criticize her trampy behavior but evidently her mama and daddy didn't teach her that was unacceptable behavior, especially when there are cameras on you every minute. They must not have explained that a DUI is not "nothing" but is a very big *something*. Oh, yeah, the first time this kind of behavior showed up, she might have just been a rebellious teenager acting up and expressing herself. That is a legitimate excuse for less-than-acceptable behavior one time. But only one time. If I had been her daddy, there would never have been a second time. Paris even made a sex tape that appeared all over the Internet. Didn't her parents teach her that when your boyfriend pulls out a video camera to tape you having sex with him that might not be the best of ideas? And why didn't Daddy find that punk and beat the crap out of him for it? I know, I know, no violence! Sorry, but she's his daughter! Some young man needed to get his butt kicked over that deal. Some even say that the whole sex tape thing was nothing but a publicity stunt to increase her fame. While it was effective in getting her plenty of publicity, if that is true, it is beyond sick.

Kim Kardashian's parents didn't teach her about watching out for a guy with a video camera either. I guess good old Olympian Bruce Jenner and his self-absorbed wife were too busy trying to hang on to the flickering flame of their fame to explain those things to their little girls. Maybe they were just too busy trying to get a reality television show so the rest of us could make fun of them and their ridiculously pitiful lives.

All of these little girls were allowed to make their own rules and set their own limits. They obviously didn't do a very good job of it based on their results. I am sure that these girls' parents are not happy about the videos and the pictures and the jail time and are sorry and embarrassed that it happened. But I believe that the parents primarily view what happened as an exploitation of their daughter's celebrity status and blame the paparazzi instead of understanding that the fault lies with their own bad parenting. More evidence that it is easier to blame someone else for your results than to take responsibility.

Some of you might be saying, "These are grown women you are talking about here, Larry." They are *now*. They weren't when the seeds of reckless behavior were planted and nourished.

When you look at all the celebrity kids who act so recklessly in so many ways, it's easy to forget that these kids have parents who should be controlling their behavior. They should but they don't. They didn't rein them in as children and teach them how to function with all their celebrity. I guess that's hard to do when you are making millions of dollars from your child.

I don't care how famous your kid is. You are the parent. You control what she does and how she does it. Even President Obama requires that his daughters make their own beds. I bet you don't require that of your kids, do you?

The same applies to your kids and the friends of your kids and the kids you see at the mall. Kids are OUT of control because their parents are not IN control.

Kids are OUT of control because their parents are not IN control.

THE FIVE BASICS
OF PARENTING

The Five Basics of Parenting

1. Communication
2. Involvement
3. Education
4. Discipline
5. Punishment

These are the five basics of parenting. Many parents already do all five of these basics. But it isn't a matter of just doing them; it is how well you do them that counts. Do them well and you end up with a great kid. Do them poorly and you will end up with something other than a great kid. If you don't master these basics you will end up with an uneducated kid who is uninvolved, undisciplined and unable to communicate—which means that the consequences will require punishment. When you do these things well, you end up with a smart kid who is involved, disciplined and can communicate.

Which do you want? Again, the choice is all yours.

CHAPTER 2

COMMUNICATION

C ommunication is the backbone of civilization. A zillion years ago, Cave Man A wanted Cave Man B to pass him a chunk of wooly mammoth, so he grunted at him to make his wishes known. (Sadly, for some that level is about as far as it has gotten.)

On the whole, we are poor communicators. We expect others to read our minds and know how we feel, what we expect from them and what our desires are. We don't tell people that we love them. We don't tell people we are mad at them. We don't talk. We don't listen.

Add to that the fact that many people just plain don't know how to speak well and the problem is compounded. Top that off with all the political correctness and the fact that no one is willing to be totally honest, open and frank for fear that someone might get their feelings hurt, and it is a wonder that we aren't still grunting at one another over a slice of wooly mammoth.

COMMUNICATION IS LEARNED.

Do you and your spouse speak openly about how much you love each other? Chances are you heard that type of communication between your own parents and now it is completely natural for you to talk to your spouse that way.

Do you allow your friends to hurt your feelings and mistreat you without speaking up for yourself and telling them that you aren't willing to let them treat you that way? Chances are this is a behavior you learned or witnessed when you were a child.

Do you scream and yell when something upsets you instead of having a calm discussion?

When someone enters into an argument with you, do you turn and run so you won't have to engage in a verbal disagreement?

Do you quietly accept lousy service from individuals or companies without complaining?

Do you sit at the breakfast table with the newspaper in front of your face while your spouse talks? Then when she is finished, you don't have a clue what she said?

Do you go to a party and find yourself standing alone in the corner simply because you don't have the skills to become involved in conversation?

I am sure you read these and at least one of them hit close to home with you. I am also convinced that a few other situations came to mind as I reminded you of your ability or inability to communicate effectively. As you evaluate your communication skills, know that you are passing those skills on to your children.

Kids will learn to communicate with the world based on how they learn to communicate within their own family.

TALKING.

That is where communication starts. Talking to one another. I make my living talking. I talk about all kinds of things and topics and give my opinion on just about everything under the sun. I am good at it. My wife thinks I talk too much. My boys spent years wishing I would shut up. But the fact that I love to talk is the result of the way I was brought up. My family talked. We talked from the time we woke up until we went to bed. We sat at the dinner table and talked about our day. My folks would ask me what I did at school and what I did when I got home from school. They asked me questions. I learned to ask them questions about their day. They always told me. It was called a "conversation." I listened to my parents talk to each other, too. I listened to them fight about things and I listened to them express their love for each other. It was never quiet at our house. We talked.

I encourage you to talk in your family, too. To have conversations. To ask one another questions. To listen and comment on the answers. It's good for you and good for your family. No subject matter should ever be taboo. It isn't what gets said that causes problems; it's what goes unsaid that causes problems.

> *It isn't what's said that causes problems; it's what goes unsaid that causes problems.*

BAD GRAMMAR, SLANG AND, YOU KNOW, STUFF LIKE THAT.

Teach your kids grammar. That means that you have to know and use it yourself. Sadly, that isn't the case among most people. We are surrounded by poor grammar on television, in movies, in advertisements, in books and in nearly every conversation. I promise you that your kid will never get or keep a good job and make any real money if he or she uses bad grammar. Would you trust your legal problems, health or finances to someone who isn't able to speak well? If you would, then you are an idiot. You want the people you do business with to use good grammar. I don't even want to buy a pair of shoes from someone who can't put one word after the other correctly.

Our language is also inundated with slang and worthless words that don't add to the meaning of what is being said. Don't allow the current slang to become your kid's only way of communicating. Eliminate *like, you know, you know what I'm saying, that's what I'm talking about,* and the current stupid word of the moment from your conversation. In fact, when someone says "You know what I'm saying?" to me, I usually reply with "Sorry, I don't have a clue what you're saying." That almost always stops them dead in their tracks.

Don't let your daughter talk like a valley girl or talk through her nose. She has a voice; make her use it. That affected way of speaking is not attractive and will not add to her credibility when she grows up and enters the real world. She talks that way because her friends talk that way. Have a conversation with her and explain. Record her and prove that she sounds like an idiot. "Like, oh my god, I like totally can't believe I sound like that!" is the response you want from her. If she looks at you and doesn't have a clue what you are talking about, you have a problem. Show her positive role models—someone on television or in her own life who speaks properly and who she respects—and have her note how they sound.

The first rule of communication: Be *able* to talk.

The second rule of communication: Listen. "Say what?"

LISTENING.

Talking is only half of the equation when it comes to communication. You also have to be able to listen to what is being said. While listening is a great skill to teach your kid, it is also maybe the most important skill to have when raising your kid. Most kids will eventually quit talking to their parents simply because they don't feel that their parents listen to them. Sadly, they are right! Parents are so busy pushing their own agendas that they fail to listen to their kid's point of view. While I agree that it is your right, even your obligation as the parent, to push your agenda, it is also your obligation to listen to your kid's point of view. Do you have to agree? No. Do you have to listen? Only if you want your kid to keep talking to you. Anyone who feels like they aren't being listened to will eventually stop talking. You want your kid to talk to you. You want him to talk to you about his friends, what is going on at school, sex, religion, relationships, smoking, health, money and everything else that is going on in his life. That will only happen if you are willing to listen to him. Even if you adamantly disagree with every word that is coming out of his mouth, you owe it to him to listen. That is called respect. Show respect for your child's words and opinions by listening to him. That is the way you teach him to show respect for your words and opinions. You talk and he listens. He talks and you listen. That is called effective communication.

One of the ways you teach kids to listen is by not allowing them to speak when someone else is speaking. Again, that means that you don't get to speak when *they* are speaking. This is all a matter of common courtesy. It's about respect. You don't have to respect what they are saying, but you do need to respect the person enough to listen to them.

A way to make sure that your distracted young child is listening to you is to ask her to repeat what you have just said to her. Tell her what you want her to do and then to verify understanding, ask her to repeat it. This habit, when started young, will instill in her the idea that your words matter and that she is expected to be paying attention. Even when they are teenagers, this is an especially helpful tool for verifying that there is an understanding—not an agreement with, but an understanding—of your wishes.

Let me recommend a great book to you by Adele Faber and Elaine Mazlish called *How to Talk So Kids Will Listen & Listen So Kids Will Talk*. These authors have written some spin-off books about talking to teenagers, too. All are good books on the subject of talking to your kids and I highly recommend them.

Talking and listening: I could spend the entire book just on those two elements of parenting. And while I might do that someday, I really want to move on from *how* to communicate to *what* has to be communicated. Even if you know that you have poor grammar, have a hard time making yourself understood and are a poor listener, it is your job as a parent to communicate the important things in life with the skills you have.

COMMUNICATE YOUR LOVE.

Want your kid to feel good about himself? Want him to act with confidence? Want him to willingly come to you with his problems, concerns and fears? Then communicate your love for him no matter what—with heavy emphasis on the *no matter what*. I always did my best as a father to communicate my love for my kids even if I was disappointed with their behavior. My approval was up for grabs based on their actions, but my love for them was unconditional. That line needs to be communicated and explained to your kids so they understand that when you disapprove of their behavior, it does not mean that you don't still love them. I have witnessed parents withdraw their love from their kid based on their kid's actions. I have seen mothers and fathers get upset over something their kid has done and tell their child that they don't love her anymore based on the kid's mistake. I heard a mother say that she was going to disown her son because he did something that made her mad. Sadly, parents withhold love, affection and attention over bad behavior. That is heartbreaking to witness. The poor kid doesn't understand a withdrawal of love over a mistake, especially from his parent.

> *Love your kid for who he is—approve of your kid's behavior based on what he does. Understand the difference and learn to separate the two.*

Kids have an incredible need to be accepted. Kids join gangs, clubs, cliques, teams, fraternities and sororities because they want to feel accepted. Let your kid know that she can always count on your love and your acceptance. Let her know you will never try to withhold it or bribe her with it.

If you are able to communicate this to your child, that foundation will give you something you can build on that will last forever.

Some people will respond with "My kids know I love them." How? Because you buy them things? Because you provide a roof over their heads and food on the table? Some parents think this is enough. It isn't. You have to say it. You have to get their attention, look them in the eyes and tell them you love them. Say it when they are little and say it when they are older. My boys are grown men and I still tell them I love them. The last words my dad ever heard on Earth was me saying, "I love you, Dad." And the last words he ever said before he passed his last breath were "I love you, too, son." That exchange means everything to me. I feel so sorry for parents and kids who can't seem to get those words out and who let them go unsaid. Don't assume that your kid knows you love him by your actions alone. Use your words, too.

COMMUNICATE EXPECTATIONS.

Kids mess up. It's what they do. I see it all the time and so do you. I lived with it for lots of years with my own boys. But sometimes I realized that my kids were messing up because they didn't know any better. That is often the case; kids don't do the right thing because no one has communicated what the right thing is. As parents, we often expect something from our kids they can't deliver because we failed to communicate to them what we expected. When that happens, and the kid messes up, it is actually our own failure, not the kid's.

"What we have here is a failure to communicate."
—*Strother Martin, in* Cool Hand Luke

Do you want your kid to act a certain way when you go to the grocery store? Did you explain that to her before you went to the grocery store? Or did you do what most parents do and go to the grocery store and then yell, scream and maybe even spank her because she didn't live up to your expectations? Expectations you never bothered to communicate.

Do you want your kid to go with you to a restaurant and sit quietly at the table and use good manners? Did you explain that to him? Did you teach the manners before you went to the restaurant?

Do you want your kid to greet strangers with a smile, look them in the eye and address them with a "yes, sir" and a handshake? I know that was always my goal for my boys. To make sure it happened, I explained that to them ahead of time. I told them what to do, showed them what to do and clearly communicated that it was exactly what I expected them to do.

It is only fair to your child that you clearly communicate in advance the behavior you expect him to exhibit. It is totally unfair for you to dump your kid into a situation with no information and then punish him for not behaving the way you want him to.

You are dealing with kids—not psychics! They can't read your mind. If you want your kid to behave a certain way, tell him, teach him and then communicate to him what will happen if he doesn't do it.

COMMUNICATE CONSEQUENCES.

When you communicate your expectations, it is important at that same time to also communicate what happens when those expectations are either met or not met.

Again, this is only fair. It is ridiculous to impose consequences when the expectation has never been communicated. Yet, we are all guilty of doing it. If you want to improve your results with your kid's behavior, get the sequence right. Communicate the expectations, then communicate the consequences.

All actions have consequences. Even non-action has consequences. This alone is a great lesson to teach your child.

When I was in college, I took a course in logic. There was a section I particularly liked that dealt with "if this, then that" logic. The idea is: If you do this, then that happens. If you don't do this, then that happens. Can you see why I would love this kind of logic? It is based on the idea that your actions actually cause all your results. I would love to rename this Larry Logic, but I fear it's too late.

This is actually very close to that universal law of physics that says, "For every action, there is an equal and opposite reaction."

Again, I like this law, too. Roll these two together and you end up with the Law of Cause and Effect. This is also known as "causality," which according to Wikipedia denotes a necessary relationship between one event (called cause) and another event (called effect), which is the direct consequence of the first.

This universal law seems to be something that most folks in our society are trying to circumvent. They don't believe that their results have anything to do with their own actions.

A timely example.

The bank is foreclosing on your home—an action that is being taken because you aren't making your payments. This is because you bought a house with a loan payment that was more than you knew you could afford. Which is based on the fact that your stated income on your original loan application had nothing to do with how much money you were really making. Which has everything to do with the basic fact that you are a liar and lack integrity. Which means your home is being foreclosed on because you lack integrity. Which means your actions caused your results. You did it to yourself.

This law and form of logic must be communicated to your kid at the level of their understanding based on their age and the matter at hand. You have to explain the sequence of events that occurs when your kid does something, because as a kid they don't always see that their actions have a consequence.

If you drive drunk, you could have a wreck, lose your license and possibly kill yourself and someone else. Believe it or not, kids don't always make that connection. They don't see the end result of their actions. They live in the moment. It is your job to educate them and communicate the consequences of their behavior. You have to slow things down and show them "if you do this, then this will happen."

Even a two-year-old can learn the Law of Cause and Effect. "If you touch this and you break it, you will get in trouble." "If you pull the kitty's tail, it will bite and scratch you."

Will your ability to communicate "if this, then that" logic change your kid's behavior? Sometimes. Not always. Sometimes she will still pull Tigger's tail and will get scratched. That's a good thing. That consequence will teach her a valuable lesson. Better that she learns these lessons from you now while it's still early and it's just a cat's scratch than learns them later and faces much harsher consequences.

COMMUNICATE REALISM.

People tell their kids, "You can be whatever you want to be." That isn't realistic. You should not be telling your kid that he can be whatever he wants to be. Why? Because he can't. Stop telling your kid that he can be whatever he wants to be. The truth is that he can be whatever he has the basic talent for being and is willing to work hard enough to become using that talent. That is a realistic statement based in fact. It doesn't sound as fairy-tale-like and it doesn't have quite the ring to it that "You can be whatever you want to be" has, but it's the truth.

If your kid wants to play in the NBA more than anything in the whole world and he's five feet six inches tall, it's not going to happen. Don't tell him it *can* happen just because he *wants* it to happen. That would be dishonest.

If your kid has no musical ability and can't carry a tune in a bucket, chances are he is never going to make it as a professional singer. A rapper maybe, but not a singer. Don't encourage him to try out for the next season of *American Idol*. You are setting him up for failure.

Instead of instilling false hope by communicating and reinforcing unrealistic ideas, encourage realistic goals based on talent, commitment and a willingness to work hard. Communicate very clearly that your kid can be whatever she has the talent and inclination to become and is willing to work hard enough to achieve. That last part can't be overlooked. You have to be willing to work hard enough to achieve it.

When I was growing up I wanted to be a veterinarian. I had that dream from the time I was a small child until I reached college. I have always loved animals. I grew up on a farm and was surrounded by many varieties of furry and feathered creatures. I loved to feed them, love them and take care of them. I was also pretty smart and always did well in school. I told everyone I was going to be a vet when I grew up. I had the talent and the inclination but . . . I went off to college and I found out very quickly after my first calculus course that I did not want to be a veterinarian. While I had the talent and the inclination, I had to face the fact that I wasn't willing to work hard enough to achieve it. I wasn't willing to study that hard, go to school for that many years and learn the things I needed to learn to make it happen. I could have—but I wasn't willing to. Big difference.

Teach your kids the realistic truth about their future.

Talent, inclination and hard work create your reality.

Drop just one of those out of the equation and you better start looking for a different reality.

COMMUNICATE WITH TOTAL HONESTY—EVEN WHEN THE TRUTH HURTS.

I don't believe in lying. If my wife asks me, "Does my ass look fat in this dress?" I tell her if it does or not. If she didn't want the truth, she shouldn't have asked me. When she gets experimental with some dish she is cooking and asks, "What do you think?" I tell her. Do her feelings get hurt? Sometimes. But we established years ago that if you don't want an honest answer, then you shouldn't ask the question. Before you decide that I am either stupid or cruel, know that it works both ways. My wife still doesn't think I can write. Many of you may agree with her. For years, I would write something and she would quickly tell me that it stunk. Even after many bestsellers, she tells me when she doesn't like something I write. Do I like it? No. But I listen because I know she is being honest with me. I value honesty more than just about anything else, even when it hurts.

I established this openness and honesty early on with my boys, too. If they asked me my opinion about something they did, I would tell them. I always found it best, though, to ask them how they thought they did first. If they thought they sucked and they really did suck, all I had to do was agree with them. If they thought they sucked and I thought they did great, then my opinion became very valuable to them. But if they thought they sucked and they really did suck, I knew I was not doing them a favor by telling them differently. That is how you end up with kids who have a false sense of well-being about their performance. I hear parents all the time telling their kids how great they are at something, when clearly they aren't. Thus they set them up for failure. Watch some of the early tryouts for *American Idol*. Watch the kid who is there with his mama who has told him his whole life that he is going to be the next Elvis. Then Simon tells him the truth: He sucks. The kid doesn't understand and walks out crying, looking into the camera saying, "That isn't true, he's wrong. I know I can sing. Everyone has always told me

I can sing!" Then he runs out and tells Mama what Simon said and Mama gets all indignant over it. Mama should be ashamed for putting her baby through that embarrassment, because anyone with ears knows her little boy can't sing! She said he could because she loved him and wanted him to know it, so she lied. And her lying set him up for pain he didn't need to go through.

Is my approach cruel? If you are a parent who coddles your kid in all that they do, then you will say yes. However, if you are a parent who wants your kid to have a realistic view of his abilities, to be able to accept the truth, to know when he hasn't done well and to be able to take criticism, then you are going to see that honesty is the best way to go. Honesty may hurt, but it is always the best policy.

Selective truth telling, saying things that aren't true just to protect the fragile feelings of another, never really helps in the long run. Does that mean that you should go out of your way to tell someone that they suck at something? No. That really would be cruel. Yet some of you will read this and immediately take this idea to the extreme and attack me for being mean to small children. Chill out, folks. Use your head.

When you have an open, honest, loving relationship with your child and she knows you only want the best for her in all situations, then telling her the truth about something won't crush her little heart. The key is that you have established that open, honest, loving relationship in which she knows you only want the best for her. If that has been done, the truth won't hurt.

I guarantee that my boys are better men today because they were told the truth. The biggest benefit of always telling your kids the truth even when it hurts is that you establish a level of trust. My boys know that I am the one guy they can come to for total honesty. Their friends and other family members might smile, pat them on the head and tell them how wonderful they are or how great their decision was, but they always seem to come to good ol' Dad for the real truth. They appreciate having someone who won't sugarcoat it for them. They value having someone who will openly say, "Son, you are screwing up." And they really enjoy having good ol' painfully honest Dad say, "Son, you did great!"

An insincere compliment may make you feel good for a while, but a sincere compliment will stick with you forever. Your kid is smart enough to know when you are being honest with him. After a while, he will discount your insincerity and stop coming to you for feedback because he knows you will tell him how great he is when what he is really looking for is honesty.

Kids want honesty. Kids respect honesty. Kids will emulate honesty when it has been modeled for them.

COMMUNICATE THAT YOU WILL ALWAYS BE THERE.

Kids need to know that there are certain constants in their life that won't ever change. I think we all need that kind of reassurance. That is why some people cling to their religious beliefs so strongly; they need to be able to have a constant that never wavers.

Kids need to know that their parents will always be there. That doesn't mean that kids expect their parents to always approve of what they do and how they do it. They are smarter than that. They do need to understand, though, that you are going to be there for them regardless of what they do and how they do it. Approval of their behavior isn't necessary—support of who they are is.

When I was young, my dad made it clear that regardless of what kind of trouble I was in, I could call him. He told me not to call a friend or anyone else; call him. He promised me that he would be there and that he would help me. He might punish me later, but the important thing was for him to be there if I was in trouble.

When I first started to drive I took a girl out on my very first car date. Being a teenager with raging hormones, I took her parking after dinner and a movie. We drove to a park and made out for a while and when we were ready to leave, the car wouldn't start. I panicked. I couldn't even get the engine to turn over. I knew very little about cars and I had no idea what to do. The girl was panicked, too, because she had no idea what we were going to do and was afraid her parents would find out. I was a bit concerned about that, too! I told her I would call my dad. She begged me not to but I promised her it would be okay. Luckily, I had parked close to the pool house at this park and there was a pay phone on the wall of the pool house. So I walked to the pool house and told my dad where I was and that the car wouldn't start. He said he would be right there. Twenty minutes later he pulled up, slid into the car and said hello to the girl. (Her face was in her hands and she was dying with embarrassment, I'm sure.) Then he got out of the car, popped the hood and, when I joined him at the front of the car out of sight of the girl, he whispered, "You left it in drive. I put it in park for you; it will start now. Now take that little girl home." I got in the car and took her home and my dad never mentioned this episode again to me. He didn't embarrass me, or her, and he proved that he could be trusted and that I could call him anytime.

I always remembered this and told my boys the same thing. They knew that if they were in trouble and someone needed to be called, they could call me. And they did. I got calls in the middle of the night to come get one or the other of them a couple of times. Their friends told them not to call me but my boys always did. They understood that I would deal with the problem and they would get their punishment later, but I would be there and handle things first.

Your kids need to know that you are the one person they can always turn to when they are in trouble. Not to approve of what they have done. Maybe not even to fix the mess they have made. But you will be there for them. You need to be the person—the constant—that your kids can always count on.

COMMUNICATE OFTEN.

Nothing replaces frequency of communication. Yet, according to a recent study, the average parent spends three and one-half minutes per week in meaningful conversation with his or her children. Two hundred ten seconds per week. Thirty seconds per day. And we wonder why our kids are a mess. We don't talk to them. Spend some real time communicating with your kid. Sometimes it isn't about the quality, but about the quantity.

"But you don't understand, Larry. We are busy at our house!"

You are so right about this one; I don't understand. I don't understand how anyone could possibly be so busy that they don't make time to talk to their kids. My boys' mother and I were divorced and they lived with her during the week. They had busy lives just like other kids. They went to soccer, had friends, were involved in school activities and all the other things that kids are involved in. Yet, even though I only got my boys on weekends, I talked to them every day. I got on the phone and talked to them about their lives. I told them how much I loved them. I was there with advice and to ask questions and listen to them. I spent time every single day with my boys even though they lived in a different city. Don't tell me how busy you are. If it matters to you, you will find the time regardless of how busy you are.

I am amazed when I get letters from parents who complain that their kids are seventeen and don't talk to them. If those parents were to take a good hard look at their history, they would know that they didn't talk to their kids when they were five either. Establish habits of talking that become a normal part of the relationship. Make time every day to talk to your kid. I talked to my boys in the car since I spent a lot of time driving back and forth with them to their mother's house. I talked to them on the phone. I spent time with them before bed. I talked to them at mealtimes. Yes, we ate together. You should try that. No excuses; just make the time to do it.

Remember this: Your time, your energy and your money always go into what is really important to you. I wrote that in my book *You're Broke Because You Want to Be* when discussing money. I asked that people track their spending to determine what was really important to them. I wanted them to know that they could track their priorities based on where they spent their money.

This same principle applies to your kids. Track your time. Find out how much of it you really spend with your kids. If you don't spend much time with your kids, then sadly, they aren't a big priority to you. Ouch! That one hurt, didn't it? Tough! It's true. If your kids are important to you, then you will find a way to spend time with them and communicate with them. Period.

COMMUNICATE LIKE A PARENT.

This is the big one. You are not your child's pal, buddy or BFF. You are his parent! Act like it. Don't talk to your kid like his best friend would talk to him. He doesn't need that. He doesn't even want that. He needs and wants a parent! He wants you to have opinions about what is right and wrong. He needs and wants you to communicate your guidance. He needs and wants your approval and, believe it or not, your disapproval. He needs and wants you to tell him what to do. You know, like a parent would!

My boys and I are friends now. But my boys are grown men. We communicate on issues like friends. We talk about politics, finances, history, religion, world issues, movies and everything else just as friends would. But even now, there are things we talk about in which I am clearly not their friend. I am their adviser. I am the older guy with all of the experience who has been where they are and has done the right thing and the wrong thing and has learned from it. I am the guy who can offer the benefit of those lessons. I can tell them what I think they should do based on my experience. In other words, I am their dad.

COMMUNICATE YOUR MISTAKES.

You aren't perfect, so don't pretend to be. Admit your mistakes. If you overcorrect, punish unfairly or yell when you shouldn't, stop as soon as you realize it and admit your mistake to your child. Apologize. The parent who acts like he is always right and never makes a mistake is an idiot and will lose the respect of his child quickly. The parent who admits his mistakes and knows when to apologize to his child will gain the respect of his child and build trust.

When you mess up in business, or with a friend, and your kid knows it, that is an excellent time to use that situation as a way to communicate to your child that you are human. Good people admit their mistakes. Teach your kid that ability. Teach her to be able to admit her own mistakes with her friends, her teachers and coaches and with her own family.

Usually, your kid already knows you are wrong so it's best to just admit it. One time, I was on a tirade about something when my son Tyler turned to me and said, "Dad, you need to listen to your own speech!" and walked away. I hated that. I hated it because he was right, I was wrong, he knew it and I was busted. Your kid knows. Be the grown-up and admit it. He will respect you for it.

CHAPTER 3

INVOLVEMENT

Typically, kids come home from school and head off to their rooms to watch television and play video games or possibly do their homework. Or they go to a friend's house after school to do the same thing. Parents come home and plop their fat butts down in front of the television and no one sees one another much at all. Few dinners are eaten together. As children get older, the problem grows.

For the most part, parents don't know much about what is going on in their kids' lives and are rarely really involved in what their kids are doing.

That's how you end up with kids who have a complete arsenal of guns in the garage without the parents' knowledge. The parents simply were not paying attention. They weren't involved.

Become involved in the lives of your kids. Know their likes and dislikes. Know their talents and their skills. Know their friends. Know their teachers. Talk to them to find out how they feel and what they are thinking. If you don't, you might end up with a kid on top of a water tower with a deer rifle.

> *Larry's Rule:*
> *Know what your kids are doing, where they are doing it*
> *and with whom they are doing it.*
> *(And a good bit of the time, you need to be the one*
> *doing it with them.)*

If you aren't involved with your kids, then you are leaving their upbringing to someone else. Either you raise your kids, or they will turn elsewhere for guidance: to their friends, their teachers, other parents or the television. Do you trust someone else to raise your kids? No? Then get involved.

GET YOUR KIDS INVOLVED, TOO.

Your kids need to be involved, too. They need to be involved in sports and other socializing activities. I was never much good at sports. I was a skinny kid, too little to play football, too short to play basketball, too slow to play baseball. I could talk. So I did things that used that talent. I debated and was in plays and speech contests. I was also in the band. Yep, folks, Larry Winget was a band nerd. But I was involved. My parents saw to it. And anything I was involved in, they were involved in. They were always there for me in whatever I did. They were present to support me in whatever way they could.

My buddy and manager Vic has great kids. We have been together for more than fifteen years so we have watched each other's kids grow up. Vic is the ultimate involved father. He told me one time that his girls didn't have time to get in trouble because he kept them so busy. That's a good idea. Keep your kid busy.

CAN YOU BE TOO INVOLVED?

Yes. There is a fine line between being involved in your kid's life and being overly involved in your kid's life. You need to let your child feel some independence. That doesn't mean you abandon him or that you aren't aware of all he is doing. You just aren't in the middle of all he is doing. You can become the meddlesome, overly involved, overprotective pain-in-the-butt parent that your kids will grow to resent. Do this and you will push your kids away. That's not what you are looking for. You are looking for kids who know that you care enough to always be there for them in any circumstance. You want your kids to know how to behave and what choices to make even when you aren't there. You want your kids to become responsible people who can stand on their own two feet but who know that if things go wrong, you will be close by.

There is a guy who lives down the street from me who puts signs in the middle of the street that say SLOW—CHILDREN PLAYING. If he is in his yard when a car drives by he rushes to the curb and waves his hands up and down indicating that you need to slow your car down. I stopped one day and told him that I was driving the speed limit and didn't need him telling me to slow down on my own street when I was driving the speed limit. I also told him I didn't appreciate the signs in the street blocking my travel. He said, "But there are kids playing out here!"

I said to him, "Then it's up to you to teach your kids to play in their yard and not in the street. Do that and there won't be a problem." This is a case of an overly protective parent who is trying to control the world instead of taking control of his children. You cannot train the world to revolve around your kids; you have to train your kids to live in the world.

I have another neighbor who still walks her two teenage children to the corner to catch the school bus. I get to witness this spectacle often as the school bus stops in front of my house. I have no problem with a parent walking their kids to the school bus stop. It is the appropriate action if the kids are young and your neighborhood is a little edgy. However, these kids are teenagers. They do not need to be walked to the corner. The bus stop is only two houses away and Mama could stand on her front porch and watch the whole trip since it only takes about fifteen seconds. And my neighborhood is far from what you would consider an edgy neighborhood. What this mother seems oblivious to is that she is embarrassing her teenagers to death by being so overprotective. You should see their body language and the looks on their faces as Mama hugs and kisses them good-bye every morning in front of their friends. Can you imagine the teasing that these poor kids get when they get on the bus? Let them go, Mama!

PLAYING.

Kids are all about playing. It doesn't matter what age they are—they love to play. I love to play, too, and I'm glad I never lost that desire to have fun and the ability to let the work go and just play. I run into so many adults who have totally lost their sense of humor and their appreciation for play. They can't even *play* golf. They may go golfing but for them, it is anything but play.

Kids and adults alike need regular playtime. Kids especially need a break from scheduled time; they need time every day to just have fun and enjoy themselves. Too many parents don't get involved in this playtime with their kids. They send the kids off to play by themselves because they are "too busy."

Kids who aren't taught to play can end up doing things that will get them in trouble. Their parents didn't show them what was acceptable play, and the kids got carried away having fun and before you know it, the kids are in trouble. You have to play with your kids to teach them the difference between good play and bad play.

The memories my grown sons talk most about are the times we spent playing together when they were kids. They remember the hide-and-seek games that I would organize with all the neighborhood kids that would last well into the night. They remember making forts out of blankets thrown over dining room chairs. They especially loved playing "sock wars" in the hallway. If you haven't done this, it is great fun. Just take rolled-up socks and get in the hallway and have a battle throwing rolled-up socks at each other. Socks don't break anything and don't hurt when you get hit with them, and hallways are pretty safe places to play. We played board games and card games, put on puppet shows and made our own movies for which the boys wrote the screenplays. And we spent a lot of time playing outside. I know that in some areas playing outside is a challenge, but I honestly believe that one of the problems today is that kids don't go outside enough.

The fact is that only 6 percent of kids between the ages of nine and thirteen play outside on their own each week. I find that sad. Kick your kids out of the house and have them play in the sunshine. It will be good for them.

As I was writing this book I asked my son Tyler for one of the more valuable lessons I had taught him. The first thing out of his mouth was "Go outside and play." I laughed and said I was being serious. He said he was, too. He told me he remembers well that I would tell him and his brother to go outside and play. When they would ask, "Play what?" I would tell them that I didn't care what they played but that it had to be played outside. He told me that he remembered going through the garage and coming in with little scrap pieces of wood and other stuff and asking if I cared if they built something with it all. He said that I never turned them down and told them to have fun and not to come back inside until I called them or until someone was bleeding. I remember going into the backyard to find a ramshackle playhouse built in the corner of the yard and Tyler and Patrick happily hammering away, so proud of what they had built. If I had allowed them to stay inside, they would have wasted those hours watching television, but because they were forced to go outside and get creative, they had a fort!

TEASING.

My boys and I have always joked around a lot. We tease, kid each other and give each other a hard time about most things. It is important to teach your kids not to take themselves too seriously and one of the ways you do that is by teasing. I am a funny guy with a quick wit and a sharp tongue. Teasing is how I show that I care about you. Trust me on this one; if I don't tease you, it's because I don't like you. I guess I am like the second-grade boy who pulls the little girl's pigtails to show he likes her.

However, teasing can be abused. There is a fine line between loving and playing and belittling someone. I have made the mistake of crossing the line in many relationships but what I regret most are the times I crossed that line with my boys. I have teased too hard. They have, too. There is a fine line where teasing becomes hurtful and disrespectful. It isn't okay to cross that line.

CHAPTER 4

EDUCATION

No one can argue that kids need to be educated. Having an education is the difference between making informed decisions and flying by the seat of your pants. It is the difference between getting a good job and getting a mediocre job. It is the difference between success and failure.

I believe that kids would do better if they simply knew better. When we are educated and have lots of high-quality information at our disposal it allows all of us to make better-informed choices in every area of our lives. How can anyone argue with that? The problem is that kids aren't getting the information that would allow them to make good decisions. Their education is lacking in nearly every area and they simply are not getting the lessons they need in order to be responsible, productive and smart.

Some of the facts are:

On average, only about 70 percent of the kids who begin high school graduate from high school. Meaning that nearly one-third of kids do not get a high school diploma. These numbers vary by state, with some states hovering around 50 percent. When that many people don't even have a high school education we have to accept that unemployment and crime are going to increase as a result.

High school dropouts are 72 percent more likely to be unemployed than high school graduates. Unemployed people cost us all money. So if you are tempted to say that these numbers don't affect you, don't be naïve. These numbers affect all of us and cost all of us money.

Only 10 percent of high school seniors are at or above basic proficiency in history and only 26 percent are at proficiency level in civics.

Only 31 percent of U.S. college graduates score as proficient in English.

The United States currently ranks 21 out of 29 countries in mathematics scores.

These few statistics are typical of how poorly we educate our children in our school systems. I could continue to list even more startling statistics about just how unprepared our kids are for the workplace. In fact, I found a survey of corporations that regularly interview globally looking for talent to hire, and one of the respondents said, "If I wanted to recruit people who are both technically skilled and culturally aware, I wouldn't even waste time looking for them on U.S. college campuses."

These numbers are the facts that represent the sad state of affairs of our country's educational ineptitude. However, I'm not citing these statistics as an indictment of our school system. That would be just too easy. Besides, there are many kids who go to public schools and come out with a great education. So the fault lies not only with the school system. While the school system may appear to be failing our kids, it is really parents who are failing by not making sure their kids learn what they need to know to be successful, healthy and prosperous.

Besides, my bet is that when a kid does well at school it is because there is discipline and support at home. My bet is that education is held in high regard within that household. My bet is that the kid is encouraged to do well at every turn. My bet is that the parents are involved in the education of their kids. Kids do well at school in many cases because it is important to the parents and they stress that importance to their child.

You may argue that many of the kids who are failing according to these statistics don't come from "traditional" homes. Many kids don't have parents to encourage them. You are right. But many do. As I stated in the beginning of this book, I can't deal with every situation or sad condition or exception. The fact is that many kids—too many kids—drop out and don't do well simply because they have no reason to do otherwise.

Parents, you need to make sure that your kids get an education whether their school does its job or not. Why? It is *your* kid, that's why! The uneducated thirty-five-year-old working for minimum wage and struggling to pay his bills won't end up the responsibility of the school system. That "kid" won't be coming back to the principal asking for help making his mortgage payment or to move into the spare classroom because he got evicted from his apartment. That "kid," your kid, will be coming back to *you*. Is that what you want? I'll bet the answer is no. So educate your kid. Make sure that your kid is involved at school and in his classes. Make sure your kid reads books on relevant subjects instead of spending all afternoon and evening watching television and playing video games. Rip the cell phone out of his hands and stick a book in his hands.

I was fortunate that education was important in my household. Not that my parents had much of it themselves. My mother graduated from high school and then went straight to work. My dad graduated from high school and went to work and then to the navy and then back to work. Yet when I was a little boy he went to night school to take a course in bookkeeping. He never became a bookkeeper but he wanted to better himself, so he took the class one night a week. He still worked all day in the warehouse for Sears and ran a chicken farm and took care of a couple of acres of garden for our vegetables, but it was important to him to get more education. My folks always took my education very seriously. They went over my grades with me in great detail and made sure that I studied.

When I was about eight years old a door-to-door encyclopedia salesman knocked on our door. He came in and my folks listened to the pitch and called me into the room to show me the set of encyclopedias. They asked me what I thought about them. I told them I liked them but tried not to show much excitement since I knew my folks couldn't really afford them. As I remember, the set cost about $300 and that was a lot of money for my parents in 1960. The man explained that they could put them on a payment plan and make monthly payments until they were paid for. I remember my dad asking me if I would use them. I promised him I would. So they bought that set of *World Book* encyclopedias. They were green and white and the most beautiful books I had ever seen. I still remember how they smelled as I took each one out of the wrapping paper it was packaged in. Because I knew how much of a sacrifice it was for my parents to buy these for me, I never took owning them lightly. I read them every night and I read nearly every word of that entire set of encyclopedias from A to Z. The emphasis my parents put on my education and the sacrifices they made for me to have the best they could afford gave me great respect for books and education. I am so fortunate that education was so important in my house.

Education doesn't just apply to typical academic subjects like mathematics, history and science. It is the responsibility of the parent to educate his child in all areas of life. Finances, relationships, ethics, health and civic responsibility also have to be taught.

HOMESCHOOLING.

I know homeschooling works out really well for some people. In fact, I have friends who have homeschooled their children and ended up with great kids who have a great education. They were the fortunate ones, because I have seen other homeschooled kids who didn't turn out so well. However, I do understand that is the case in public schools, private schools, military schools and church-sponsored schools as well.

I only have two issues with homeschooling. First, you are turning your child's education over to an untrained teacher. Did Mom go to school and get a degree in elementary education? No? Then what makes you think she is qualified to teach? Because she read a book on how to do it? I read a book on surgery one time; want to let me cut your appendix out? Why not? Or maybe she attended a homeschooling class for mothers. I went to a class one time on how to install granite tile. Want to turn me loose in your house? No? I don't understand why you wouldn't. Is it because I'm not trained? Is it because I am not qualified? Bingo! Leave something as important as your kid's education to the trained educators. Not that they are perfect by any stretch of the imagination—but the odds are certainly better.

My biggest issue when it comes to homeschooling is the socialization aspect. Your kid needs to be around other kids. Kids need to get punked on, be bullied a bit and made fun of by their peers. They need to win in a crowd of their peers and they need to lose in a crowd of their peers. They need other kids around them so they can work (yeah, that's what school is for a kid: his job) in a real work environment, just like when they grow up! They need to see people do well and get rewarded and do poorly and get punished.

The real world is full of adults who will punk you, make fun of you and bully you. You will have to learn to handle it in the real world so you better learn those skills as a child. If you don't, then I would hate to be your supervisor the first time you have an issue with a coworker on the job. You need to be able to handle the praise of an outsider and you need to be able to handle the criticism, too. And guess what? There is a lot more criticism than praise in the real world.

READING.

There are many ways to teach children. Placing an importance on school is only one of the ways. Reading to your children and encouraging them to read is another. I always made sure my kids had plenty of books and every night before bed, we read something together. Twenty-five years later, they can still quote passages from *Alexander and the Terrible, Horrible, No Good, Very Bad Day* because they loved it and had it read to them so much.

Sadly, not nearly enough emphasis is placed on reading. Here are a few statistics that back that up:

58 percent of the U.S. adult population never reads another book after high school.

42 percent of college graduates never read another book after college.

80 percent of U.S. families did not buy or read a book last year.

The reality is that most people just don't spend much time with books in their laps. I believe most of that is because they were not read to as children and then they didn't learn how to read well in school.

I love to read. My love of books was instilled in me when I was a small child. A high value was placed on books and reading in my house. I watched my mom and dad read before bed every night. My dad always had a Louis L'Amour western with him. My mom usually had a paperback in her purse. Both of my parents read to me at night when I was young before I went to sleep. I was given books as presents and they became my prized possessions. I first learned to enjoy books as an escape from reality. I was able to solve crimes with the Hardy Boys and float down the river with Huckleberry Finn. Then I learned to read for information. I desperately wanted to change my life and books held the keys for me to be able to do that. They still do. I have read over four thousand books in the past twenty years. I will forever be grateful to my parents for creating my love of books.

SPEAKERS, THEIR CDS AND THEIR DVDS.

I have always believed in exposing children to great speakers, teachers, lecturers and writers. My own life has been shaped by listening to speakers, and I believe it is important to give kids a chance to learn from these folks as well.

Zig connects with my six-year-old.

When my own boys were about six and ten years old, I took them to Dallas, Texas, for a weekend to go to Six Flags Over Texas. This was a big deal at the time. I was living in Tulsa, Oklahoma, and had just gone through bankruptcy a few months earlier. I was emotionally beaten, financially devastated and physically worn out. I spent all my time trying to fix my situation. I sold nearly everything we owned. Our living room and dining room were empty because I sold our furniture. I was scrambling, doing anything I could to make a buck to pay my bills.

I needed a break and I knew my kids could use one. We couldn't afford for my wife to make the trip, too, so I piled the boys in the car, broke open my piggy bank (literally, I broke into my change jar to finance the trip) and off we drove from Tulsa to Dallas. We spent Saturday at Six Flags, stayed in a Motel 6 that night and ate a pizza in our room. The next morning, I took them to First Baptist Church of Dallas, Texas, because Zig Ziglar, the legendary motivational speaker, taught a Sunday school class there in the sanctuary. I had been listening to Zig's tapes and doing my best to stay positive about my situation. I really admired his style of speaking and knew that if given a chance I would love to be in that business, too. So I was thrilled to give my boys a chance to hear Zig. They had listened to his tapes in the car and while they were far from fans, they were willing to put up with Dad's request and go hear him in person.

At one point, Zig said, "You can be whatever you want to be, do whatever you want to do and have whatever you want to have as long as you believe in yourself." I didn't think much of that line at the time because I had heard it from him so many times that the words rolled off me pretty quickly. But my boys had never heard those words and they stuck in the mind of my younger son, Patrick.

A few weeks after that experience, we were taking our dogs, Elvis and Nixon, on a walk before bed. As we walked along, Patrick asked me a simple question: "Dad, what are you going to do?" I guess he had noticed that I wasn't doing very much. I didn't have a job. I couldn't figure out what my next step would be. I had sold most of our stuff. I was scrambling and it was obvious. So his question was a fair one. I said, "Patrick, I just don't know what I'm going to do." He said, "Dad, why don't you do what Zig said?" I will admit that at that point, I didn't have a clue about one thing Zig had said. When I asked him what Zig had said, he reminded me, "You can be whatever you want to be, do whatever you want to do and have whatever you want to have as long as you believe in yourself."

The words hit me in a way they never had before. I said to him, "Patrick, do you believe that?"

He said, "Sure, Dad, why don't you?" I didn't have an answer for his question. But I had the answer to my own situation. I had forgotten to believe in myself. At that very moment, my life changed forever. Zig's words that day in the church had little impact on me. But hearing those same words from my son made a complete difference in the rest of my life. And it all happened because I had decided to expose my boys to the words of a great speaker.

Note: I don't actually believe you can "be whatever you want to be, do whatever you want to do and have whatever you want to have." While that message sounds good and can be motivating for the naïve, it doesn't hold much water in the real world without action and hard work. In this case, a naïve six-year-old heard some inspiring words and was able to repeat them to his troubled father. I was inspired by my son's belief in me to take action, get back to work and accomplish something.

Here is another bit of proof of the influence of speakers that I will admit humbled me. I received this letter as I was writing this section of the book and I got its author's permission to include it.

Dear Larry,

I will try and make this short because I know you're busy. I will try and not kiss your ass too much either.

My name is Rob Hunter, I'm 23, and I live just outside of Toronto in Canada. Eleven years ago, when I was 12, I was going through some very typical adolescent problems—I don't want to say I was depressed, because everybody at that age is "depressed" at some point, but I didn't think too highly of myself, I was overweight, and I wasn't accomplishing as much as I could have.

Something very lucky happened to me around that time. My uncle, John Wyne, gave me your "Success Is Simple" tape set. To paraphrase something you said on that set about exposing young people to good speakers—I didn't understand it all, I certainly didn't appreciate it all at that age, but Larry, I have to tell you, it made a hell of a difference in shaping my adolescence and putting me on the path to become the man I am today.

I would be surprised if there is someone who has listened to that tape set more times than I have. It was a weekly ritual for at least a year or two. It encouraged me to start reading and listening to books and tapes on success that were designed for people beyond my young years—Zig Ziglar, Dale Carnegie, Robert Kiyosaki, and many others. Most importantly, the message that impacted me the most was—be yourself. Be proud of who you are and don't worry what other people think of you. Adults have heard lines like that a million times—but to a lost 12-year-old boy who wasn't overly confident about himself, it meant the world.

Larry, I don't want to brag, but I wanted to share with you a few of the things I have accomplished since being a "depressed" 12-year-old.

—I have been enjoying long-distance running for 10 years now, and have completed five marathons—my baby fat is long gone.

—When I was 14, I opened my own online sales company, selling videotapes and DVDs of rare sporting events to customers all over the world. I was making about $35,000 a year doing this part-time as a high school senior, and was able to pay my way through university as a result.

—I attended the top business school in Canada for my undergraduate years, and got involved with real estate investing during my time at school.

—Right now, I own four franchised Marble Slab ice cream stores throughout Ontario. Despite the recent turn in the economy, our sales have been fantastic. In all candor I anticipate being a millionaire within the next three years if things continue at the pace they have been going at.

Larry, I don't want to give you too much credit here, but I do strongly believe that my good fortune in receiving and listening to your tapes at such a young age played at least some role in all of the accomplishments I have enjoyed.

At the end of the day, I am the only one responsible for my success—but I'd be wrong if I didn't give you credit for getting me off to a good start. THANK YOU for being who you are and doing what you do—and CONGRATULATIONS on your own success and growth over the last few years.

All the best,
Rob Hunter

I like this letter. Why wouldn't I? It compliments me and makes me feel good about what I do. But that isn't really why I wanted to include it. I wanted to show you one more piece of evidence of what can happen when you get your kids to listen to great speakers. Start with someone who has a real message and delivers it with humor. Kids will put up with it if it's funny. And while they might complain about it, they will hear more of the message than you expect they will.

TRAVEL AND SOCIALIZATION.

Both of these are also critical teaching experiences in the life of your child. I dragged my kids to museums, old buildings, churches, to see the giant ball of twine, the World's Largest Free Outdoor Municipal Concrete Swimming Pool (in Garden City, Kansas) and more. I was like Clark Griswold in all of the National Lampoon's vacation movies. In fact, my wife and kids even jokingly referred to me as Clark Griswold, though I'm not sure it was really a joke. I believed in taking my kids places. We didn't always have a lot of money, but I usually didn't take them places that cost a lot of money. I took them to places we could easily drive to and pack a lunch and be back in our own beds the same night. I'll bet you there are dozens of things you could show your kids that are cheap and don't require overnight travel where you could spend time and learn something, too. Do an Internet search and find them. When I got more money and was speaking all over the country and even internationally, I took my kids with me whenever possible. Those travel experiences shaped the way they now view the world. They relate better to people from other countries and other cultures. They appreciate other foods and customs. And they know things they would never have learned otherwise.

Kids also need to be socialized. Take them to church if you are so inclined and teach them how to behave in that environment. Take them to the movies and teach them how to behave by sitting quietly and not talking during the show so everyone can enjoy the movie. Point out to them the inappropriate behavior of the other people in the theater and use the experience to teach a valuable lesson. Teach your kids how to behave in restaurants. I used to say that I would rather eat at a fine restaurant with my little boys than I would with most adults because my boys had better manners. That came from taking them to restaurants, explaining ahead of time what was expected of them and then rewarding or punishing the behavior they exhibited. After only a few restaurant visits, they were better behaved than most adults. Allow your children to attend dinner parties at your house, at least long enough to greet the people at the door with a smile, an introduction and a handshake. Then you can send them to their rooms or hire a babysitter or whatever so they won't be bored to death by your boring adult guests! The key is to expose your kids to situations in which they will learn how to act and behave. Again, kids would do better in all situations if they just knew better what was expected from them.

The entire second half of this book, called "What to Teach Your Kid," is about education. In this section I will cover the principles I believe every child must learn to become a responsible, productive adult. But we are not there yet, and these principles have to be given in order since they build on each other.

CHAPTER 5

DISCIPLINE

Most people automatically think I am now going to talk about punishment. Punishment is not the same as discipline. Discipline is a code of conduct by which you live your life. Punishment is what happens to you when you deviate from the code of conduct.

I am going to talk plenty about punishment, that's for sure. However, it is important to understand that much has to happen before you ever get to the point of punishing a child for her behavior.

CODE OF CONDUCT.

Establishing a code of conduct within a household is the responsibility of every parent. There has to be a set of rules by which all members of the family must live.

Businesses have a code of conduct.

The military has a code of conduct.

Even churches have a code of conduct.

Families must also have a code of conduct.

Sometimes the code of conduct is a written set of rules. Sometimes the code is an "understood" set of rules.

For instance, you would not think of walking into a beautiful cathedral and spitting on the floor or cussing. Refraining from that kind of behavior does not reflect your religious beliefs as much as it reflects your understanding that spitting and cussing in a church is inappropriate behavior. You simply know better.

When I was growing up, I knew how my mom and dad felt about cussing. My folks didn't cuss and I knew that I was not allowed to cuss. Therefore, it never even crossed my mind to do it in front of them. I understood that cussing was inappropriate behavior.

My boys knew that I would not tolerate disrespect of my wife, Rose Mary. My wife was their stepmother but they knew without me ever saying a word to them about her that I respected her and thus they had to respect her. Not once did they ever show any disrespect toward her. They might talk back to me when they were feeling particularly brave, and they would talk back to their own mother because they could get by with it, but they would never even think of talking back to Rose Mary. It wasn't a rule that was written down or even discussed; it was an unwritten rule that became a code of conduct within our family.

We had many things within our family that fell into our Winget Code of Conduct. We never lied to each other. We stuck up for each other. We never let anyone else put a family member down. We expected the best of each other. We believed in each other. The family union was based on honesty, integrity, love, responsibility, trust and humor.

Any code of conduct you establish will be challenged. That's what kids do—they challenge authority and push the limits. Prepare yourself by knowing that sometimes the code of conduct you establish will be broken. When that happens, punishment for breaking the rules should be imposed. But before I talk about punishment, let's look at two more elements of the family dynamic.

CHAIN OF COMMAND.

There is a chain of command within a family. It works like this and it is very simple to follow: parent, child. Period. See? I told you it wasn't complicated. The parent is in charge. The parent is the boss. The parent *should* be in control. The parent makes the decisions and the kid lives with the decisions. The parent is the leader, the manager, the decider, the one in charge . . . NOT the child. This is a simple chain of command that is in effect from the moment the child is born until he packs up and moves his stuff into his own place that he is paying for with his own money.

If there are two parents in the home, then the chain of command works like this: The one who is closest in proximity is in charge. Not the daddy or the mother, the one who is closest to the kid physically. One of the worst things you can do to a kid, in my opinion, is to abdicate your role and say something like, "You just wait 'til your father gets home!" The kid shouldn't have to wait; you as the parent who is standing there should deal with it right then. So many great opportunities for discipline are lost by asking the kid to wait until later. The same goes for the father who says, "Ask your mother." No, your kid asked you; be a man, be the father and deal with the issue!

MY ROOF—MY RULES.

Somehow this idea became passé. It shouldn't have. If I feed you, clothe you and let you live in my house, then you live by the rules I establish. Those rules exist to protect you and take care of you. I have made those rules because I love you.

When you are of legal age and can feed yourself, clothe yourself and provide your own shelter out of your own earnings, then you can establish your own rules to live by.

What's wrong with that? It's fair. It makes perfect sense, it is grounded in love, caring and respect and it reinforces the chain of command.

BECAUSE I SAID SO.

Didn't you hate that line when you heard it from your parents? I know I always did. I wanted an answer and an explanation for everything. I wanted to know why I couldn't go out with my friends. I wanted to know why they got to do things and I didn't get to do those same things. I wanted answers.

Sometimes I got them. But many times I heard that line that I know you also heard from your parents: "Because I said so."

Know what? It's a good line. Not every issue needs to be explained, discussed or debated. Sometimes, the appropriate answer simply is "Because I said so."

> *Your family is a kingdom, not a democracy.*

Your decisions about your child's welfare are not up for a vote.

Yes, you will take some lip from your kids over it. You will hear things like, "You don't love me." The appropriate response is, "Yes, I love you enough to make sure that I always do my best to take care of you. I love you enough to take care of you, look out for you, protect you and keep you safe."

Will your kids hate you for punishing them? Of course they will—but not for long. You may even hear the words "I hate you." In fact, that might be an indicator that you are doing a good job as a parent. If your kid doesn't hate you for imposing your will, then chances are you aren't doing much of a job imposing your will. When hearing these words from their little darling, many parents will crumble and say they are sorry. Big mistake. Never apologize to your child for wanting the best for her. Never apologize to your child when she is the one who broke the rules. You only enforced the rules. So don't crumble when little Jennie screams, "I hate you!" She'll get over it. Don't retaliate either by screaming back, "I hate you, too!" I have seen this happen. Great, now we have two emotional out-of-control babies. Let your kid scream and gripe and get it out of her system. Then make her apologize to you for saying she hates you or for screaming at you. Let her know that you have no intention of tolerating both her bad behavior and her disrespect. Be the bad guy when the situation calls for it. Remember, you are the parent; it's your job to be the bad guy. She will respect you for it in the long run.

Principles for Handling Conflict with Your Kid

Listen to your child's explanation of his behavior.

Explain your decision and then let him know that your decision is final and it is up to him to live with it.

Don't argue with your child. There is no need to defend your position.

Keep your cool even though he has lost his.

Never inflict punishment when you are angry.

Never apologize for having rules or for enforcing those rules.

Move on. Once the decision is made, it isn't up for discussion. There is no reason to keep the emotions of the moment alive by rehashing the issue.

BEHAVIOR CANNOT BE IGNORED.

Too many parents seem to live by the idea that if you ignore it, it will go away. That might work with a bear in the woods, but it won't work with bad behavior. All bad behavior must be recognized and dealt with in order to establish the habit of good behavior.

What gets rewarded gets done. I wrote about that principle in my book *It's Called Work for a Reason!* regarding employees. In the workplace, any behavior that is rewarded will be repeated. The key is to recognize the behaviors you would like to see repeated and reward them. This is a very simple and effective approach for molding behavior.

It works in the workplace with employees and it works at home with kids. Catch your kid doing the right thing and reward her for it, and that behavior will be repeated. Do it often enough and the behavior will become a habit. But that means that you have to be paying attention to all of the behaviors your kid exhibits.

This principle works with good behavior and it works with bad behavior. That's right, bad behavior will be repeated as long as it is rewarded. Now your immediate response is probably, "Who would reward bad behavior?" Nearly every parent rewards bad behavior every single day. How do I know? There is so much bad behavior. If the bad behavior wasn't rewarded it would cease to exist. Just look around at all the bad behavior and know that somewhere that behavior is being rewarded, otherwise it would go away.

Your kid throws a tantrum because he doesn't get his way. Why is the kid throwing the tantrum? To get your attention. He falls on the ground and screams and cries and you grab him up and yell at him and scold him and threaten him. You may even give in to his demands and let him have what he wants in order to get him to stop his bad behavior. Bingo! He wins. You have rewarded the behavior. Whether you give in or not, the minute he got your attention, which is all he wanted by throwing the tantrum in the first place, he won. You rewarded the behavior and you taught him a valuable lesson: If I throw a tantrum, I'll get Mama's attention. If I scream and cry, Daddy will give in. Because you taught this lesson to your child, you can expect to see it repeated often. That little darling of yours is going to throw a tantrum every time he doesn't get his way because when he does, he becomes the center of attention. The minute that doesn't work any longer, that behavior will stop. So next time you tell your kid no and he throws himself on the floor, walk away and don't pay any attention to him. Is that hard to do? It can be. But if you want to alter the behavior, you need to remove the reward. No reward—no behavior.

However, remember what I covered in the communications section. Sometimes kids act inappropriately because they have not been *shown* the appropriate way to act. Ask yourself: Has the appropriate behavior been explained? Demonstrated? Enforced? Or did I just expect my child to know how to behave in every situation? Granted, you can't teach every appropriate behavior ahead of time because you don't know every situation that will come up, but good behavior that is taught, explained, demonstrated and enforced will spill over into other new situations.

But don't expect your child to be a mind reader. And don't expect your child to demonstrate the correct behavior when you continually act as a role model for bad behavior.

DISCIPLINE IN THE REAL WORLD.

Kids require discipline at home. They have to learn what is allowed and what isn't. They have to learn what the boundaries are at home in order to be able to handle the boundaries put on them by the rest of the world. If your kid can't handle the laws of your household, how will she react to the laws of the land? If your kid isn't able to handle discipline as a child at home, how will she handle discipline at school? Or as an adult in a work environment? Answer: She won't. Ill-behaved children who abuse or disrespect the authority of their parents will disrespect the authority of their teachers and their bosses. If you don't impose and enforce compliance with your wishes as a parent you are dooming your child's future at school and ruining her chances of being productive in the real world.

CHAPTER 6

PUNISHMENT

Woo-hoo! We've reached the part that most parents feel is the most time-consuming part of parenting. Excited? Why? Is it because you see punishment as your biggest parenting job?

If you are one of those parents who honestly believe that the bulk of your parenting has to be consumed by punishing your kids, then you are sadly mistaken. When you have performed all of the other elements of parenting well, punishment will be the smallest part of your parenting role.

Parenting is primarily about the other elements I have talked about: communication, involvement, education and discipline. Punishment is what happens when you have a breakdown with one of the other elements. When you have failed in one of these other areas, your kid will exhibit bad behavior and punishment may be required. Sometimes, you will have done it all right and your kid will still do wrong simply because he is a kid. At those times, you will need to impose some punishment.

You might also be one of those parents who has a hard time with punishment and believes in letting your children behave any way they want with no correction. That is certainly your choice, because they are your children. But when they end up in prison, in bad relationships, broke, on drugs, undisciplined, disrespectful, jobless, homeless, selfish, bad-mannered and more, just remember that your kids are your own fault! You allowed them to become irresponsible adults because you were an irresponsible parent. You have hurt your kids because you didn't inflict punishment when it was necessary.

Many parents also think that their kid will end up not loving them because of the punishment. Wrong. You kid will love you more if you punish them. You won't lose his love, but you will lose his respect if you don't enforce punishments. Your children won't respect you if you are a pushover.

I know that enforcing punishment is one of the toughest parts of being a loving parent. Some parents dread the confrontation and hate the idea of punishing their child. But it is a necessary part of parenting. The key is to always remember that when all of the other elements of parenting are done well, the time you spend punishing will be kept to a minimum.

DIFFERENT KIDS REQUIRE DIFFERENT PUNISHMENTS.

My mother could snap her fingers and I knew I had better straighten up. We would be in church on Sunday morning and I would be across the church sitting with my friends and I could hear her fingers snap and I knew I needed to be quiet and pretend to listen. I also knew if I heard those fingers pop a second time, I was toast when I got home. One snap of the fingers was all the warning I needed to alter my behavior. I'll bet as you look back at your own childhood that you can remember some signal that was the line you knew you shouldn't cross. I also am betting that if you had brothers and sisters, it was different for each of you.

My boys were not perfect little boys. They pushed every boundary and every button I had. At times, they were little monsters requiring a heavy hand to keep them from killing each other and from growing up to become felons.

With Patrick, my younger kid, I could have spanked him until both my arm and his butt fell off and it still would not have changed his behavior. He might have cried over it, but little else would change. Instead, Patrick responded better to being talked to. You could use words to make him realize that he had messed up and should change his behavior. I could make him cry, admit he was wrong and get him to apologize all with a few short minutes of quiet conversation.

On the other hand, Tyler didn't really respond to much of anything. When he messed up, he was normally well aware he had done so and was willing to accept any punishment I decided on. He did stop me once when I was having a serious talk with him about his behavior and said, "Dad, why don't you just spank me? I don't really want a seminar." Therefore, I realized that the best punishment was a good talking-to simply because he hated it so much.

So does this mean I am pro-talking and against spanking? Hardly. I think a good spanking is a great way to punish a kid. Sometimes. Not often, but sometimes. My son Tyler says that he can remember actually being spanked by me only one time. I think I probably did it more than once, but he can remember only one time. Guess it was a good one that had a lasting effect since he still remembers it!

I know there is a huge segment of society that is totally against spanking. That's fine. It's your kid. You get to decide what works and what doesn't work. The key is, it really has to work.

There are people who call spanking child abuse. No, it isn't. It could be if you get carried away and do it when you are angry, emotional or out of control. However, no punishment should be carried out when that is your mental state. Certainly, no physical punishment should ever be administered when you are angry. Other than that, however, it is my opinion that not utilizing any effective tool to punish your child is shirking your parental duty.

There are also people who believe "hitting" your child teaches them to hit. Sorry, I can't get there from here. I don't believe you teach your kids it is okay to hit other people when you effectively use spanking to alter behavior.

Personally, I think that a well-placed swat on the butt is an effective means of altering behavior. Notice what I just said: a well-placed swat on the butt. The butt is where you spank. Not the arm. Not the face. To slap a kid is totally uncalled for and anyone who does it should be ashamed. I have also witnessed parents pinching their kid. Disgusting!

The butt is covered with plenty of meat to absorb a swat. Notice again that I said swat. You don't have to bare their butt and go to town on them to get your point across. Besides, you spank to alter behavior, not to hurt the child. That is the goal of all punishment: to alter behavior, nothing more. Certainly, you shouldn't leave a mark or a bruise. You just need to give them a firm, well-placed swat on the hiney to make sure you have their attention.

Spanking is an effective tool with some kids. In fact, I have yet to see a kid who couldn't benefit from the effective use of a good spanking from time to time. When I see a kid running around a restaurant yelling, screaming and making all of the other diners miserable, I know that one well-placed swat on his butt would fix that. Of course, a little parental counseling is also in order when something like that occurs. The problem with spanking is that it is overused. It is also the easiest form of punishment to administer. Which is probably the reason it is overused. That is actually the problem with any form of punishment. Any single form of punishment loses its effectiveness when it is the only form used. Spanking is just one tool. So is talking. So is grounding.

It is really all about when to use the appropriate tool. You can't use one tool all the time or it loses its effectiveness. Just like you can't yell all the time. Or talk all the time. Or ground your kid all the time. You have to mix it up. You have to use all of the tools in your parenting toolbox.

WHAT DOES YOUR TOOLBOX LOOK LIKE?

There are lots of great parenting books out there that will tell you exactly what to do in every imaginable situation. From potty training to picky eating to talking back, you will get the answers. Some of them are excellent. Of course, some of them aren't worth the paper they are written on, but that applies to every genre of how-to book out there.

I wish many of these books had been around when I had little kids so I would have had a few more tools in my parenting toolbox. I believe that you can't have too many tools . . . ever! I like tools. It's a guy thing! And I love that old saying "If your only tool is a hammer, all of your problems look like a nail." My problems cannot always be solved with just a hammer; therefore I want other tools. So I have a big toolbox.

When you are raising a kid, there is a wide variety of problems that can come up and one tool just won't fit every situation. Some parents only have one tool in their toolbox. They always spank or they always give "time out" or they nag or ground their child. No matter what inappropriate behavior they witness, they pull out that one tool and use it for every situation. That just doesn't work.

In order to know which tool works best for a situation, you have to know your kid. When a child is small, a swat on the butt may work well. When they get older, the tools must become more sophisticated: grounding, taking away the car, not allowing them to go someplace they want to go, cutting down on their allowance, and any other reasonable alternative that makes them feel the pain of their mistakes.

Let me give you one tool to drop completely from your toolbox: threatening.

DON'T THREATEN YOUR KID.

"Do you want me to leave you here? I am going to leave you here if you don't behave." I hear this stuff all the time and I bet you do, too. Why would you want to instill the fear of abandonment in your child? And do you really expect your child to say, "Sure, leave me here"? Though as I look at some parents, I think the kid would have a better chance if they did.

How about this one? "Do you want me to call the police? I'll have the police come get you if you don't behave!" Again, why would you want to instill fear of the police in your children? Police are your child's friends!

Or how about this one? "Don't make me take you outside!" Although I will admit this one is effective. Your kids do not want you to take them outside. Outside, there are no witnesses!

Remember the old line "Is that a threat or a promise?" That is what you want to do with your kids. Don't threaten them; promise them. If you say something is going to happen, then make sure it happens. I remember when I was about six years old my parents took the whole family on a two-week vacation. It was a big deal, as we just didn't do that kind of thing. On the first day of the vacation, I did something wrong. I don't remember what it was, but I remember what happened as a result of doing it. On day one after I messed up, my dad told me, "When we get back home, you are going to get a spanking." I thought to myself, "I am golden. That is two weeks away and he will forget." We then had a great two weeks of vacation. And the minute we pulled into the driveway and parked the car, my dad pulled me aside and told me to wait for him in the barn. I asked why and he reminded me that he had promised me a spanking when we got home and now we were home. Cruel? It sure seemed like it to me. But as I look back, while it seems pretty harsh, it taught me a valuable lesson in keeping your word to your child. As a result of that experience, when I became a father, I always kept my word to my boys. If I promised to issue some form of punishment, I kept my word. Never give your word unless you plan on keeping it.

NO SCAPEGOATS.

Years ago, I was driving my car with some friends in the backseat. Their three-year-old daughter was behaving badly, jumping up and down and screaming at the top of her lungs. I was truly about to lose it. The father just sat there like nothing was going on. The mother finally said to her daughter, "Jessica, you shouldn't be acting like that because it makes Larry nervous." I stopped the car and said, "No, she shouldn't be acting like that because it is inappropriate! It has nothing to do with me and don't bring me into this. Instead, control your child." They stopped being our friends. I never really missed them much.

We had some other friends over recently for dinner. They told their little boy to eat the dinner because Larry would be mad at him if he didn't. I immediately told the little boy that wasn't true, Larry would not be mad at him. I then told the parents to leave me out of the discussion when it came to getting their son to eat dinner. It wasn't fair to me or the kid.

The father said, "Whatever works!" No. It's not whatever works. It's about using the right tool for the job. Parents who resort to the "whatever works" approach are lazy parents.

Don't use someone else as an excuse for your child's behavior.

Larry's Rules for Punishing Your Kid

1. Consistency. If it is wrong today, it will be wrong tomorrow. Wrong is wrong every time and must be dealt with whether you are tired, frustrated or busy. There may not be time to run to the grocery store but there must always be time to deal with inappropriate behavior.
2. Don't punish when you are angry. This one is challenging but try hard! Kids can drive you crazy and frustrate you beyond all rational thinking, and you will lose your temper. However, don't punish while you are in that emotional state as you may end up regretting what you've done.

    My all-time worst parenting moment was when my son Tyler threw a ball over the neighbor's fence and I told him to go get it. The yard had two barking dogs in it and he was afraid of them and didn't want to climb the fence to go get the ball. I got mad. I yelled, threatened, screamed and made a complete ass of myself while belittling him until he cried and crawled over the fence. He was afraid and trembling and the instant he started over the fence I regretted it all. The dogs were harmless and getting the ball was not a problem. But the afternoon was ruined and I had ruined it with my anger. I apologized to Tyler and have felt bad about my behavior on that day for over twenty years. I mentioned it not long ago to Tyler and he didn't even remember the incident. I never forgot it. That was the moment that taught me to cool down before administering any kind of punishment.

Get mad if anger is an appropriate response to the offense, but wait to administer the punishment. Just like in a court of law, there is a wait time between being found guilty of a crime and when the sentence is passed down. You need a wait time, too, in order to cool off and administer punishment that is appropriate and will teach the lesson you want to teach.

3. Make the punishment fit the crime. To ground a kid for a week because they were playing and spilled the milk is ridiculous and it's overreacting. That's why you need to wait and cool down until you are ready to consider the appropriate punishment. This also relates to my toolbox example; you can't spank a kid for every infraction. Think before punishing and use the appropriate tool— one that fits the crime.

4. Listen to your kid's side of the story. This shows you respect your child and are a reasonable person regardless of the situation. This is important behavior to model for your child. Plus, it allows you

to get to the heart of the bad behavior to see what the motivation was behind it. That way you can deal with more than just the bad behavior itself. And it allows you time to consider the punishment you are going to inflict.

5. Make the punishment about the behavior—not the person. When your child does something bad, it doesn't mean he is a bad kid, it means he did a bad thing. Don't belittle him and call him a bad person. Instead, deal with the behavior.

6. Watch your mouth. That's right, be careful of what you say. Words said in anger to a child are going to be hard to take back. Remember, this is your child and you love him, even though you may hate what he has just done. Your goal is to maintain a relationship with your child that will last a lifetime. Too often that relationship is damaged by one stupid thing you say while you are mad.

7. Remember whose side you are on and remind your kid of that, too. You are on your kid's side. You ultimately want to issue a punishment that will help him to learn and exhibit appropriate behavior. The goal is for your child to become a better person. Be sure the punishment includes a lesson that does that.

8. Don't apologize for punishing your child. You are the parent. The authority figure. The person in charge. The adult. You know best. You laid out the rules and your child broke them. Which means you have nothing to apologize for when inflicting an appropriate, meaningful, well-thought-out punishment.

Punishment is something you do *for* the child, not *to* the child.

THE BEST NEWS OF ALL.

They grow out of it.

That is about the best news I can give you about many of the things your kids will do that are going to drive you crazy. They will grow out of it. Not everything, that's for sure. But a lot of it. Does that mean you should just ignore the behavior and they will grow out of it without your help or punishment? Absolutely not. It just means that eventually, your work will take hold and they will get it. It might also mean that age won out over their rebellious spirit and they won't feel the need to push as much any longer. It might also mean that they are just giving up one form of bad behavior so they can take on another. Oh well, at least you will have something new to work on.

My son Tyler looks back now at the way he was when he was fifteen and says, "Dad, I would have killed me!" Believe me when I say there were many times that I wanted to do just that. I once told him that there was only one cure for our relationship: euthanasia. I seriously wanted to just put him to sleep—at least for a while.

At one point when Tyler was at the peak of his rebellious teenage years, he stood up to me and said he didn't have to do what I told him to do because he was bigger than I was. I responded to him with, "Yeah, you are bigger, but I'm smarter, I'm meaner, I have all the money and I know where you sleep!" He thought about it and realized I was right and backed way down.

I remember myself at the age of sixteen when I did the same thing to my dad. I wasn't ever bigger than my dad but I was at the age when I thought I knew everything. He and I got into it over something and I mouthed off (I've always been good at that) and he said he was going to whip me. Not literally with a whip, but he was using an Oklahoma expression that meant I was going to feel the pain of my mistake, administered with his belt across my butt. I told him I was too big to get a whipping. He went on to prove that I wasn't. That was the last time he ever whipped me. I didn't get smarter or less mouthy but I never challenged my dad's authority like that again. I realized that at any age, it wasn't worth it.

Give your kid a chance to spread his wings, be rebellious and feel the pain of his consequences. It's good for him and it's a test for you to prove how much you care about him by bothering to punish inappropriate behavior.

And then realize that as he grows older and more comfortable with who he is, what he believes and what you believe, his behavior will settle into a much more acceptable place.

SECTION THREE
WHAT TO TEACH YOUR KIDS

Before I even presume to tell you what you should teach your kid, let me make it clear that these are my personal opinions about what you should teach your kid. You can teach your kid whatever you want; after all, it's *your* kid. And because it's your kid, you don't even have to teach her a damn thing if you don't want to. I want to be clear about that. You can choose to let her learn by accident, hit or miss, from experience or observation or any other method you choose. You can even read this section on what I think your kid should be taught and say to yourself, "No way am I going to teach my kid any of that!" Fine. Again, it's your kid.

But be aware that it isn't always about you. It's about your kid. You can teach your kid only what you are comfortable with him knowing, but realize that you may leave him ill-prepared to face the world. You have to go beyond teaching your kid what you want him to know and move over to teaching your kid what he needs to know to be happy, productive and prosperous.

I am about to give you all of the things I believe your kid needs to know in order to become the kind of adult you want her to be. I came up with this list of things I think your kid needs to be taught based on observing what is wrong in society today.

After studying what is happening in the world, I determined that most of it could have been avoided if we had just taught our kids differently. I looked at our economic mess, our business problems, our health issues, our governmental problems . . . every kind of problem I could come up with and realized that these problems are the result of a lack of learning. Ignorance (a lack of knowledge) and stupidity (not applying the knowledge you have) are to blame. Therefore, I have created a list of things that we should all teach our kids so we can avoid adding to these problems in the future.

We all tend to teach our kids what we want them to know based on our own biases, beliefs and prejudices. In some cases, we teach our kids only what we are comfortable with them knowing. While this is natural and somewhat to be expected, it is a mistake. Our own vision of the world may be skewed in such a way that we cheat our kids of the total experience.

Many parents pass on their fears without even realizing it. When I met my wife, she was terrified of thunderstorms, which amazed me because I never had been afraid of a storm. Growing up in Oklahoma, I would stand in my yard with my dad and watch the tornadoes approach with fascination, but never fear. How did we have such different views of thunderstorms? Because of the influence and teaching of our parents. My dad was fascinated; her mother was terrified. Passing down a fear of thunderstorms to your children is not really that big of a deal. Passing down your fear of success, wealth, vegetables, exercise, people of a different color, travel, sushi or other truly good things can be. You may not like something but there is no reason to pass that on to your kid.

When teaching your kids what they need to know, it is important to go beyond what you are comfortable with. You have to move past your own fears and prejudices so you can free your kids from your past. It's important not to saddle your kids with your history.

A BACKWARD APPROACH.

If you want to know how to be successful, find out what successful people are doing, then repeat that behavior. That principle can't be beat. It works every time and in every area of life. It is a formula that just can't be argued with and no one can disprove that it is effective. It's been around forever and is a guaranteed formula for success.

It's how you get rich: Duplicate the behavior of rich people. It's how you run a better business: Find out what successful businesspeople do in their business and duplicate it in your own business. It is how you live healthfully: Find out what healthy people do and duplicate it in your own life. The same principle applies to parenting: Find out what successful parents do and duplicate it.

It is simple to find out what rich people, successful people, healthy people and good parents do. The information you are looking for is everywhere. The information is contained in books. It's on video and audio and even on television. The information has been around for years and yet for the most part, our behavior has not changed all that much. Why? The idea is so simple. That is why it gets either overlooked or ignored. And some people simply don't learn from good examples. Therefore, I want you to completely reverse your thinking and take a backward approach.

If you want to be stupid, find out what stupid people do, duplicate it and you will end up stupid. If you want to be broke, discover what broke people do, duplicate it and you will end up broke. Want to be fat? If you are fat you must want to be, because you are doing what fat people do. Want to raise stupid, selfish, irresponsible kids? Then do what the parents of stupid, selfish, irresponsible kids do and you will indeed end up with horrible children.

Watch some reality television for one week and you can learn everything you need to learn about what it takes to parent the wrong way.

Watch these television shows (once):

The Real Housewives of Orange County

The Real Housewives of New York City

The Real Housewives of New Jersey

The Real Housewives of Atlanta

Keeping Up with the Kardashians

Paris Hilton's My New BFF

Jerry Springer

The Simple Life

Supernanny

Nanny 911

Wife Swap

Trading Spouses

My Super Sweet Sixteen

The Bad Girls Club

Charm School

I know that a couple of these shows are no longer aired but chances are you have seen them at least once. Even if all of these shows go off the air, a dozen more similar shows will replace them. Shows that display the train wreck our society has become by showing people at their worst are always going to be popular. Each of these shows is a prime example of how not to raise your kid. So if you ever want to know what not to do, turn on the television and tune in for an evening of bad parenting.

Then go to the next level with it. Watch *The Bachelor* or *The Bachelorette*. What do these shows have to do with parenting? Would you be proud of your son or daughter parading his or her stupidity on national television in order to snag a lifelong spouse? I would be ashamed if my daughter ever did any of that crap in order to end up with some wannabe celebrity who had to resort to a television show to find love. Not fair to these fine upstanding bachelors? After all, they are doctors and military officers and one was even a single father! Too bad. No man who is serious about finding real love with a real woman would ever go on a television show like *The Bachelor* to find the mother of his children. These guys are not interested in finding love; they are interested in finding "celebrity." They are idiots.

Then turn the station over to what your kid watches. Watch one episode of *A Shot at Love with Tila Tequila* and *Flavor of Love* with Flavor Flav and *Rock of Love with Bret Michaels*. Funny how each of these shows uses the word *love* and yet I don't see any love going on. I see a lot of stupidity going on, but no love. Your kids watch this stuff and are led to believe that the way you attract a long, deep, meaningful relationship is to act like either a complete idiot or a complete whore on national television.

Don't get too upset by your kid watching these shows because you have already set the example by watching your slightly toned-down version of the same. That's right, *The Bachelor* is just a dressed-up version of *Rock of Love*. And Bret Michaels, without the guy-liner and the do-rag, is no better or worse than the guy in the suit on *The Bachelor*. In fact, he is actually more honest. He's in it for the publicity and the booty and he doesn't hide that fact.

All of these reality shows are meant to be entertainment. And in some loose, sad, sick sense of the word, they are entertaining. However, like it or not, we all learn from what we watch on television—we just don't always learn the right thing. We don't expect the shows we watch to teach us lessons, but it happens. If nothing else, we become desensitized to moronic behavior, and that turns out to be the lesson we have learned.

In our voyeuristic, star-struck society we make television characters our role models. Our kids believe that if they see a kid on television disrespecting his parents or teachers or authority or society in general then it must be cool. It isn't. This misperception must be addressed by parents. These shows should not be used to model behavior—if anything, they should be used as an example of what *not* to do.

The moral of this story? If you aren't willing to learn from people who are doing it right, then at least learn from people who are doing it wrong.

CHAPTER 7

THE MOST IMPORTANT LESSONS FOR PARENTS TO TEACH THEIR KIDS (AND THE MOST IMPORTANT THINGS THEY DON'T)

TEACH THE RIGHT STUFF.

What are the lessons you are going to teach your kids? Have you decided what they are, how you are going to teach them and when you are going to start? Like it or not, aware of it or not, you are teaching your kids lessons every day that will stick with them for a lifetime. It's time to start being more deliberate about teaching the lessons you want them to learn.

The principles I have based my life on began as lessons I learned from my parents. Some of those lessons are the basis for the principles I teach in all my books.

Things my parents taught me:

Smile, it don't cost nothing. (Bad grammar, good lesson.)

Two ears, one mouth: Listen twice as much as you talk.

When a man hires you to work, you work. He's the boss and you do what he says whether you like it or not. That's how you get paid.

When you give your word, you keep it no matter what. A man is only as good as his word.

Never let anyone disrespect your mother.

Never hit a girl.

Hold the door for people—men and women alike. It's polite.

Be nice to old people; you will be old, too, someday.

Say "please" and "thank you." And always say "sir" and "ma'am."

Look people in the eye when you talk to them.

Stand up for yourself. Better to nurse a bloody nose than your dignity.

Be good to animals.

A deal is a deal.

You can't borrow your way out of debt or spend your way out of debt. I once asked my dad, "So how do you get out of debt?" He said, "You have to work harder and pay your way out."

Share with people who don't have as much as you do. And never forget that no matter how little you have, there is always someone who has less.

If you borrow something, return it in better condition than when you got it.

My dad taught me how to shake hands, how to use a hammer and other tools, how to make a fire in the woods and how to make my bed. And he taught me how to clean a fish, plant a garden and make a pot of coffee.

When walking with a girl, walk on the side toward the street.

When going up the stairs with a woman, follow her up the stairs in case she falls.

You can always do a little more than you think you can.

When shopping, look with your eyes, not with your hands.

Read something every night before you go to bed.

WHAT IS THE SINGLE BEST THING YOUR PARENTS TAUGHT YOU?

I asked this question of my Facebook friends and got hundreds of responses. I want to share a few of these with you.

If you want to pass, go to class. If you want an A, study every day." My dad used to say this to me all the time—from a pretty young age. I applied it pretty well throughout my academic career and as I have gotten older I realize that this idea applies to everything I do in my life. If you want to get by, you show up, sign the attendance sheet, sit in the back and do the minimum amount of work required. You'll get a C and that will be fine. However, if you want to be successful, to earn the A, you have to put in the effort. You can't just show up and expect things to be handed to you. You have to put in the work and the time and maybe a little brown-nosing and yes, even the sweat, to get what you want, whether it's a perfect GPA or a promotion or weight loss. We all choose to get by or choose to be great—the difference is in the effort we make.

—Elaina M. Osteen

The single best thing my parents taught me was that there was nothing out there that I couldn't learn, do or become. I was capable of doing whatever I wanted in life and they supported me, and continue to support me, in everything I do. I saw early on that wasn't the way things were done in a lot of my friends' homes.

—Skip Kanester

"Look it up, William!" That was always my mother's answer. No matter how simple or complicated the question, I was always directed to look up the answer. That lesson has served me well as I've made my way through this thing called life. And now, I diligently pass it on to my son with this other bit, "It's not what you know, it's do you know how to find the answer to what you don't know?" My soon to be thirteen-year-old has become a master of the Internet search engines!

—Bill Parry

The only two helping hands you will ever have are attached to the ends of your arms. Don't expect other people to pick up your pieces.

—Marsha Petrie Sue

If you mess up, apologize, see how you can fix it, don't repeat the action, and carry on; don't dwell on it.

—Sara Reese

The single best thing my parents ever taught me was to get to know someone before you judge them. I say that because I remember growing up, I had a friend who would run away from me whenever she saw her mother coming. She finally told me that she ran away because her mother did not want her daughter to play with me because she hated my race. Granted, I was a child and knew nothing of racism, but I stopped being friends with the girl in question because I didn't want her to feel like she had to hide the fact that she was my friend.

—Shavon Green

To be polite, respectful and kind (saying "please," "thank you," "yes"—instead of "yeah"—"sir" and "ma'am" go a long way) and to SMILE.

—Pam Hunter

That no matter what you do in life, do something. It will always be better than doing nothing. Even from our biggest mistakes we can learn, and if you do not try, you will never know. AND, love what you do for a living and the money will follow.

—William Bradley

A little hard work never killed anyone.

—Kevin Vinicombe

No one owes you anything. You must work for what you want and anything worth having is worth working for.

—Stan Gaither

If you fail, it is your fault! You cannot place blame on anyone else.

—Tracy Mallary

The single best thing my parents taught me was to respect my elders. The wisdom I gained from spending time with and listening to them has been an irreplaceable, positive factor in my life.

—Jan Pitchford

If you don't have time to do it right, how will you ever find time to do it over?

—John Keuffer

Do the best you can in everything you do without expecting a special reward. Giving it all is the reward.

—Eric Chung

The single best thing my parents ever taught me was that if I wanted something, like a new bicycle, I could have it. All I had to do was go out and mow some lawns or work at the grocery store, save my money, and I could buy the bicycle or anything else I wanted. Don't get me wrong, they were generous and gave me everything I needed and some of what I wanted. But the lesson was clear: If you work, then you get all the things you want.

—Joe Calloway

Take responsibility for your actions, NO MATTER WHAT.

—Michelle Cary Palmer

Be polite, respectful and always keep your word.

—Aunty Lynn

Don't be afraid to do what's needed to get through tough times.

—Steve Wignall

Integrity.

—Lauren Starsiak Fisher

The single best thing my parents ever taught me was to live within my means.

—Yana Donovan

The discipline to spend much less than I earn.

—Rick Francis

My mom taught me about the Golden Rule, which still serves me well.

—Greg Leavelle

To be strong and believe in my own ability to make the right decision and if not, to be strong enough to deal with the consequences.

—Tina Rosengren

You have to be willing to accept responsibility for yourself and your actions, including your failures.

—Nancy Miciag

It doesn't cost a thing to be friendly, and it's no reflection on me if the other guy doesn't feel like being friendly back. There are always more hands to shake in the world, and many of them are willing.

—Sharon Lensky

Kindness.

—Kim Wright

My dad taught me that any bad moment, outside of serious illness or death, will pass. He taught me to remember that whatever was breaking my heart or worrying me to death last year was something I was completely over now and probably couldn't even remember.

—Isabelle Baker

The most important thing my parents ever taught me was that you can lose everything you own, but no one can take away your education.

—Richard McAroy

Whatever you do, do it to the best of your ability.

—Aimee Newman

My father had a saying, "Non illigitamus carborundum." That is Latin for "Don't let the bastards get you down."

—Stephanie Menning

Engage brain before mouth.

—Ira Leary

THE WINGET BOYS WEIGH IN.

I asked my sons to weigh in on what they learned growing up with me as their father. They get asked that question quite a bit. Nearly every time they travel with me, someone comes up and asks what it was like growing up with Larry Winget as their dad. People want to know if I was different as a father than what they have witnessed onstage or on television or in my books. They always smile and say something like, "That's how he is all the time." Which is a great compliment, in my opinion. I wanted them to tell all of you, with absolutely no influence from me, what they learned from me as their dad. Here are their responses.

Tyler Winget, Police Officer, Phoenix, Arizona

My dad asked me to write a page in his new book. I am not a writer. That being said I found this to be a great opportunity to prove that my dad practices what he preaches!

The number one thing my dad taught me growing up is RESPONSIBILITY!

My dad taught me that if I messed up . . . I should just admit it. I never got spanked for messing up. I got spanked for lying about it. And I can only remember one occasion where he turned my rear end red. My brother, on the other hand, was another story.

When I was eighteen I was horrible. I was so horrible that I had to leave home to try to figure things out. So I joined the United States Army. Hands-down the best decision I have ever made. My dad supported me 100 percent. Of course there wasn't a major war going on in 1996. Shortly after arriving at my first duty station I was given the honor of participating in a ceremony for a senator visiting our base. My job in the ceremony was to shoot a 75 mm cannon during the 21-gun salute. I would stand behind the breach of the cannon holding on to a lanyard. My attention focused only on my squad leader standing about five yards in front of me. When my boss pointed at me, I had to jerk that lanyard with everything I had and then the loader would load another round and I would prepare to be pointed at again. Everything had to be perfect. There were seven cannon crews and I was in the first. They even lined up the cannons with string. I would be the first to shoot and start the whole thing off. This was quite an honor for an E-2 (private second class). We practiced for probably a month straight. We practiced morning, noon and night. We practiced in the rain, sleet and snow. We were going to make our unit proud and perform a perfect 21-gun salute. The night before the ceremony I polished my boots for hours. I would rub cotton balls soaked in water over my boots until I could see myself in the shine. I blew through two cans of starch on my uniform! That thing would stand up on its own! This ceremony was probably the biggest deal I had been involved in thus far in my military career. I wasn't nervous though. We had practiced until it wasn't cool anymore. We practiced until it was second nature. We even practiced what to do if one of the cannons didn't go off. These were Vietnam-era cannons reconfigured to shoot only blanks for ceremonies like this. Sometimes the firing pin would break and they wouldn't go off. Sometimes if the guy pulling the lanyard didn't pull hard enough the cannon wouldn't go off. When your squad leader pointed at you and your cannon didn't go off he folded his arms in front of him and put his head down, a signal to the rest of the cannons that his crew would be skipped. This was embarrassing if it happened to you. All of the other guys pulling the lanyards would laugh and make fun of you. You didn't want this to be you.

The morning of the ceremony I was looking sharp. I looked like one of the recruiting posters. When we got to the parade grounds where the ceremony was being held I couldn't believe how many people were there. There were at least four or five hundred people sitting in the bleachers. We got our cannons all lined up with the string and we were told to take our places. The national anthem played and we all stood at attention giving our most crisp salute. Then came time for the 21-gun salute. We were given the command to take our positions and get ready. My attention focused on my squad leader, waiting for his hand to drop. When his hand dropped it was like slow motion. I pulled the lanyard and nothing happened. The worst feeling was watching my squad leader fold his hands and put his head down. I just stood there as if nothing happened like I was trained. All the other cannon crews picked up the slack and nobody in the crowd knew the difference. While the other cannons fired I was thinking about what could have gone wrong. I had checked the breach like we always did before the ceremony. The firing pin wasn't broken, everything was lubed, everything worked perfectly. I was the one who messed up. I didn't pull the lanyard hard enough. I felt like crap. When the ceremony was over my squad leader told me that the commander wanted to see us. The commander asked me what had happened. I said that I hadn't pulled the lanyard hard enough. The commander asked if I had checked the functioning of the cannon prior to the ceremony and I told him that I had. He asked if I thought the firing pin had broken. God, I wish that was it. Then it wouldn't have been my fault! I could have explained that the pin had broken to all the other cannon crews and everything would be good. But I couldn't. I knew that I had just messed up. I'm not going tell you that I heard my dad's voice in my head telling me, "Just admit that you messed up, son." I didn't have to hear his voice because that was just the way I was raised. I grew up admitting my mistakes. I told my commander again that I was the one who had messed up and the cannon was fine. My commander told my loader and squad leader to take the breach apart and check it. I told him that it wouldn't matter and that I was the one who messed up. I was then placed in the front leaning rest position (push-up position) and told to wait. I waited in that position until the breach was checked. And sure enough, it was fine. My commander told me to get up and then he talked with my squad leader. Nothing more was said about the incident. Two weeks later I was promoted to private first class. Taking responsibility ultimately pays off.

Patrick Winget, Fashion Designer, Los Angeles, California

My dad asked me to write about how he has influenced me in my life. I could go on and on about this topic but I will save that for my own bestseller one day. As I am sure you can imagine, it's not easy having a financial adviser, life coach, self-help guru, and motivational speaker as a dad, but his advice has helped me out more than once.

When growing up I saw that my dad never gave up. When life dealt him a bad hand he was always persistent and creative enough to make the best of it. I never heard him complain about anything ever. I didn't even know that we were broke and that he had gone bankrupt when I was a kid until I got older and my dad explained it all to us. Seeing my dad push through tough times while growing up has helped me get through all of the day-to-day crap I have had to deal with on my own.

When I was twenty years old, I wanted to start my own company. I thought I knew everything about the fashion industry and I wanted to take it by storm. I started a company that was immediately successful but as it started to grow I didn't know how to shift gears and move to the next level. All I wanted to do was design and make cool clothes. When the business got overwhelming and I wanted to give up and quit, my dad said, "Stick with it, suck it up and you will get through this." At the time I thought he was full of it, but as it turned out, he was right. Before every trade show I was in, I would call my dad and tell him that there was no way I would get all of my samples made in time for the show. He would laugh and say, "You say that every time and every time you get it done; shut up and go back to work!" I hated hearing that but sure enough, every time, I went to the trade show with every piece finished. My dad taught me that there is no other option except to succeed. Maybe monetary success didn't come every time, but I was always there with my collection finished and that was accomplishment enough to prove I could do it no matter what odds were facing me. I was taught that failing was not an option and that you have to do whatever it takes to get to the finish line. I am still going and living by that philosophy and I haven't hit the finish line yet.

While I have moved on and my original start-up company is history, I still find myself going that extra mile to make sure that I always finish what I start, no matter how hard it is and no matter how much I want to give up.

THE LESSON OF THE DOG BISCUIT.

I told this story in my first book, *Shut Up, Stop Whining, & Get a Life*. It always gets a ton of comments from readers so I want to include it again. I consider it to be one of my finer parenting moments.

My boys and I used to play a game called "What would you do for how much money?" It was based on stupid stuff like how much money would it take to get you to eat a worm? Or bite the head off of a live chicken? I know it's gross, but hey, we're guys. It was harmless fun that we could laugh about and use to one-up one another while testing our personal gross-out limits. By the way, my price was always much lower than theirs. I know what it takes to make big bucks and somehow eating a worm or biting the head off a chicken doesn't seem like such a big deal to me compared to having to put in some actual work for the same money.

When the boys were about five and nine years old, we were out walking our dogs. I had some dog biscuits in my pocket and I asked my older son, Tyler, what it would take for him to eat a dog biscuit. He laughed and said that he would eat one if I would eat one. I immediately popped one in my mouth, chewed it up and swallowed it with a smile and handed him his dog biscuit. He said he was just kidding and refused to do it. Oops. Big mistake.

That is when I taught my son one of life's most valuable lessons: A deal is a deal. I made it clear to him that he would eat the dog biscuit because he said he would. He had laid out the conditions of the transaction and I held up my end of the bargain and he would, too. I explained that when you say you will do something you must do it whether you want to or not. I explained that you don't have the option of changing your mind after giving your word. I explained another valuable life lesson at that point: Don't let your mouth write a check that your ass can't cash. I explained that we would stand right there all night if we had to but that he was going to eat that dog biscuit before we went home. Finally, after a lot of moaning and groaning, he realized that he had no other choice but to eat the dog biscuit, so he reluctantly ate it.

Some would say that I am a harsh father after hearing that story. I respectfully disagree. Tyler learned two valuable lessons that day that he never forgot. Few people ever learn that a deal is a deal and most folks write checks with their mouths that their asses can't cash nearly every day. As an adult, my son laughs about this story and brags that he learned those lessons the hard way.

YOUR TURN TO PLAY.

WHAT IS THE SINGLE MOST VALUABLE THING YOUR PARENTS TAUGHT YOU?

_____

_____

_____

_____

_____

_____

_____

_____

_____

While it is always valuable to look back on the lessons we learned from our parents and to pay homage to them for those lessons, we all know there are things they didn't prepare us for. This is one of those "Hindsight is 20/20" things. Which leads us to the next question.

WHAT DO YOU WISH YOUR PARENTS HAD TAUGHT YOU?

It is important to recognize the good things your parents taught you. I believe it is also important to reflect on what you wish they had taught you but didn't. You do this not so you can blame them for your mistakes. As an adult, it is too late to lay blame. At some point, you have to look around, recognize what you don't know and go about learning it on your own. You look back so you can reflect on the difference that lesson might have made and so you can be sure to teach your kid that valuable lesson you missed as a child.

In my case, my parents did a good job teaching me the principles for building a good moral life. But when it came to money, my parents let me down. We talked a lot about money, but most of the talk was about how we didn't have much and how we always had to be really careful with the little we had. We would take drives through the "rich" part of town and look at how the "other half" lived. It was always clear which half that left us in. I learned to be embarrassed by what we didn't have. I was taught that those with money were "lucky." This left me feeling "unlucky." While my parents taught me to enjoy what we did have when we had it, there was always an underlying sense of scarcity and lack. Thus, it made me approach money with fear. I wish they had taught me that having money was not based on luck or birthright.

When I asked my Facebook fans the single best thing they learned from their parents, I also asked them what they wish they had learned. Here are just a few of their responses.

The one thing I wish my parents had taught me was to laugh more. We could have used a little more laughter in our house.

—Joe Calloway

I wish they had taught me that you don't have to hit your kids to get them to listen.

—Michelle Cary Palmer

I wish they had taught me to take the time to smell the roses as time waits for no man.

—Karl Doelle

But the overwhelming response to this question was the same:

I really wish my parents would have taught me better money management skills.

—Chris Deringer-Sykes

The one thing I wish my parents had taught me is how to handle debt.

—Mary Condit

The one thing that I wish my parents would have taught me is how to use credit and pay it off every month. I had to learn this the hard way, and now I do.

—Therese Livermore

I wish they would have taught me how to manage my finances and invest wisely.

—Aunty Lynn

I wish they would have taught me to handle my finances better.

—Christine Webster

The one thing I wish they had taught me was money management and how to have a healthy relationship with money. But you can't teach what you never learned, so I'm learning that one myself.

—Skip Kanester

What lesson do I wish I had learned? Simple financial lessons. It's really hard to learn those at forty-plus when you're stacked up behind the 8-ball.

—Bill Parry

The one thing that my parents did not teach me is to listen to my instincts when someone tells you to just pay the minimum on a credit card statement.

—Andi Bennett

I wish they had talked to me more about finances.

—Steve Wignall

The thing I wish my mom and stepdad would have taught me would be about money and how to save it and spend it.

—Greg Leavelle

When it came to finances, it was considered none of my business and never discussed. We were well taken care of and did not go without, however, simple financial lessons learned about money, at an early age, would have me in a much better position than I currently am. Simple lessons like how much income is needed to run a household, how to save, to respect credit cards, etc.

—Bill Alty

At age almost fifty-three . . . I wish my parents had talked to me more about finances and investing. Coming from a southern culture, I was taught it was impolite for a woman to talk about how much money you made, had or spent. My mother had a checkbook that never had a balance in it because my father handled all of the finances.

—Clare Rice

I should have been told the value of money and to understand how families make money and spend it.

—Marsha Petrie Sue

How to be financially responsible (i.e., smart and dumb ways to spend your money, how to SAVE money).

—Pam Hunter

The one thing I wish they had taught me was the power of compounding when saving.

—Eddie Zwerko

Money doesn't fix relationships in the family.

—Eric Chung

What I wish my parents had taught me was to save more and shop more wisely. I also wish my parents had taught me better about avoiding impulse purchases, and maximizing money.

—Cathy

How to make money and how to invest money in order to create more of it!

—William Bradley

The one thing I wish my parents had taught me better was how to talk about money and finances. They seldom talked about money, except to say whether or not we could afford something. Beyond that, they felt it was in bad taste to discuss money.

—Erin Foster

YOUR TURN AGAIN.

WHAT IS THE ONE THING YOU WISH YOUR PARENTS HAD TAUGHT YOU?

Based on the answers I received, you can see that the most common thing people wish they had learned from their parents and didn't were money principles. In fact, I received hundreds of responses to my question and only 1 percent of the people who responded actually said their parents taught them anything about money. One percent. Pretty pitiful, isn't it? Is it any wonder our society is in the financial mess that it's in? People never learned how to handle money as children and as adults they are in a financial mess. Based on that, let's deal with money lessons first.

CHAPTER 8

MONEY

Our society is in an economic mess. If you pick up this book ten years from now, that statement will still be true. If you pick up this book in England, China or Bulgaria, that statement will be true. The reason that statement will always be true is because there is a huge portion of the population that doesn't understand the basic concepts of money: how to earn it, how to spend it, how to save it, how to invest it, how to share it and how to enjoy it. Until those things are learned, money is going to be a problem.

Sadly, many parents think they can teach their kids about money only if they themselves have a lot of money. That's just not true. Some of the best memories my kids have come from when we had the least amount of money. And the lessons I learned from those experiences allowed me to teach them valuable principles about money.

The Christmas that my boys remember as their best Christmas ever came at a time when I had the least amount of money. I had just filed for bankruptcy. I was barely hanging on to my car and my house. And it was Christmastime. I remember my wife and I facing Christmas with almost no money to spend on gifts. My boys were aware of the fact that I no longer had a company and I had thoroughly explained to them that our lifestyle was going to be much different for a while. The evidence of our lifestyle change was clear because we were no longer going out to eat, no longer going to the movies, and no longer buying anything. But it was still Christmas. You can live a pretty lean lifestyle with kids and if you do it right, they will barely notice. However, at birthdays and at Christmas you have to get creative if you are going to make it work. My wife and I had $50 to spend on Christmas for the boys. That's all we could eke out. Mind you, we could have spent much more if we had done what most people do and shirked our responsibilities, skipped a house payment or a car payment or gone deeper into debt on our credit cards. But that wasn't our style. We believe you pay your bills first and that you don't go deeper in debt when your finances are already in trouble. We believe that even Christmas and birthdays have to be dealt with responsibly. So fifty bucks was it for us. Tyler was ten and Patrick was six and both were typical boys. They loved the outdoors, they loved playing army and they loved stuff they could use their imaginations with. So it hit me that we should try the army surplus store. I dug through boxes of worn-out stuff they were selling for almost nothing. I bought old army shirts and hats. I got dozens of patches and sewed them myself all over the clothes. I got canteens and old grenades and belts and old army blankets. I was able to get a cheap tent for $14. On Christmas Eve, we cleared the dining room out and set up the tent. When the boys got up, they saw a tent and lots of presents that all together added up to only $50. The boys loved all of it. To this day, they say that was their best Christmas ever. We spent little but we created an event out of it. We also got creative. Add that to the fact that we actually knew our kids and what they liked and bundle that up with lots of love and it all worked out great.

One of the lessons it's important to teach kids is not so much about how much money you have but how you use the money you have. Sadly, that lesson is rarely taught. Even when I was growing up, with parents who didn't have very much, we always managed some kind of vacation every summer. In the fifties and sixties, the typical work schedule for most people was that you worked fifty weeks of the year and you got two weeks' vacation. My folks always planned great vacations for our family even though they didn't have much money. One year, we went to Disneyland. My mom, dad, and sister, along with my dad's father and my mom's mother, all piled into a 1960 Chevrolet Biscayne with no air-conditioning and started the long drive from Muskogee, Oklahoma, to Los Angeles. We had relatives in L.A. so we'd be able to stay for free once we got there. We ate sandwiches packed in ice chests the whole way. We stayed in two cheap motels on the way there and two on the way back. This was a huge treat as these little motels always had a concrete hole in the ground filled with murky water called a swimming pool. Believe me, those were the only swimming pools I ever saw growing up. It was a hard trip and a hot one as we drove across Texas, New Mexico and Arizona in July with no air-conditioning and a car filled with two kids and four big, overweight adults! But I remember those vacations well and how much fun they were to this day, and it has been nearly fifty years. I remember them because I knew they were special times. Today, I would shoot myself before I would consider repeating that kind of a trip. But as a kid, I thought it was great fun. One of the things I remember about those trips now is my mom and dad sitting at the kitchen table figuring out the money for the trip. They would work through what it all would cost daily and would scrimp and save and do without to make sure we would have enough to make it. My dad worked for Sears but he also owned Henry's Bantam Ranch (a chicken farm) with hundreds of chickens and other assorted farm animals. He would sell some of his chickens and eggs and whatever else he could to make these vacations happen.

That one trip to Disneyland was our biggest trip in all the years I was growing up. All other vacations were spent at the lake. My dad had purchased an old ski boat, and he sanded it, patched it and painted it along with rebuilding the engine until we had a working ski boat. We spent every summer at the lake with my dad dragging me behind this old beat-up boat on water skis. We lived in a tent for two weeks and cooked all our meals on an open fire or on a Coleman stove. Again, these vacations were relatively cheap but they were fun because they were breaks from our normal lives and we were together as a family.

Looking back on these family vacations, I realize that I was learning the importance of budgeting, saving and sacrificing and the joy of just being together as a family.

THE OTHER SIDE OF THE COIN.

In some families lack of money isn't the issue, it is the irresponsibility that comes from having too much money. Notice I didn't say that the problem is having too much money, as I don't think it is possible to have too much money. I am saying that irresponsibility is the problem. If you have plenty of money and don't teach your kids to respect it and be responsible with it then you are guilty of a form of child abuse in my opinion.

On my A&E television show, *Big Spender*, I worked with a woman who had serious spending and shopping problems. The root of her problem was an obsession with her appearance. She always had to be wearing a brand-new outfit that no one had ever seen before so she could be the center of attention among her friends. She lived for the oohing and aahing that came with every new outfit, new pair of shoes, new piece of jewelry and new shade of lipstick and fingernail polish. She drove a new Mercedes and publicly looked like a million bucks, which is about what it was costing her to keep up this appearance. However, the home that she shared with her husband was a five-hundred-square-foot apartment with no furniture except for a couch and a bed and a dresser. No dining room table or chairs—not a big problem since they ate out every meal. No television. Bare walls with not one painting or picture. Why? Because no one ever saw that stuff, so why bother? When I asked her about it all she told me that her father had told her that as long as she drove a new Mercedes, wore a gold Rolex watch and dressed like a million bucks, what happened behind the scenes didn't matter.

I told her that was child abuse. She cried. I was right and her dad was clearly wrong. He had money yet he never taught her to respect it, how to use it, how to invest it, how to save it or even how to spend it wisely. In this family, the money used them instead of the other way around.

Too many times, parents with money don't take the time to teach their children how to earn money or use it wisely. They spoil their children and they think they are helping them by not allowing them to "suffer" and do without any little thing their heart desires. What they are actually doing is crippling their children's future by teaching them to take wealth for granted. They are building a sense of entitlement, showing their children that they don't have to work to be taken care of. Kids raised in this environment usually end up with financial issues as they grow older, ending up with way too much debt and credit card abuse simply because they never learned the value of earning.

Whether you have a lot of money or very little money, you must teach your kids how to earn it, invest it, save it and spend it wisely.

What lessons are you teaching your kids about money? Do you talk openly with them about earning, the cost of things, how to budget and how to save? Why not? Scared?

WHERE TO START.

Begin by giving your young kids an allowance. This money should be given on the same day every week just like your paycheck is given on the same day each week. Even if you get paid monthly, a month is too long for kids to think about, as they don't yet have a great grasp on time. Weekly is better.

Tell them that their allowance is the money they get for holding up their end of the family responsibilities. Those responsibilities include keeping their rooms clean, keeping their stuff picked up, hauling their dirty clothes to the washing machine, putting away their own clean clothes, and helping with the food preparation and the dishes and taking out the trash. Every one of these chores can be done by even the smallest of children. Even at two years old, every item on this little list can be done to some degree. This teaches a sense of earning from a very young age. It's a simple lesson: You are expected to work and that work will be compensated.

This allowance is paid regardless of how well the job is done. Just like your salary. If your job isn't done to the boss's satisfaction, he doesn't withhold your salary; instead he talks to you about your performance and works with you to improve your performance. But you still get paid. Just like if your child's job isn't done to the boss's satisfaction (that's you), then you don't withhold the money; you talk to your child about his performance and work with him to improve it.

This is unlike payment for special jobs like washing the car and other projects. When those projects come up, you should agree on a price, set the level of expectation of the quality or quantity of work required and then pay according to the agreement. In those cases, if the job is not done according to the agreement, then you have the right to withhold payment. Also in these cases, I am a big believer in written contracts in which both parties sign. This is a great lesson that teaches kids that work is usually performed with a written agreement and that even deviation has repercussions. This teaches them that their signature has meaning. (More on that one later.)

As the child becomes a teenager, you might consider opening a checking account for your kid with a debit card. Based on the child's age and your own finances, you can put an amount of money in the account each month and allow the kid to use the account to withdraw cash and to use the debit card to pay for the things they want to buy. This is a great way to teach independence and how to use banks and credit cards and how to budget.

In fact, the whole goal of an allowance is to teach your kid how to budget based on their priorities. When you give your child their allowance, talk to them about what responsible people do with their money. In this case, it would be helpful if you were actually being responsible with your own money so you would have something of value to teach. If that is a problem for you, read my book *You're Broke Because You Want to Be: How to Stop Getting By and Start Getting Ahead.*

Don't just hand your kid the cash and say, "This is yours, you can do whatever you like with it." While it is true that it is hers and she can ultimately do whatever she likes with it, it would be irresponsible not to show her what she should do with it.

THE 10-10-10 RULE.

Save 10 percent. Invest 10 percent. Give 10 percent.

Begin by telling your children that they should save 10 percent of all they receive. These savings are for a "rainy day" or an emergency. You do that by first teaching them what 10 percent is. If the child is very young and the allowance is one dollar, pay them with ten dimes. Teach them that they need to put one of the dimes in a bank. A piggy bank is fine. Then you teach them about investing 10 percent. This is hard for a four-year-old but you can help them with this concept by telling them that if they will put away a dime now, in a year, you will give them two dimes back. Let them decide, but advise them to invest. Then explain the importance of charity with another 10 percent. This is not a religious concept unless you decide in your family to make it one. It is, however, a smart concept to teach from a young age. Explain that some people need help for a variety of reasons and explain that organizations exist to help these unfortunate people. Young children have big hearts and will willingly help others when given the chance. Then show them their 70 percent. Explain that they get to use that money any way they want. They can save up until they have more money and then buy something they really want. Or they can blow it now and wait until next week.

This is the point where you start talking about goals and priorities.

Is there something that your kid really wants? A special toy or some event they would really like to attend? Resist the temptation to pay for it yourself and allow your child the privilege of saving for it. Teach them to put away extra money above their normal 10 percent. The 10 percent savings is for a rainy day and not for something they want to buy. Have them write down the goal amount and determine how much money they want to put toward that amount on a weekly basis. This teaches goal setting, prioritizing and saving, and it builds anticipation that will make the thing you want mean more to you because you sacrificed to get it.

Note to parents: This is probably something you can afford to learn as well. Instant gratification is a toxic condition in our society. Just because you can buy it now, doesn't mean you should buy it now. Learn to wait. Learn patience. Don't go into debt because something looks good now and causes you to make a spur-of-the-moment decision that you will later regret.

The 10-10-10 principle is important to teach when your child is very young. Don't be naïve and think that your child is too young to understand savings and investing and being charitable. They aren't. It can be explained and taught if you are diligent and patient. And please don't think that your child shouldn't have to worry about saving a dime or giving one away when they only get ten of them to begin with. This kind of thinking is what has led to the mess we are in today. Look back at the list of things that adults wish their parents had taught them. Money is number one. You are never too young to learn money lessons. If you learn solid financial principles when you are young and don't have much money, those principles will serve you well when you are older and do have more of it.

Saving, investing and giving are all habits. Habits are best formed when young.

HOUSEHOLD FINANCES SHOULD NOT BE A SECRET.

It is a good idea to involve kids in the finances of the household. This is done for the purpose of teaching your kid that households have expenses that they never considered. They need to know that the lights don't just come on when you flip the switch; you have to pay for that privilege. They need to understand that there are many expenses that are never even seen, like insurance. They need to understand that some money spent and enjoyed is not very glamorous, like when you have to buy a new hot water heater. They need to see that everything they enjoy has a price tag attached and they should understand how those expenses are budgeted and paid for.

ENCOURAGE ENTREPRENEURSHIP.

At some point, your kid will hopefully want to earn more money than his allowance. If he doesn't, you might want to examine how much money you are giving him. You may be paying him so much that he doesn't need any more money. Or he may not know how to set goals and plan for something he really wants. Or you may be buying him whatever he wants so he doesn't have the need to work. If any of these are the case, adjust your actions.

When a kid has the desire to earn money, encourage him to do so. When I was a kid, paper routes were popular. I picked up pop bottles and sold them. I also picked vegetables from our huge garden and put them in my little red wagon and went door to door. Kids can still mow lawns and rake leaves and put up lemonade stands and babysit, pet-sit, dog-walk and all kinds of other things to earn money. Work with them and encourage them to stick to the 10-10-10 rule with everything they earn.

You will also need to educate them about their little business. You will need to teach sales, customer service, pricing, cost of goods sold and how to keep the boss happy. You will need to teach negotiating skills and profit and loss. Of course you have to do this with your child based on her age and how complicated her little business is, but any wage-earning opportunity is really more of an opportunity for her to learn about business and life than it is about the money she will earn.

While my son Patrick was in junior high school, he started a little business selling junk jewelry and other trinkets. Early in my speaking career I used these kinds of things in seminars so I always had plenty of catalogs that were full of this stuff. He saw that he could buy something from the catalog for a quarter and sell it for a dollar to his school friends and it would still be half of what they were paying for the same thing if they bought it full retail. I fronted him twenty-five bucks, which I made him immediately repay from his profits. He took one of my old briefcases, loaded it up and started selling this stuff before school and at lunch and recess. Things were going great until his principal called me to complain and say that Patrick was not going to be allowed to run a business at school. I pointed out to the principal that drugs were sold on his campus and that my kid's jewelry seemed pretty harmless by comparison. He didn't appreciate my comparison. I also pointed out that Patrick was learning valuable lessons about running a business. He still said no. I then suggested that maybe the principal was feeling threatened because Patrick was making more money than he was. That cinched it: Patrick was out of business. At least on the school grounds. He continued the business for a while off school grounds and made a nice little chunk of change for himself.

Kids should be encouraged to look for ways to make money. There are many great Web sites that can help. Just do a Google search on ways kids can earn money and you will find many Web sites with creative, doable ideas.

As soon as kids start earning money of their own, they should be taken to the bank to open a checking account and a savings account. Don't do it for them, do it with them. They need to experience the bank. Then you should teach them how to write checks, track their deposits and expenditures and reconcile their account.

LOANING MONEY TO KIDS.

It can be done as long as you enforce the repayment of the loan. Again, the smart thing to do is draw up a simple document that outlines the agreement, including the repayment schedule. Then you enforce the repayment. Too much for a kid? No. It's a lesson in how the real world works. You borrow money and you have to repay the money. In the real world that is how it works and one of the problems with adults is that they never learned this lesson when they were children.

BAILING KIDS OUT WHEN THEY MAKE A MISTAKE.

You should. Once. If they continue to make the same mistake over and over, and you continue to bail them out over and over, the only lesson that is learned is that you will bail them out. You are only making sure that the unwanted behavior will be repeated.

My son Tyler wrote a check for eighty cents when he was eighteen years old. It bounced and bounced again and finally bounced a third time. The bank fined him every time it bounced. It finally got turned over to the bad check division of the district attorney's office. That eighty-cent check quickly became an eight-hundred-dollar criminal problem. I was unaware of the problem as my son, out of stupidity, embarrassment and fear for his life, was doing a good job of hiding it from me. Finally, he sat down at my desk with tears running down his cheeks saying, "Dad, I have f'ed up!" My reply after reviewing all of the documents was "Yes, you have indeed f'ed up!" He told me if I would help him out of this mess, he would get his life straight and fix things. He thought he was going nowhere, which was true, as he had just flunked out of his first semester of college. He made the decision to join the army. We weren't in a war, he was a mess and it seemed like a great idea to me at the time. So I gave him the cash to fix his mess and off we went to the army recruiter's office. My son turned his life around in the army and is now one of the most disciplined people with his money I have ever encountered. He knows how to save, prioritize, invest and enjoy what he earns. He understands the importance of a good credit score and what it can do when you want to buy a new truck, and he knows how important it is to pay your bills when you are eighteen years old if you want to be able to buy a house when you are thirty.

Bailing him out was the right thing to do because he took personal responsibility and brought me a plan to turn things around. If he had not come in with a plan and had only whined about how unfair it all was, I would have let him suffer the consequences of his stupidity.

Bail your kid out. Once. But make sure that the lesson has been learned, that he has taken personal responsibility for his mistake, and that he has a plan for avoiding the same mistake again.

TEACH MATH SKILLS AND THEIR RELEVANCE TO MONEY.

There is a good chance that your kids will learn basic math skills in school but won't really see a lot of real-world relevance to those math skills until you teach them how the ability to add, subtract, multiply and divide relate to money.

Addition is important so you can add up what you have and what you owe.

Subtraction is necessary so you can subtract what you owe from what you have.

Think that is too basic? I promise you that most adults have never done the basic tasks I have just outlined. Teach your kids to do this stuff.

Percentages and multiplication.

A recent study I read said that when asked the question "If something costs $300 and it is on sale for half off, how much will it cost?" less than half the people asked were able to come up with the correct answer of $150. That is pitiful. Is it any wonder why we are in the mess we are in?

My parents both worked in retail so I learned how percentages worked at a young age. We would walk through a store and something would say "30% off" and I could immediately tell you how much it would cost. How? My mom taught me that if something is 30 percent off, you just multiply what it costs by 7. This is why multiplication tables are so important. If it costs $20 and it is 30 percent off, you don't have to calculate 30 percent of $20 and then subtract that amount from the $20. You can simply multiply the $20 times 7 and you know it costs $14. (Of course you have to tell your kid to slide the decimal point or drop a zero but they will get that pretty quickly if you practice with them a few times.) This may seem like a silly thing to go over, but I'll bet you that not one-fourth of the people asked (that's 25 percent) know this shortcut.

You also have to understand percentages when it comes to credit. Teach your kid what a 6 percent interest rate really means. Don't know? Go online and there are plenty of sources that can teach you. Teach your kids that when you have a credit card balance of $1,000 at an interest rate of 18 percent and you only make minimum payments, without charging one more dime on the card, it will take you 153 months to pay off that $1,000. Go to www.bankrate.com/brm/calc/minpayment.asp and play with balances and rates to see how it works.

I had a college senior on my A&E television show, *Big Spender*, who had no idea what a mortgage was. Her mother had to take out a second mortgage to pay her daughter's credit card bills and keep her in party money. When I explained to this girl (twenty-two years old) that her mother had taken out the second mortgage, her question to me was, "What's a mortgage?" I will admit, that one caught me off guard. Her mother should have taught her what a mortgage was. But then again, her mother should have taught her not to buy everything she saw and not to party every night. Mostly, her mother should have taught her not to go on national television and prove what an idiot she was.

Teach your kids that when you pay $250,000 for a house, the house doesn't really cost $250,000. Show them that $250,000 at 6 percent fixed interest over thirty years makes the house really cost $539,000. How do you come up with that? Google "mortgage rate calculator" to figure it out.

CREDIT.

Possibly one of the worst forms of child abuse would be to neglect teaching your kids about credit.

Teach them what a credit score is and explain that those are the three most important numbers they will ever deal with. Show them how quickly they can ruin their score by not paying their bills—even one bill—on time. Show them your credit report and explain every ding that appears. Show them how their credit score determines how much they will pay for a loan and whether they will get a loan, and that it can even determine their future employment.

WANTS VS. NEEDS.

Teach your kids the difference between wants and needs. This might be a problem if you don't know the difference yourself. Sadly, most people don't. You don't *need* four ESPN channels, six HBO channels, three Starz channels and two Showtime channels. You don't *need* a sixty-inch plasma-screen TV. You don't *need* to go out to eat four nights a week. You don't *need* a new car. How do I know you don't need these things? Because you can survive without them. Is there anything wrong with having them? Not at all. I have all of these things and more. But I don't have them out of need. I have them for the same reason other people have them—I want them. But, I can also afford them. There is nothing wrong with having everything you want if, and it's a big IF, you can afford it.

How to do you know you can afford something? Take this test:

Are your bills and obligations paid?

Do you have money (cash) saved and readily available?

Have you set aside a portion of your income for investing?

Have you been charitable with a portion of your income?

Do you have secure employment?

If you can answer yes to all five of those questions, then you are good to go. Have fun. Buy what you want as long as you can afford to pay for it without going into debt. Enjoy your hard-earned money.

If you teach your kids to answer those five questions before they spend their money on things they want, they will be okay forever as far as their money is concerned.

YOUR MONEY WILL BE SPENT ON WHAT IS IMPORTANT TO YOU.

If looking cute is important to you, your money will be spent at the mall. If being cool is important to you, you will spend your money on a cool car or a big-screen television. If having a financially secure future is important to you, then you will put your money toward having a financially secure future.

It's all about priorities. Teach your kids to prioritize the things that really matter to them and after their priorities are funded, to have fun with what's left over.

BE CHARITABLE WITH YOUR MONEY.

I have already mentioned charity as one of the 10s in my 10-10-10 rule. But it's time to talk more about its importance. Being charitable with your money is as important as saving and as important as investing. Why? Because it is simply the right thing to do. It's important to take care of people who don't have anything. When I was sixteen, my dad sat me down and explained that a girl who worked with him at Sears was having a hard time. Her husband had left her, she didn't have any family and she had three little kids. He explained that those kids weren't going to have any Christmas presents to open. He said he wanted to help, but that would mean he would have to cut back on presents for me. I told him I was fine with that and didn't care. I told him I was proud of him for wanting to help. The next day, he came home with a bunch of toys and a nice sweater for the mother and my mom wrapped them all. He didn't want to embarrass her so he asked if I would mind delivering the presents to her since she didn't know me. I was honored. I took a big box full of wrapped presents to her house on Christmas Eve, rang her doorbell and handed it all to her. She cried and hugged me and asked me who I was and who sent the presents. I just said Santa Claus and quickly left. That year my dad gave me the greatest Christmas gift ever—the gift of giving to those who need it more than you do. My dad never made more than $17,000 per year in his life. Yet he always gave to others no matter how little he had.

I always tried to live with that spirit of charity and teach it to my kids. When my boys were ten and fifteen, we took a trip to Washington, D.C. My boys, coming from Oklahoma, had never really seen homelessness up close. So seeing the homeless people begging on the streets was a new experience for them. Patrick, then ten years old, took some of the money he had saved for the trip and got a bunch of nickels and gave every homeless person he passed a nickel. Yeah, a nickel is a ridiculous amount, I know. And his big brother gave him a hard time about giving people a nickel. In fact, his brother was more apt to tell people to get a job. (They really are a unique mix of my qualities!) While you and I both know that the nickel didn't make much difference to the homeless folks, it made a big difference to Patrick. He felt like he was making a difference. And he was! He was making a difference in his own life by tapping into his charitable spirit. Even as a grown man, when he didn't have much, he was always dropping a dollar in the bucket of some guy on the street, or buying him a cup of coffee or a sandwich.

Don't think that you have to wait until you have a lot of money to be charitable. It is very easy for someone to say they will give away some of their money once they have a lot of money.

But I have my doubts about that. When you have a dollar, a dime doesn't seem like so much. Even when you have a hundred dollars, a ten spot doesn't seem like such a huge sacrifice. But when you have a million dollars, giving up a hundred thousand is tough. It's best to establish the habit of being charitable when the amounts are small.

Another thing to keep in mind is that when you exhibit charity when you have only a little money, your chances of having more money will go up. How does that work? Beats me, but it always works. I think it primarily works because giving is the right thing to do. And doing the right thing always has its reward.

AND . . .

Teach your kids how to balance a checkbook—both online and on paper.

Teach your kids about taxes, why they are paid, how they are paid, what they pay for and the importance of paying them.

THE MOST IMPORTANT THING TO TEACH YOUR KIDS ABOUT MONEY.

Money is good. Money can bring you great happiness. Don't ever let anyone tell you differently. The people who tell you that money can't make you happy don't have any money. Money will allow you to live in a great house, own cool stuff, travel places and do things that people without money can never enjoy. There is nothing wrong with having money.

There is more wrong with not having money than with having money. Poverty is the enemy, not prosperity. There is nothing noble or honorable about doing without or not having enough. Never let anyone, including any religious organization, communicate that message to you or your child. Money is always a good thing. It feeds people, takes care of sick people and is a measure of your own service to others. It is a reward for your efforts. Notice that I didn't say it was a measure of your worth, but of your service and efforts.

To have the ability to earn money and not to make use of this ability is dishonorable. It is a waste of your talent and an insult to yourself. To waste the opportunity to make money and take the very best care of your family is immoral. Teach your kids to do their best. To serve others well. To earn as much as they can, save as much as they can, and spend well so they can enjoy life as much as they can. That would be serving your child well.

However, with all of that said, it is important to teach these things, too:

Money is not more important than people.

Money gotten dishonestly is never worth it.

Money carries responsibility. Don't shirk those responsibilities.

Money is freedom. The freedom to do what you want, the way you want, when you want, with whom you want. That is the ultimate benefit of having money.

HOW ARE YOU DOING SO FAR? WHAT LESSONS HAVE YOU TAUGHT YOUR KID ABOUT MONEY?

WHAT LESSONS ARE YOU TEACHING YOUR CHILD BASED ON YOUR OWN BEHAVIOR?

WHAT LESSONS DO YOU STILL NEED TO TEACH YOUR KID ABOUT MONEY?

CHAPTER 9

SEX

Money is the area most wish their parents had talked more to them about. That evidence came from my own personal polling. But I didn't have to take a poll to know that parents aren't doing much of a job teaching their kids about sex. Proof? Let's go to the facts:

The average age a girl loses her virginity at is 15.

About 16,000 pregnancies are recorded annually among 10-to-14-year-old girls.

46 percent of high school students in the United States have had sexual intercourse.

46 percent said they had sex because they felt they were ready to have sex.

Over 50 percent of teens have unprotected sex.

25 percent of teenage girls have an STD.

50 percent of African-American girls who are having sex have an STD.

24 percent of the girls who have an STD are still having unprotected sex.

14 percent of teens have sex in school. That's right—*in* the school.

Got teenagers? Scared yet? You should be. Not just because your kids are having sex, but because they are having unprotected sex. You should be terrified because they are being STUPID!

Kids are going to have sex. Period. Don't argue with me on this one. Teenagers have been doing it since the beginning of time. I did it. Chances are you did it. Am I saying that makes it right? Not at all. I am just saying that it is reality. The reality is that kids have sex.

Chances are very good that you aren't going to stop your kid from doing it. Once you tried it when you were a teenager, did you give it up? My advice is to teach your kid about sex. Not how to do it—I am betting they already have that part down pat. I don't think they really have any issue figuring out how to put Tab A in Slot B. How to do it is not the issue; how to do it responsibly, respectfully and safely is the issue.

You read above that nearly half of all the kids having sex reported they felt ready to have sex. Where did that feeling of readiness come from? Not from their parents, I am guessing. Kids are getting their readiness information from their friends. They are also heavily influenced by television, as you have read elsewhere in the book. But they are not getting their readiness information from their parents. Why? Because parents are embarrassed to talk to their kids about sex. Instead they leave it to their kid's school to do their work.

Okay, back to the facts.

Abstinence-only sex education is taught in twenty-eight states. Responsible sex isn't part of the curriculum. Birth control isn't taught. In these states abstinence is the *only* thing taught. The primary argument behind abstinence-only sex education is that teaching birth control promotes sexual activity. Can you say "head in the sand"?

I am a guy who always goes straight for results. And the results of this approach are abysmal. Of the twenty-eight states that teach abstinence only, ten of those rank highest in teen pregnancy. How's that abstinence-only thing working? The results prove that teaching abstinence doesn't make kids abstain.

Those who promote abstinence argue that abstinence is the only guaranteed way to make sure you don't get pregnant and don't get an STD. That is 100 percent correct. Abstinence works! *When* people abstain. But people don't abstain. They never have and they never will. People have sex! It's why you and I are both here: People had sex.

You can't effectively teach people not to have sex. You can legislate against it and you still won't keep anyone from having it. You can try to use guilt to keep people from having it, which is what most churches do with virginity agreements and abstinence contracts, but that doesn't work either. It has been found that teens who take those virginity pledges varied little from those who didn't when it came to waiting to have sex. Pledges about a lot of things work, I am sure, but when it comes to sex, it takes more than a pledge. It also takes more than a purity ring like the Jonas Brothers wear. Disney loves these guys and the churches like them because they wear purity rings and say they won't have sex until marriage. I am just jaded enough to consider that to be a great marketing ploy to enhance their celebrity and sell records. It must be, since I have heard their music and it's not their musical talent that is selling records!

THE TRUTH: SEX IS AMAZING!

That's the real issue here. Sex is the coolest thing on the planet. And if you don't think that's the truth, you aren't doing it right. So what makes you think you are going to keep your kids from doing it? You aren't. It is the natural thing to do.

I had two healthy, heterosexual, testosterone-rich teenage

boys who loved girls. I knew there was no way in the world I was going to be able to say with a straight face that they should never have sex until they were married. In fact, I think that is a dumb idea. Wait until you are married? I have had buddies who did that with their fiancées. Then on their honeymoon their brand-new wife discovered she hated sex and didn't let them do it again. Soon they were divorced. Wouldn't it have made more sense to find out your wife hates sex before the wedding? For the record, I am for premarital sex between consenting adults. That line will cause many of you to stop, throw this book in the trash and run to your computers to say I am going straight to hell! But I will stand by that statement. If more couples did it before they got married there would be fewer divorces, fewer bad marriages and fewer affairs. But I digress.

I sat my boys down and had a good long honest talk about sex. I first explained about diseases, including herpes, AIDS and other STDs. I explained what they were, how you got them and that a bad one could rot your penis completely off. Want to scare a boy into using a condom? Show him pictures of pus-laden boils and a rotting penis and he will have a pocket full of rubbers from then on! I explained that AIDS would kill you. Then I explained that getting a girl pregnant was stupid and was completely unacceptable. I explained that the girl's father would find them and beat the crap out of them for knocking up his little girl and that I would stand by watching it happen, with the only help being that I might choose to hold his arms while the daddy smacked him.

Then I taught them the important stuff.

RESPECT—RESPONSIBILITY—SAFETY.

Respect. No means no. Always and without exception. "I don't think so" means no. "Let's wait" means no. "I don't want to" means no. "Can we slow down?" means no. "Let's talk about this more" means no. "I'm not sure" means no. "Wait" means no.

"Unh-uh" means no. A slight push, the shaking of the head, pulling back, any resistance at all—it all means no.

Responsibility. It is up to both partners to take responsibility for the situation and the experience of having sex. And if things go wrong, it is the responsibility of both to figure out the next step.

Safety. It is the responsibility of both parties to take precautions and stay safe. That means if you have a disease like 25 percent of all teenage girls, you have to tell the other person. That means that both parties need to carry condoms.

Don't let passion, darkness, hormones, peer pressure, sweatiness and fogged windows get in the way of logic. These things will—but try not to let them.

Bottom line time.

Kids are going to have sex. I have made my case. Am I condoning it? Am I saying that they *should* have sex? No. I am only saying that kids are going to have sex. Teach them responsibility, respect and safety. Talk to them. Communicate with them. Talk to them about your values and beliefs. Talk about the embarrassing stuff. Will you be uncomfortable? Sure you will. Will they be uncomfortable? I guarantee it. That's why most people don't do it. Don't let embarrassment be an excuse for shirking your parental responsibility. Do your job, Mom and Dad; have the talk.

When do you have the talk? You start when they are young. Elementary school. Don't think that is too young. They know about sex. They see it on television. Their friends talk about it. They even have elementary school friends who are having sex, so wake up and have the talk. Make the talk age appropriate but use the correct words and give it to them straight. Talk about my big three: respect, responsibility and safety. Encourage them to come to you with their questions. Promise them that you will be honest and there is no reason to be embarrassed to talk about sex. Keep your word on this and talk to your kids so you don't end up getting caught in a tough situation.

"I'M PREGNANT."

Every parent of every little girl fears hearing this. Why wouldn't they? I just gave you the statistics and you can see that lots of kids are having sex and that a lot of it is unprotected. And if you honestly think your child is the exception and not having any sex, you are an idiot. In all likelihood, your little angel is having sex in the backseat of some car with a pimple-faced punk who you don't even know. Reality time!

Chances are that you didn't do as I have suggested in the last few pages and talk to your kid about responsibility and safety. Chances are that you hid your head in the sand and denied that she was having sex or refused to believe that she would ever do that. Or you felt safe because she wears a purity ring and signed an oath that she would remain a virgin until marriage.

Regardless of whether you openly discussed sex or not, let's say you are now facing the problem. It won't do much good to point the finger of blame in her face, his face or your own face. And it won't do you any good to scream, "How did this happen?" Duh. You know how it happened. It was that Tab A in Slot B thing. The reality is that it happened.

Now what? Love her. Support her. There will be plenty of time for anger and yelling later, but at the moment you find out, tell her you love her and will help her and be there for her. After the shock has subsided and some of the emotions have calmed, talk. Talk about options. This part is not up to me to advise you on. Keeping the baby, adoption and abortion are your decisions. I couldn't even begin to tell you how to make these decisions. However, I will tell you what not to do. Don't throw your daughter away. She is still your little girl and now more than ever she needs you. The rest can be worked out and worked through.

"I'M GAY."

How can you have an intelligent conversation about sex and not bring this up? Yet parents rarely talk about this with their kids. The only thing most kids hear about this subject from their parents is when one of them makes a derogatory comment about a gay person they see on television or while out and about. This is where your kids' prejudices are born. They listen to you and your prejudices and model themselves after those thoughts, words and behaviors. Many kids witness these prejudices and at the same time are trying to cope with the fact that they are gay. Is it any wonder that kids are so confused and that they hide who they are from their families?

I believe people are born gay or straight. I don't believe sexual orientation is learned. I don't think it is a choice. You can't catch it from others. It is just the way people are at birth. Straight parents have homosexual kids. Duh. Of course they do. Homosexual parents who adopt raise straight kids. It is who you are: straight or gay.

Understanding that means that you love and accept your child the way he is. If your child were born with nine fingers instead of ten would you love him less? Of course not. If your child were born blind, you might be disappointed but you would love him just as much. And if your child is born gay, while that might not have been your choice for him, you don't love him any less. You accept. You love him unconditionally. That is your job as a parent. Not to love your child over something they have no control over makes you a pitiful excuse for a parent and human being. (And please don't think from the comparisons I just made that I am insinuating that being gay is some sort of birth defect. I am not.)

Denying your child's sexual orientation won't help either. I have friends who have a gay son in his thirties and they still think he just has a hard time finding good girls to date because his relationships never last. I have another set of friends who have a son who is forty-five and has lived with the same man for the past twenty years and his parents laugh about the fact that he is just too set in his ways to find a woman who will put up with him. Could it be that most women don't want to date a gay man? Nah, that couldn't be it.

Your little boy is what he is. Your little girl is what she is. If your kid is gay, it's because that is who he is. You can't control it. And you shouldn't judge it. Your job is to help him be who he really is. Your job as a parent is to accept him and love him.

Another big part of your job is going to be helping him live in a world that is still way too full of hate, prejudice, stupidity, ignorance and bigotry.

I know this is a touchy subject that will fire people up. And I must say that I just don't care. I don't believe that God hates gays. I could never believe in a God that hated anyone. I don't believe that being gay makes you less of a man or less of a woman. But if you do believe these things, I don't want to hear about it. I also don't believe that the rest of the world needs to hear about it either. And I hope that you don't have a gay child who your ignorance can influence and belittle.

WHAT LESSONS HAVE YOU TAUGHT YOUR KID ABOUT SEX?

WHAT LESSONS ARE YOU TEACHING YOUR CHILD BASED ON YOUR OWN BEHAVIOR?

WHAT LESSONS DO YOU STILL NEED TO TEACH YOUR KID ABOUT SEX?

CHAPTER 10

RELATIONSHIPS: YOURS AND THEIRS

We all want our children to grow up and have great relationships with their significant others. Whether they get married, don't get married, have a long-term partner or don't, we want them to find love and happiness with another person. In order for our kids to find that, we must first model a happy, loving relationship for them so they will know what that kind of relationship looks like. We must also teach them the skills it takes to be in a successful relationship with someone else.

LOVE YOURSELF.

I like myself. I like my wife, Rose Mary. Rose Mary likes herself. Rose Mary likes me. We both like us.

When Rose Mary doesn't like herself very much, it is very hard for me to like her. When I am not happy with myself at the moment, it is nearly impossible for Rose Mary to be happy with me. The goal for every individual is to first be happy with yourself. If you aren't any good for yourself, you are never going to be any good for anyone else.

In order to be happy and secure with another person, you must first learn to be happy and secure with yourself. The old, "you complete me" line has sent the wrong message for too many years. No other person can complete you because you are not incomplete to begin with. When it comes to relationships, I don't believe that two halves make a whole. Teach your kid that she is whole all by herself and it will serve her well when it comes to being in a relationship. Teach her that she doesn't *need* any other person to be happy. Teach her that she must first be happy all by herself. Other people only add to and enhance the happiness you already have.

This approach will bring much more satisfaction to all of your relationships.

MARRIAGE.

If you want your kids to have a good marriage, then you need to show them a good marriage. This of course depends on you having a good marriage. If yours is a mess, then you might want to change it, fix it or leave it. Those may seem like drastic steps but I assure you that your kid will emulate the relationship you demonstrate for them.

And please don't be naïve enough to think you can hide the kind of relationship you really have from your kids. Have you ever walked into your friends' house and been able to sense that they had just had a fight? The tension was in the air. They were all smiles and laughing, but you knew there was trouble right below the surface. And you couldn't wait to get out! Some kids grow up for eighteen years in that kind of household. They feel the tension, the unhappiness and the resentment that lives right below the surface. Never think you can hide what is really going on from your kids; they are much smarter than you are ever going to give them credit for and they know what's really going on.

Demonstrate the behaviors in your marriage that you want your kids to emulate in their own. Show affection. I have always hugged my wife and kissed her in front of my boys. We hold hands and laugh together. I don't throw her down on the couch and make out with her in front of them, so don't misunderstand me here. I am affectionate with her. Therefore, my boys are affectionate with their wives. Is that how it works? You bet it is.

If you openly show a full range of emotions with your spouse in front of your kid, your kid will learn to exhibit the full range of emotions in his own relationships.

LET THEM SEE YOU FIGHT.

Too often parents try to protect their kids from the fact that they disagree. They go into the bedroom and argue in private. There are certainly times when that is a good idea, as not all topics should be discussed in front of the children. However, I believe you should let your kids see you disagree and argue over many things. Why? Because people in a healthy relationship disagree. Trust me when I tell you that my boys saw their share of fights at my house. I am not an easy guy to live with. I am loud, opinionated, sarcastic, argumentative and caustic. And those are my good qualities. She is also a strong-willed, intelligent, opinionated woman herself. Therefore, my wife and I disagree often and about many things. Does it mean we don't care about each other? Of course not. Does it mean we shouldn't be married? Not at all. What does our disagreeing mean? It means we are individuals who have opinions. It also means we respect each other and our relationship enough to work it out by communicating until we reach a resolution. That lesson should be taught to children.

When I hear a couple say they never fight, then I know either they are liars, one is a domineering jerk or they have a very boring relationship because they are very boring people. Arguments are healthy and can teach your child many things. They teach that you can love someone and still disagree with him. Arguments can teach kids that marriage is a relationship that contains all of the emotions. They should see that you love each other, can be happy together and can be sad and mad. They need to witness all of that. It's healthy. Disagreements also teach your kid that there is a wrong way to fight and a right way to fight. They will witness plenty of the wrong way at nearly every turn, so it is important for you to exhibit the right way. The wrong way is for a fight to ever become physical. The wrong way is to belittle the other person for disagreeing with you.

The right way to fight is to keep it fair. The main ingredient to a fair fight is keeping it about the issue. Disagreements should be about things instead of about people. While I have made my share of mistakes in arguing with my wife, I have always tried to keep it about what she has done that I didn't like instead of about who she is. That is also the way I have always tried to argue with my boys. I attack their behavior instead of attacking them. I don't always succeed but that is my goal. When it works, it's been a productive disagreement. When it doesn't, I know I need to apologize and start over.

It is important to show your kids how to fight fairly from the time they are very small for many reasons. One is so they will know how to fight fairly. Duh! But it is also so they won't end up in an abusive relationship.

LARRY'S IDEAS FOR MARRIAGE.

These are the rules I told my boys about how to stack the deck in your favor if you want to have a good marriage. First, I believe that no one should be allowed to get married until they are thirty years old. I think we should pass a federal law to that effect. I don't think anyone is really clear on who they are until they are at least that age. I also think that up to that age, people are spending most of their energy on school and career. People who get married at eighteen, sorry, but the odds are against you. And parents who stand and smile and say how proud they are about the marriage, wake up! Ask yourself this question: Would you trust any eighteen-year-old to make a decision for you that would affect you every day for the rest of your life? No? Then what makes you think that eighteen-year-olds can make a well-informed, intelligent, lifelong decision about the rest of their lives? Encourage your kid to wait and wait and then wait some more. I know Congress will never pass my law, but hopefully every parent can encourage their own kid to wait.

Second, I don't think any two people should marry until they have lived together for one year. That will fire some of you up, I know. "What? You want people to live in sin?" No, I want people to know each other before they make a legal commitment to being together forever. I want them to smell each other's farts and have to put up with their bad breath in the morning and their stinky laundry and see how they really live instead of how they behave on a date. I want them to put up with it day in and day out and know that they can do it for the next fifty or sixty years before they sign a sheet of paper committing to do it. I want couples to get past the passion and the lust that happens at the beginning of every relationship and get down to what marriage really is: spaghetti and dirty socks.

You don't know anyone until you live with them for a year. Never kid yourself about that. Get off your moral high horse on this one and allow your kid to live with someone before marrying.

If the world followed my idea on this subject I can promise you that we would have fewer divorces. But it isn't going to happen so let's go ahead and talk about divorce.

DIVORCE.

Divorce is not the end of the world for your kids. In fact, many times they won't be bothered by it that much at all. You may even get the response that Ricky Bobby got in the movie *Talladega Nights* when he and his wife told their kids they were divorcing. Their kids responded with, "Oh boy! Two Christmases!"

I don't mean to make light of divorce. I wish it didn't happen. But I promise you that a good divorce is always better than a bad marriage. A bad marriage does much more harm to your kids than divorcing ever will. In fact, we often hear parents say that they are staying together "for the kids." I actually got divorced for the kids. I didn't want my boys to grow up with the marriage I had as their model. It wasn't healthy, wasn't loving, wasn't communicative and wasn't a partnership. We didn't like each other and didn't get along on any level. Divorce was the solution for us and the best thing I could do for my boys.

If you are worried about getting divorced because your children will have to grow up in a broken home, get over it. Are you as sick of the term *broken home* as I am? I can assure you that the home I had made with my boys' mother was broken, not the home I made after the divorce. The home I made after the divorce was completely whole. I remarried and was able to model for my boys a marriage that was a loving, friendly, fun, communicative, healthy partnership. Even though my boys alternated between living with their mother and me, their home was not broken. They just had two houses. They had a home with their mother and another home with me and my wife. They never lacked for loving parents who wanted the best for them.

If you are faced with divorce or are divorced, be sure to talk openly with your kids about it. Tell them why you are divorcing. Be fair about it. Don't throw the other party under the bus to make yourself the hero. There are no heroes in any divorce. It always takes two. Don't kid yourself: Both of you had a role in the disintegration of the marriage. So be fair. If you can't say anything nice about the other person, this is the time to practice not saying anything at all. I spent many years, until my boys reached the age of eighteen, never saying one bad word about their mother. I never trashed her. We could be in the middle of a major legal battle over visitation or money or whatever, and I still didn't talk trash about their mother. Could I have? Of course I could have. But I didn't because regardless of how I felt, she was their mother. That alone deserves respect.

The key in any divorce that involves kids is to keep the kids free of guilt. The fact that you and their other parent can't be married any longer is not their fault. They need to understand that. The other thing to remember is never to put the kids in the middle of your disagreements with your ex. That isn't fair to them at all. Keep them above the fray.

Kids can survive just about anything with enough love, honesty and open communication. Those three elements will give them all they need to make it through.

DATING.

The main question when it comes to dating always seems to be "What is the right age to start dating?" The answer depends on the individual maturity level of your child. Some kids could easily date much earlier than others because they are more mature and responsible. There is no magic number. Know your kid, know when your kid is ready and know who your kid is going on his date with.

Parents need to establish firm guidelines about when their children are allowed to date. They even need to establish some rules about when it is okay to call another child his girlfriend or her boyfriend or when he or she can wear something that belongs to the other kid or when he or she can "go steady." Elementary-school-age children are too young to be engaged in any of this. The reality is that some children are "hooking up" as young as fourth and fifth grade. Parents should not encourage or even stand in a neutral position on exclusive relationships at this age.

Your biggest battle when it comes to your child dating is going to be peer pressure. You are going to hear a million times, "But Heather's mommy lets her." "Biff's dad lets him take the car!" (If that happens, drive to Biff's house and slap his daddy for naming his kid Biff. That's a joke.)

You are going to hear that "everyone is doing it" and that you are the *only* parent who won't let their kid do something. Hang tough. Don't bow to peer pressure. Openly communicate to your child why you have established rules regarding where they go and who they can go with. Tell them you love them and want the best for them and that they are yours to protect and that you intend to do it. Don't be crazy strict or a stick in the mud about all of it. Just be reasonable and responsible.

TO THE PARENTS OF GIRLS.

If some bozo pulls up in your driveway and toots the horn for your little girl to run out, then she isn't going out. He can come to the door, greet you, spend a minute being uncomfortable with you and then make a promise to treat her with respect and to return her at the agreed-upon time. If he isn't man enough to do that, then he can't take her out. Old-fashioned? Maybe. Will your daughter roll her eyes and whine about it? Probably. Should you care? Not one bit. It is evidence of your good parenting that you would require that behavior of your daughter's date. It is also evidence of the boy's good parenting when he does it. So if you are the parent of a boy, teach him to knock on the door and meet a girl's parents politely before taking her out.

Teenage boys want sex. If they say they don't, they are liars. If they pledge not to have it, they are liars. Do they want to have sex with your little girl? Absolutely. Prepare your daughter. Equip her to handle the situation. Don't soft-sell it. Get down to the nitty-gritty and tell her the truth about boys. When she says, "But he's not like that!" try not to laugh too hard, because she honestly believes that he really isn't like that. You and I know better. He is exactly like that. Just say that you hope she is right and then go ahead and give her the talk.

Later in this book I will give you my opinions about making your little girl dress appropriately. This also should be emphasized when it comes to going on a date. Chastity belts are no longer readily available but clothes that cover the interesting parts are available. Make sure they are covered when she walks out the door. The interesting parts may not stay covered for long but you can see to it that they start out that way.

Teach your daughter that she doesn't have to give it up to be popular. I have watched little girls on various talk shows say that if they don't have sex then they won't be popular. Your little girl wants to be popular more than anything in the world, but you have to teach her that it is okay to say no.

Teach your daughter not to tease. That is different than

flirting. Teach her the difference between being flirty to attract wanted attention and teasing that will result in unwanted attention.

Go back to the section I wrote on sex and go over my Big Three: responsibility—respect—safety.

TO THE PARENTS OF BOYS.

Some little girls are gold diggers. They may only want your son for what he can buy them or where he will take them or what dating him might mean to their popularity. This really only applies if you are rich or really good-looking or a football or other sports star. But if you are the parent of a boy like this, give him the heads-up. By the way, this works both ways. There are plenty of boys who only want to date a girl because of her looks, popularity or money. Superficiality is not gender specific.

Girls like to be treated like girls. Teach your son to hold the door for women of all ages. Teach him to be polite. Teach him not to fart in front of girls. Teach him to be nice to them. Teach him to listen to them even when he couldn't care less about what they are talking about. Teach him to talk to them with respect and to treat them with respect. Girls are the best thing in the world and will love you forever if you will treat them well.

Teach your boys that it is never acceptable to mistreat a girl. You don't get to hit her or touch her in any way that she doesn't enjoy or welcome. Abuse against teenage girls from their "boyfriends" is on the rise. And some boys believe this is acceptable behavior. Parents must make it clear to their sons that it is never acceptable to mistreat a girl under any circumstance.

Teach your boy loyalty and honesty. If he is dating Heather exclusively, then it isn't okay to date other girls when Heather doesn't know about it. If he wants to date other girls, which I think is an excellent idea at a young age, then he should be man enough to tell Heather that he wants to date others.

Boys like to drink. As teenagers they don't know how to have one or two beers. They typically drink until they get drunk. Teenage boys don't always make good decisions, especially when they are full of testosterone and beer. Put them on a date and now they have an adoring, sometimes encouraging audience. At that point, they are ten feet tall and bulletproof. Talk to your son about drinking, driving and dating. These three activities don't go together. Tell him if he combines these three, you will have him by the balls for the rest of his life. Let him know that he will grow old and look like Howard Hughes on his deathbed waiting for you to push food under the door to his room.

TEENAGERS AND LOVE.

All teenagers think they are in love—usually about a hundred times before they actually have a clue what love is. You and I both know this but they don't. They actually believe they are in love and that it's the real thing. Don't belittle them for having these feelings. Just understand that it's normal and help guide them through this roller coaster of undeveloped emotions and out-of-control hormones.

They will get their hearts broken. You did, too. You were devastated and couldn't eat or sleep. You may have forgotten it by now, but it happened. You lived through it and they will, too. Let them cry it out and talk for hours on the phone with their friends and be slightly stupid. It's all they've got.

Some rules about dating:

Know who your kid is dating. No excuses. Embarrass him if you must, but know who your kid is dating.

No one touches your child in anger. According to teenwire. com, it is believed that 25 to 40 percent of all teens either are or have been in an abusive relationship. Does that number shock you? It should. Teach your kid not to touch another in anger or to allow herself to be touched in anger. Abuse doesn't stop. Abusers don't change. Teach this to your child.

Talk to your kid about who she is dating. According to the Centers for Disease Control and Prevention, one in three teens experiences an abusive relationship and 40 percent of teen girls know someone who has been hit or beaten by someone she is dating. Fewer than 25 percent of teens talk about dating abuse with their parents.

Synchronize your watches. "But, Daddy, my watch says it's midnight right now!" won't fly if it's fifteen minutes after midnight. "I had to stop and get gas, Mom, and didn't realize it was twelve-thirty" is a lie.

Enforce curfews. Ten o'clock on a school night. Midnight at most on weekends. Remember that nothing good goes on after midnight. Being late for a curfew must have consequences. Establish what the rules are in advance and then enforce them.

If your daughter's date doesn't respect your rules, then he can date someone else's daughter.

Encourage double dates. While kids have a tendency to get in trouble in packs, there are certain things kids are less likely to do when there are witnesses around.

If you are a single parent who is dating, model good dating behavior for your child.

No closed doors. I am amazed when parents tell me about their kids having dates over and how the couple goes into their kid's bedroom, shuts the door and studies or listens to music. Are you kidding me? The only subject they are studying is anatomy. They are bumping uglies in there! No closed doors—ever!

WHAT LESSONS HAVE YOU TAUGHT YOUR KID ABOUT RELATIONSHIPS?

WHAT LESSONS ARE YOU TEACHING YOUR CHILD BASED ON YOUR OWN BEHAVIOR?

WHAT LESSONS DO YOU STILL NEED TO TEACH YOUR KID ABOUT RELATIONSHIPS?

WHAT TO TEACH YOUR KIDS ABOUT GETTING ALONG WITH OTHERS.

The ability to get along with others is going to be critical to your child's success. You need to teach your children how to do it. Explain to them that other people are going to do stupid things— things that make them mad and things that are wrong. People will be rude, inconsiderate and irresponsible. You have to teach your kid that all of those things are normal and he has to learn how to respond when it happens. Sometimes, it is necessary to call people out for their behavior. Teach your kid how to do that calmly, politely and logically. Also teach your kid when to laugh it off, shake his head, roll his eyes and move on. Teach him how to choose his battles and how to know when it's worth it and when it isn't. These are valuable lessons he is going to need every day of his life.

Teach your kid to listen to others. Teach her to respect others for who they are even when she can't respect them for what they do. Teach your kid to be kind. Teach your kid that she can't always be right, and when she is, she doesn't need to be a jerk about it. Teach her to win with humility and lose with graciousness. These lessons will help her get along with others and be the kind of person others enjoy.

SIBLING RIVALRY, PLAYING FAVORITES AND HOW TO KEEP YOUR KIDS FROM KILLING ONE ANOTHER.

Siblings fight. It's natural. You can't stop it, so don't drive yourself crazy trying. All you can do is teach them how to do it so no one ends up hurt too badly. My boys fought constantly. They still do quite often as grown men. They are very different men with very different jobs, skills, likes and dislikes. They have very different views on politics and religion and most other subjects. How they both came from one source is a mystery. I bet it is the same with your kids, too.

The rule I used with my boys was to let them work it out on

their own and leave me out of it. I told them to close the door and figure it out and not to hurt each other. I didn't want to see any bruises or blood. And if you think I was kidding when saying "no bruises and no blood" then you were either an only child or you now have only one child. Little boys and girls play rough with each other and don't kid yourself by thinking that they don't smack each other when you aren't looking, because they do.

My boys never liked my approach. They wanted a parent to rule in favor of one or the other. Sometimes it is necessary to mediate a dispute, especially when one child is physically dominant, smarter, older or more devious than the other, but most of the time, it's best to let them work out their differences on their own. They need to learn how to negotiate with each other and how to find a resolution without interference from a grown-up. If this doesn't work, chances are that your house has more than one room. Separation is a great mediator.

It is perfectly normal and acceptable for your kids to fight with each other. They need to learn how to work out their differences with others within the safety of their own household so they will know how to do it in the real world. Let them feel anger, resentment, envy, jealousy and all the other emotions and coach them through how to handle those emotions at home before they rear their ugly heads at school or in other public places.

There are also some things you can do to make sure your kids aren't constantly at each other's throats.

Don't make comparisons between your children. "Your sister always made A's in math; why can't you be as smart as she is?" "Your brother was star quarterback and you can't throw a ball at all." Statements like these cause problems that don't need to be there. Kids are very self-critical anyway and they get plenty of criticism from their peers, so comments like these only hurt and cause more problems.

Don't play favorites and be sure to balance your time between your kids evenly. This can prove challenging. If you are a sports guy and one of your kids loves sports and the other has no interest, it may be challenging for you to connect with the child who doesn't share your interests. Do it anyway. I went on more camping trips, freezing my butt off in a stupid sleeping bag lying on the cold, hard, rocky ground, than I can count simply because I had a son who loved it. I hated it, but I did it because it was important to him. Often your children will feel your love and your interest based on the amount of time you spend with them, so make sure you show impartial interest among them.

CHAPTER 11

HEALTH, WEIGHT, FOOD AND EXERCISE

For the first time in history we are raising a generation of children who may not outlive their parents.

Those nasty facts again.

WEIGHT.

The percentage of overweight children is growing at an alarming rate. Today, one out of three kids is now considered to be overweight or obese.

More than 10 percent of toddlers are overweight.

The United States has the highest number of overweight adolescents of any country.

50 to 80 percent of overweight teenagers become overweight adults.

If your child is overweight at the age of eighteen, she is one-third more likely to die prematurely.

OVERFEEDING.

If your kid waddles side to side instead of walking with his feet going front to back, he is fat! You probably don't recognize that he is waddling though, since I am betting you waddle, too. If your kid's pants wear out between the legs before the knees wear out because his thighs rub together, your kid is fat!

I see a lot of reports on television of parents starving their kids to punish them. I know we all agree that this is despicable behavior and is certifiable child abuse. These parents should be jailed and experience a little of their own treatment in my opinion. However, we rarely see the opposite applied. While feeding your kid too little is child abuse, feeding your kid too much is also child abuse. Do parents who feed their kids until they are fat little tubs of lard go to jail? Rarely. Oh, yeah, sometimes when the kid is four years old and weighs one fifty, social services will step in, but that doesn't happen too often. But feeding your kid too much food or the wrong kind of food is clearly abusing the health of your child.

I was giving a speech at a casino in Louisiana. The only place to eat in the hotel/casino was their big buffet. Don't get me wrong, I was enjoying myself. I love those big buffets, especially in the South. Fried chicken, fried okra, fried catfish, gravy . . . my oh my, I was in heaven! And it is fine to eat all that fried stuff from time to time; you just can't make a habit out of it! While I was sitting there eating my one plateful of food, in came a family. The father weighed at least four hundred pounds. The mother weighed in at about three hundred. Their five-year-old was about eighty-five pounds, which is about twice what a five-year-old should weigh. But here is the kicker. They had a baby about a year old that was nothing but a huge ball of fat. You could hardly see its face or eyes because it was so fat. When they got their food, they sat at a table about ten feet from me. They pushed two tables together and she parked herself with her kids while the father brought food. He ended up with over a dozen plates of food on the table before finally sitting down. The plates were heaped with everything except salad. When he sat down, they all went facedown in the food like starving hogs at a feeding trough. The mother was stuffing fried chicken and french fries in the baby's mouth when the baby started to cry. The mother said to the father, "No wonder she is crying, she doesn't have anything sweet to eat between bites of her good food. Go get her some ice cream." At this point, I had completely lost my appetite but was glued to my chair watching this abomination of parenting. The father pushed and sweated and heaved his lard ass out of the chair and waddled off to get a bowl of ice cream that would feed three adults. The mother would then feed the baby a french fry and a couple of big bites of ice cream between bites of chicken. The baby was cooing and giggling the whole time. I had to leave for fear I was about to get arrested. Sadly, this scene is played out every day in every city in America. Not to this extreme, of course. But parents still stuff their kids' faces with what they call food and create grease-dependent, obese kids who are doomed to a life of obesity-related illnesses.

Pay close attention here!

Having a fat little kid is inexcusable. You control his diet and you control his exercise. Those are the two main ingredients for having a height-weight-proportionate child. His intake and output are in your hands. Don't make excuses. Don't be lazy. Care enough about your child to feed him right and to make sure he gets the right amount of exercise.

EXERCISE.

Sixty percent of kids between the ages of nine and thirteen do not participate in any physical activity during non-school hours.

Most kids don't get much exercise during school hours either. Many schools don't have physical education programs for kids and of those that do, studies indicate that they only actually produce about thirty minutes of vigorous activity per week.

The benefits of exercise are many. It not only helps kids lose weight and be healthy, but according to researchers at the Medical College of Georgia, less than an hour of daily exercise reduces depressive symptoms and improves self-esteem in overweight children. Yep, exercise improves self-esteem and has an impact on childhood depression. Doesn't that make more sense than drugging the child? It would seem!

FOOD.

The first rule I have regarding food is to feed your kid. Sound like a no-brainer? It isn't. According to Parenting.com, 10 percent of kids do not get a hot meal at home in the mornings and 11 percent don't get any food at all before school. Too busy to feed your kids? Not buying it. This is negligence. Of course when you consider that 44 percent of kids don't brush their teeth regularly either and that 36 percent of parents have dropped their kids off for school in their pajamas, it isn't all that surprising. And yes, those are real numbers.

Feed your kid. I don't mean hand them a soda and a donut before school. I mean a meal.

Now on to some of the basics about food, eating at home and eating at a restaurant.

Eating at home.

Kids eat what you put in front of them to eat. It really is that simple. Don't let your child be in charge of meal planning and dietary selection.

I recently heard a "loving" mother on television say that her freezer was full of chicken nuggets because that is all her four-year-old daughter would eat. Really? Could the truth actually be that she only eats chicken nuggets because that's what you cook for her when she complains about not getting her way? She would eat other things if other things were put in front of her. She might complain about it. She might even cry or throw a little fit about it. And she might also need to be sent to her room to skip dinner tonight. What? Actually send a child to her room and not feed her? Exactly. Trust me, when she is hungry enough, she will eat what the rest of the family eats. Besides, she is four years old. What kind of parent gives in to the whims of a four-year-old? I know, a weak, irresponsible parent.

You are the parent. You decide what your child eats. You should be planning and serving healthy meals based on the nutritional needs of your child and not based on what your child wants. Feed your child what she needs, not what she wants. Would you let your child play on the roof of your house? No? Why not? Because it wouldn't be good for her. Even if your child whined and cried to do it, you wouldn't let her do it because it would be stupid and irresponsible. You wouldn't care how much she wanted to or how much she begged and cried to do it. It wouldn't be the right thing to do. Feeding your child only what she wants is just as ridiculous.

> *"As a child, my family's menu consisted of two choices: take it or leave it."*
> —Buddy Hackett

Meals at home are also the time to teach manners and how to behave at a table. You ask people to pass things to you. You learn to say "please" and "thank you." You also learn to help clean up.

Home is where you teach your kid to chew with his mouth closed and talk once his mouth is empty. I drove my kids crazy with my "don't smack when you chew" rule. One day one of their little friends was over and I heard them both say to their friend, "Don't smack, it's annoying and rude." At that point, I knew I had won the battle. You should also teach them how to hold their utensils correctly so they don't look like they are stabbing their food.

These habits are learned at home so when your kid goes out to eat at a restaurant, he knows how to behave.

Eating at home is also a great way to teach your kids how much fun it is to plan meals that are nutritious and where everyone gets to have their favorites from time to time. Mealtime can be used to teach your kids how to cook or even when you and your child learn to cook together. And it is the perfect chance to get your child to participate in various chores like setting the table, cleaning up after the meal and washing the dishes. I did all of these things as a boy in rural Oklahoma. My dad taught me as much about it as my mom did and I am a better man for it.

Most of all, eating at home is where you sit down together as a family and talk to one another. No television. No telephone interruptions. No texting. In fact, no phones can come to the dinner table, whether carried by the kids or the parents. It doesn't take long, the world won't fall apart while you are eating together. Give the electronics a rest and let them cool off while your food is still hot!

Eating out.

Most kids have a lot of experience eating out. Many get their meals almost exclusively at places other than their own home. McDonald's, Wendy's, Arby's, KFC and the like have become the norm for many kids. To allow your kid a steady diet of fast food is irresponsible parenting. Of course, to allow your kids to eat a steady diet of soda and sugar-laden cereals and prepackaged, processed foods at home is also irresponsible. The main excuse for this style of eating is time. Really? By the time you load the kids in the car, listen to them argue about which fast food place to go to, drive there, order a couple of times because the pimple-faced putz taking your order can't stop talking to his coworker long enough to pay attention to anything you have said, then pay and get the wrong change back because he can't count even when the cash register tells him how much to give you back, then drive back home so your family can all eat this highly nutritional (sarcasm) feast, you could have cooked a real meal that was actually good for you. Saving time is not the reason you go to fast-food restaurants.

Then people talk about saving money. Are you kidding me? I promise you can cook nutritious meals at home—really good meals—for much less than it takes to buy a meal at a fast-food restaurant.

This is not an indictment of fast-food restaurants. I like almost all of them. But I know what a steady diet of that high-calorie, high-fat food can do to your health, your waistline and your bank account. Fast food is fine from time to time but that's it. More than once a week is too much.

If you are going to take your kids out to eat, take them to real places. Not necessarily expensive places. There are some great diners, delis and little hole-in-the-wall restaurants that serve nutritious meals at great prices and that have some character. These experiences are much better for your child than the sameness of the typical fast-food experience.

When my son Patrick was about twelve years old, he went to Europe for a school trip. When he came home, I asked him all about the food. He told me that all of the other kids would get off the bus and immediately run for the local McDonald's. Which was really sad since they were in Rome and Athens and other great cities across Italy and Greece. I asked him what he did and he told me that he bought bread, cheese and meat from street vendors and sat on the curb outside the McDonald's while his friends were inside eating their Quarter Pounders. I hugged his neck. He stood independent from a crowd of his peers and enjoyed the country to its fullest.

How was he able to do that? I'll take the credit for that one. My boys were exposed to every kind of cuisine I could afford to expose them to. They were exposed to dives and really great restaurants alike. That's how they learned about food and how to act when eating out. My wife and I never catered to their whims about what they didn't like when we went out. We went where we wanted to go and they learned to eat food wherever we went. We weren't mean about it but we weren't going to let a little kid who didn't have a developed palate decide what we were going to eat when we went out. If we wanted Mexican food, they learned to eat Mexican food or they were going to have a very hungry evening. The same applied to Italian, Thai, Vietnamese, Chinese and Japanese. It didn't matter where we went; my boys ate from the menu like regular people. As a result of this exposure, my boys now love every kind of food. They love great restaurants and they find great joy in discovering some out-of-the-way dive with great food. I find it very annoying when I hear a little kid saying that he doesn't like sushi when he has never tried it. Or when a kid thinks Italian food is Chef Boyardee spaghetti from a can. Expose your kids to various kinds of food and to a variety of restaurants in a variety of price ranges.

> *"Ask your child what he wants for dinner only if he's buying."*
> —Fran Lebowitz

Behave!

Nothing is more annoying to me than being in a restaurant and witnessing bad parenting. You know what I mean. Some little monster running around the tables because his parents won't make him sit quietly at the table while the grown-ups finish their meal. Crying, whining, screaming in a public place because the mama or daddy doesn't have the gumption to walk the child outside and deal with the issue appropriately. Is it the kid's fault though when he does this? Not really. Kids can be taught to act differently. They can be taught to behave. When they don't behave it is because they haven't been taught to behave. And that's because they have lazy, irresponsible parents.

Kids can learn to behave in restaurants. They can learn to

order their own food, eat their food quietly, have good conversation, finish their meal, then sit quietly while others finish theirs. They can learn to say "please" and "thank you" and treat servers with respect. Kids can be pleasant dinner companions at the finest restaurants. They can learn these things when they are taught these things.

I want to expand on one thing I just mentioned about eating out with your kids. Make your kids order for themselves. Teach them how to read a menu, select something they would like and order it from the server. Teach them to look the waiter in the eye and to speak up and to say "please" and "thank you." Then teach them that they have to eat what they order. Even if it turns out they don't like it. As a child, there were many times that I didn't love the meal I ordered but I still ate it. I ate it or I did without. Your kids need to understand that, too. There are no do-overs because you don't like the choice you made.

When my son Patrick was about eight years old, we went to a restaurant for dinner. I had always taught my boys to read the menu and place their orders themselves by looking at the waiter or waitress and speaking politely and distinctly. When the waitress took my order she then asked me what Patrick would like. I told her to ask him. She turned toward him and said, "What would you like?" He looked at her, smiled and said very clearly, "I would like the liver and onions and a cup of coffee." She looked at him, then looked at me and said, "Can he have that?" I said, "He ordered it and he can have it and he will eat it when you bring it." She shook her head and walked away. I never said a word to Patrick about what he had ordered. I didn't need to. They brought the food, he ate the liver and onions and drank the cup of coffee and we went on our way.

Eating disorders.

I am not an expert and won't pretend to be. My way of dealing with most issues is to teach prevention. I believe it is best to have loving, open, honest communication with your child and to teach her to hold herself in high esteem. I believe that you do your best to teach your kids the right way to live and act and you hope you have taught those lessons well enough that they will go on to make good decisions. But sometimes they don't. Sometimes your kid will have emotional, psychological and physical problems. When that happens, deal with it quickly by involving a true professional.

Eating disorders are a problem for our kids today. Much of it comes from placing too much emphasis on appearance and not nearly enough emphasis on substance. Our society's shallow obsession with physical perfection contributes to problems with body image. Another reason problems develop is that we allow our kids to have role models who exhibit behavior that is anything but "model" behavior. Many of these problems can be nipped in the bud at a young age when parents place proper emphasis on the truly important things.

That said, watch your kids (especially teenage girls) carefully at mealtime. If they skip meals often, play with their food rather than eat it, weigh themselves daily, talk about dieting and seem obsessed with their weight, you may have a problem. Get professional help.

SMOKING.

Each day 6,000 children under the age of eighteen start smoking. Of those, 2,000 will keep smoking. That is 800,000 new teenage smokers every year.

60 percent of smokers start before the age of thirteen.

According to the Centers for Disease Control and Prevention:

Nearly a quarter of high school students in the U.S. smoke cigarettes.

8 percent of high school students use smokeless tobacco.

People who start smoking before the age of twenty-one have the hardest time quitting.

About 30 percent of youth smokers will continue smoking and die early from a smoking-related disease.

Teen smokers are more likely to use alcohol and illegal drugs.

Teen smokers are more likely to have panic attacks, anxiety disorders and depression.

So why do so many kids smoke? One, they watch their parents do it. Two, they watch their friends do it. Three, they want to look and act older than they are. Four, they don't fully understand the harm in it.

If you don't want your kids to smoke, then you have to work hard to teach them about the negative health effects of smoking. You also have to set a good example, so don't smoke yourself! If your kids don't listen to you and smoke anyway, you have to impose consequences that will curb the activity.

DRUGS.

This is another area where I don't have the expertise to help you. I can't tell you how to get your kids off drugs. I can tell you, though, what I believe on the subject of drugs.

First, from what I have read on the subject, most parents don't openly communicate with their kids about drugs. Funny how most problems come down to communication, isn't it? Drugs are no exception. Talk to your kids about drugs when they are young. Give them your feelings, express your fears and talk about the facts. Don't just threaten and tell them what you will do to them if you catch them with drugs. I think that does exactly the opposite of what you want it to do. You only end up with kids who will be afraid to talk to you and will learn to hide their behavior so you won't catch them. Instead, talk! Do that thing where you talk and then you listen. Ask questions. Find out what they know. Learn what is going on in their school and with their friends. Find out what they are learning at school. Ask them what they think. If you do this, you will be far ahead of what most parents do. Most parents avoid the subject, stick their heads in the sand and hope for the best. That's a stupid approach with anything but especially with something that can be as devastating as drugs.

Second, if you discover that your kid has a drug problem, love him. Screaming, yelling, hitting him, grounding him and the like are going to be your first impulses because you will be angry. You will probably be more angry at yourself than at him—at least you should be. But those emotions are mostly a reflection of your fears because you know what lies ahead for you and for him. You know how hard it is going to be to deal with the problem and chances are he hasn't taken the time to figure that out yet.

But the key is going to be that you communicate your unconditional love for him. You have to tell him you love him, hug him, comfort him and listen to him. Then you have to get him help. No one gets off drugs alone. Get professional help. Love him enough to make the tough choices for him. Whatever you do and whatever happens, never let him wonder whether you love him or not. Make it clear that you hate what he has done and is going to have to go through but that you love him completely for who he is and that you will be there to support him in any way you can.

Privacy.

I am not a big believer in snooping, spying or going through a kid's stuff. Your child has a right to her privacy. Except when it comes to her safety. If you believe that your kid is doing drugs or something dangerous, then you are obligated to investigate. To be fair about invading their personal space, all you have to do is communicate your intention to do this clearly in advance as part of your parental rights. You should have already told your child what is acceptable behavior and what isn't. She should know that you will strip-search her and do a better job than CSI on her room if you suspect her of any illegal or unsafe practice. You will interrogate her friends and follow her around like a bloodhound if you suspect any drug activity. If you have communicated that in advance then all is fair. However, just to snoop around in your kid's stuff because you are nosey is flat-out wrong.

If you find a problem, deal with it. Get it out in the open. Talk about it. You don't have to apologize for keeping your child safe. It is better to make her mad and keep her alive and healthy and safe than to turn your head and ignore a situation just because you don't have the guts to address it or deal with it and end up losing your child.

WHAT LESSONS HAVE YOU TAUGHT YOUR KID ABOUT HEALTH, FOOD, EXERCISE, SMOKING AND DRUGS?

WHAT IS YOUR OWN BEHAVIOR TEACHING YOUR CHILD ABOUT FOOD, SMOKING AND EXERCISE?

WHAT LESSONS DO YOU STILL NEED TO TEACH YOUR KIDS ABOUT THESE TOPICS?

CHAPTER 12

APPEARANCE

CLOTHES.

Kids use clothes for two things: to fit in and to stand out. Yes, the irony is that they want both and that they use their clothes to do it. Most kids just want to fit in so they want to dress like everyone else, especially if that "everyone else" is famous. That is why when they see Miley Cyrus or another favorite teen idol wear a certain brand or style, they simply *have* to have it. Because they want to fit in. They don't want to stand out.

On the other hand, some do want to stand out. My son Patrick never wanted to look like anyone else. (Gee, wonder where he got that?) If he had something and then saw another kid wearing the same thing, he didn't wear it again. If he did wear it again, it was because he had modified it in some way. He would paint or draw something on it, cut a sleeve off it, staple something to it, or make some other modification to again make it "one of a kind." I should have figured out then that he was destined to be a fashion designer.

Other kids dress all in black, call themselves Goths and think they stand out. Actually they just stand out from one group while trying to fit into another group.

Just understand that kids are only trying to express their

individuality. Every kid does it. They do it by finding strange ways to dress. I certainly did it. I still do it!

When I was a little boy, I wore red socks. Yep, I loved red socks and my folks indulged my weirdness. In fact, I used to say that my tombstone would read, "He was a red-sock guy in a brown-sock world." Was there a problem with me wearing red socks? No. I may have looked like an idiot to everyone else but that was my problem and not theirs. It made me different and I felt good about it. No harm done. I moved from red socks to other things all throughout my life until I finally ended up in wild embroidered cowboy shirts and brightly colored cowboy boots. But that desire to stand out and be an individual never left me.

What is the harm in allowing a child to express his individuality? None, as long as it doesn't lead to any harm. That is the key. If they only look weird, what difference does it make? They won't always want to look weird—or maybe they will—but what difference does it make? The key is, does it lead to them experiencing any harm? Sometimes it does.

FOR GIRLS.

Little girls are trying to grow up to be big girls way too quickly. Society is helping them. Girls as young as six years old are being targeted with ads for beauty products. The fact is that girls between the ages of eight and twelve spend on average $15 per week on beauty products. These little girls (called tweens) will spend $40 million this year on makeup, spa treatments, waxing and the like. Yes, girls as young as eight years old are getting bikini waxes. Come on! Why do little girls want to do this stuff? To make themselves look older. Why do parents allow it? They are weak! They give in to the child's whining that unless she does these things she won't fit in.

Many mothers are getting their little girls' hair bleached or dyed when they are in preschool. Preschool? The saddest part of this is that it conveys to the little girls that they aren't good enough just the way they are. In fact, that is the whole message behind the marketing efforts to sell beauty products to young girls: You aren't good enough the way you are!

And beauty pageants for little girls? This is one of the sickest phenomena in our society. Sick mothers (for the most part) and daddies parading their little girls in makeup, false eyelashes, wigs and spray-tanned little bodies in slutty clothes for the purpose of what? Exciting the pedophiles? Television shows like *Toddlers and Tiaras* only perpetuate this abomination. I pity these little girls and I am disgusted by their parents.

Parents, please get a grip on this stuff. There is way too much external pressure for your little girl to grow up quickly but it is your job as the parent to slow it down. There will be times when they hate you for it—for a while—but they will get over it. Don't give in! And don't add to the problem.

Your daughter can be trendy and fashionable and not look like a ho. What? Did I really just say that? Yes. In fact, let me make it even clearer because this problem needs to be addressed in an open and frank way. Don't let your little girl dress like a slut. How's that for open and frank? And please, don't pretend to be shocked or act like you don't know exactly what I'm talking about.

I live in a very trendy place: Scottsdale, Arizona. I go to the mall and see ten-year-olds wearing push-up bras with low-cut tops and skirts so short you can see their panties and more eye makeup than a geisha girl. Did their mamas and daddies not see them before they left the house? These little girls run in packs and look like tramps and stand around giggling hoping to get the attention of an older boy. Believe me, it works. It always has and it always will. These little girls get plenty of attention. Boys and even grown men notice women, including little girls, who dress like sluts.

Am I being too harsh here? Too bad. Teach your little girl how to dress stylishly without showing off her goodies. All of that attention she is so interested in getting is going to get her in trouble. And while I will get in trouble with this next line, I am going to say it anyway: She is *inviting* trouble. Calm down. I know that no woman is ever *asking* to get raped or attacked or molested or sexually abused or taken advantage of. But little girls who are allowed by their parents to dress like this are inviting trouble. Don't bother to argue this point with me, because I am right and you know it.

I am certainly not saying that any little girl deserves any kind of abuse. They don't. But when a little girl dresses too provocatively she is clearly sending a signal. That signal has consequences. Consequences that she is not mature enough to deal with.

When she is of legal age and out in a bar and wants to flirt with some guy or attract the attention of the opposite sex, then that signal may be exactly what she is intending to send. That's all fine with me. A grown adult can make that decision. It is all part of the ritual of dating and attracting the opposite sex. After all, that is why they manufacture makeup, high heels, sexy lingerie and short skirts. But when a preteen girl is allowed to dress that way, the signal that she is available as a sex object is unacceptable.

Daddies, is that honestly the message you want your little girls communicating to those nasty little boys and men out there? I am betting the answer is no. Then it is up to you to stop it. When your wife steps in and says, "Oh, honey, it's not that big of a deal," stand firm, because it *is* that big of a deal. When your daughter says, "All the girls dress that way," remind her that she is your daughter and will *not* dress that way. She can cry, say you don't understand and throw a hissy fit but you have to hold your ground. Don't let your daughter dress like a tramp unless you are willing to have everyone think she is a tramp.

Remember the old saying "If it looks like a duck, walks like a duck and quacks like a duck, chances are, it's a duck"? Apply that saying to your daughter. "If she looks like a tramp, walks like a tramp and talks like a tramp, chances are, she is a tramp."

By the way, I want to make it clear that I am not being prudish here. Nor am I out of touch with girls' fashion. I go to the mall and I see how girls dress. The school bus stops right in front of my house and I watch the kids get on it. I read magazines, watch television and go to movies. I have friends with preteen and teenage daughters. My son is a fashion designer. I am fully aware of teenage fashion and am completely up to date on women's fashion. Let me sum up the point of this tirade with two words: age appropriate. If your little girl is under eighteen, she is too young to be walking around with her boobs and her butt hanging out. When she is old enough to buy her own clothes and lives under her own roof and you are no longer financially supporting her in any way, then she is old enough to dress the way she chooses. By that point, your parental influence when she was a child will influence the decisions she makes as an adult. You need to hope you have done a good job and that her decisions are good ones. But at that point, they are her decisions. Until then, she has to live with your decisions.

FOR BOYS.

This section isn't as long as the section for girls. Boys are easier. In fact, after much observation I have concluded that I could fix most of the fashion issues of boys with one thing: a belt!

None of us want or need to see your butt or your underwear, so pull up your pants, boys.

TATTOOS.

Tattoos are for grown-ups. That is why you have to be eighteen to get them. If your kid comes home with a tattoo from a tattoo parlor and he or she isn't eighteen, call the cops and throw the bastard who did it in jail. Tattoos are not for kids. Mainly because kids aren't smart enough to pick out artwork that they are going to want to live with until they die. My experience indicates that most grown-ups aren't smart enough to do that either.

Just look around at some of the stuff people have inked permanently on their bodies. A guy showed me his arm the other day and I asked him why he had tattooed a crucified Willie Nelson on his arm. He said it was Jesus. Could have fooled me!

I have tattoos. Several of them. I have them in places that you can't see unless I am wearing shorts or don't have my shirt on. Luckily for the people who see me, I only wear shorts when it is really hot and rarely take my shirt off except at the pool. When that happens, you can see lots of tats. I tell you this because it is hard for me to say, "Tattoos BAD!" My sons both have lots of tattoos. Both sons have sleeves. One son also has his hands tattooed, a leg tattoo, a chest piece and a back piece, too. Is that too much? It would be for me—I don't like the pain. But it isn't for him. He is a grown man and got all of these after he was legal and paid for all of them with his own money. Would I have chosen differently? Of course. But he is a man, not a kid, and he is willing to live the consequences of having that many tattoos.

Hear are my rules for kids and tattoos:

Don't let your kid get a tattoo until he is of legal age.

Make him spend his own money.

Encourage him to think long and hard about what he is going to put on his body for the rest of his life.

Advise him to *never* put anyone's name on his body because as we all know, people come and go, but tattoos are forever.

As in real estate: location, location, location. No tats anyplace that you can't cover up with pants and a long-sleeved shirt. Girls, none on your chest, neck or boobs. You don't want your tats showing when you wear a dress to your granddaughter's christening.

PIERCINGS.

Let's begin with an interesting statistic: 13 percent of teenagers have piercings that their parents don't know about. When this is the case, the piercing is not the issue. Trust, honesty and communication are the real issues. This statistic might be a clue that you should ask your teenagers some questions to find out if they have piercings you don't know about or don't want to know about.

In some cultures it is common to see babies with their ears pierced. And many little girls have pierced ears. Turn on any football game or ESPN show and see the big football players with the diamonds in their ears. Go to a bike rally and see the bikers with the pierced ears. Pierced ears are everywhere these days on all types of people of all ages.

My ears are pierced. I know that it may seem strange for a grown man in his fifties to have pierced ears, but for me, it works. I don't dress up and put on a suit every morning and trot off to the office like many men. If I did, I probably wouldn't wear earrings. But because I wear earrings and have since I was forty, my boys wanted their ears pierced. It was a little hard for me to tell them no because I had it done. There is no age limit for getting your ears pierced at the mall, so my boys both got pierced ears. Patrick got his pierced at about age fourteen and Tyler at sixteen. Patrick wore his for a couple of years and Tyler wore his for a couple of weeks. They decided it wasn't for them. That often happens. The good thing about piercings is that you can take them out and the holes close up. So it's not really a big deal unless you have holes the size of a coffee cup in your lobes like some kids end up with.

But ears aren't really the issue any longer when it comes to piercings. Now you have nipples, lips, eyebrows, navels, tongues and noses. And those are just the beginning. Now kids are moving to the penis, scrotum and clitoris. Ouch!!!! Experts say if a kid gets a piercing on his face, it is usually done for effect and as a form of self-expression. If a kid gets a piercing on her nipples or clitoris, it is a sexual gesture. This applies mostly to girls as it is a fact that very few teenage boys actually get their penis or scrotum pierced.

Luckily these types of piercings do require that the person getting them be of legal age. Which means that if your kid gets one and isn't of legal age, it was either done illegally or it was done by a friend—unless your kid has a fake ID, which is a totally different problem.

The biggest physical risk with any piercing is infection. So take all necessary steps to control the infection. Past that, there is a bigger issue: Why did they get the piercing in the first place? To fit in? I get that. I may not approve but I at least understand it. However, if your daughter gets her nipple pierced, the question is who does she plan on showing her nipples to? The only reason to pierce genitalia is for sexual pleasure, which should tip you off that your little princess is having sex and it would appear that she has some experience at it.

I have no issues with piercings. I don't really care what you get pierced. Even if it were my own child I wouldn't care. Seriously. I would only want to make sure that he was old enough to make an informed decision and that it be done legally.

Again, regardless of what has been pierced, when they tire of the look, the hole will close up.

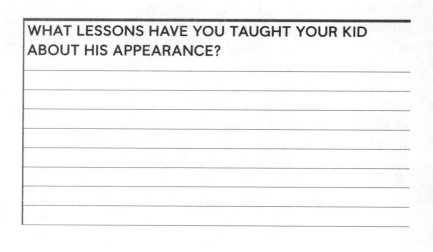

WHAT LESSONS HAVE YOU TAUGHT YOUR KID ABOUT HIS APPEARANCE?

WHAT LESSON IS YOUR OWN APPEARANCE TEACHING YOUR CHILD?

WHAT LESSONS DO YOU STILL NEED TO TEACH YOUR KID ABOUT APPEARANCE?

CHAPTER 13

SCHOOL

You have a job. Your kid has a job. School is your kid's job. When you go to work, you have to do your own work. No one does it for you. You do your work because your work is your responsibility. That's the way it works with your kid's job, too. It's her work and you need to let her be responsible for it.

Which means that your kid's homework is her responsibility. It isn't your homework. It is her job to complete it, not yours. If she needs help, you should be there to help, with heavy emphasis on help. You shouldn't do it for her; you should only help her figure out what she needs to know to do it herself. Don't badger and nag your kid to get it done. She knows it should be done. If she doesn't do it, let her suffer the consequences for not getting it done. Every nine weeks, there is a report card. That report card is your kid's job evaluation. If she does well, she gets a promotion. If she doesn't do well, then she fails, gets left behind and experiences the consequences of her failure. Sadly, we don't fail many kids these days, which doesn't do the kid any good at all. In fact, it is a huge disservice to keep passing a kid through the system when she hasn't learned. However, our school systems have a tendency to pass kids whether they learn the material or not. Which means that if the school doesn't impose consequences, it is your responsibility to do so.

Allow me an aside right now to talk about the new movement to get away from letter grades. I am a big believer in A's, B's C's, D's and F's. No E's! There are no E's for effort in the real world. I don't believe in "needs improvement" and smiley faces and frowny faces and all that happy crap. Some of the new psychologists and parenting groups say that giving a child an F that represents failure will hurt their delicate psyche and lead them to believe they are a failure. Guess what? If your kid gets an F, it means they failed! They failed to do the homework, do well on the tests and gain the knowledge so they could move forward. The world is full of circumstances in which you fail and children need to learn at a young age what that feels like. When a salesperson doesn't make the sale it's because he failed to convince the customer to buy. When a lawyer loses a case, he failed his client. There are thousands of circumstances where people fail all the time. Let your child experience and learn from failure when she is young so she can learn how to correct her behavior in a safe, nonthreatening environment. Better to fail at school than in the real world.

There is also the competitive nature of grades. When you see another student get an A and you know you could have worked a little harder and gotten an A as well, that is a good thing.

While I am on grades: When it comes to getting all A's— take a chill pill. I made a lot of A's when I was a kid. But then I got to high school and I made a lot of B's and some C's. What happened? I got busy. I worked, was in all the high school plays and the band and was involved in lots of stuff. My parents were understanding and knew that it was important to have a well-rounded kid with varied interests. More important than straight A's. The moral is, don't beat your kids up to get A's all the time. Let them have a life and make *good* grades. Have them do their best. Expect them to do their best. But raise a kid who can have a lot going on and still get good results with a healthy amount of stress. You know, kind of like real life.

Years ago, there was a book by Wess Roberts entitled

Straight A's Never Made Anybody Rich. Wess was right. So am I. The practical principles I am teaching here will make you rich and successful much quicker than straight A's on a school report card.

WHAT LESSONS HAVE YOU TAUGHT YOUR KID ABOUT SCHOOL?

WHAT DOES YOUR BEHAVIOR AT YOUR OWN JOB TEACH YOUR CHILD? (REMEMBER, SCHOOL IS YOUR KID'S JOB.)

WHAT LESSONS DO YOU STILL NEED TO TEACH YOUR KID?

_____

_____

_____

_____

_____

_____

_____

_____

_____

_____

_____

_____

BULLIES.

I don't mean to make light of the bullying that goes on among kids. It can be painful. I get it. Kids are being humiliated and in some cases they are being hurt physically. Some kids are even afraid to go to school because they are so afraid of the bullies. Again, every issue has extremes. I can't deal with all of the extremes and I am not qualified from a psychological standpoint or a legal standpoint to address all of the issues surrounding bullies. However, most of the bullying that goes on between kids could be handled with a little common sense and some good parenting.

I know that bullying has been covered on all the talk shows and I have seen the videos of kids being bullied. I have also seen mothers drag their kids on Dr. Phil and the morning talk shows to tell the story of how their child was made fun of for any number of reasons. Their kid was called Fattie. Guess what? The kid was fat. Whose fault is that, Mom? Or the kid was called Unibrow. Get out the tweezers and fix the problem. And did these parents ask themselves how that kid was going to be treated when he went back to school after appearing on one of these television shows? Don't they know they are essentially taping a KICK ME sign to the back of their kid's shirt?

What should happen in most cases of bullying? Some parental intervention might be appropriate. The parents of the bully should bust that kid's butt for making the lives of other kids miserable.

Then the parents of the kid getting bullied should look at their kid and ask themselves why their kid is the "victim" of such vicious attacks. Are they asking for it? "No kid ever asks for it, Larry." Bull. Yes, they do. Have you lost your memory? When I was in school, there were any number of kids who were begging to get their butts kicked every day. They were annoying little punks who drove the regular kids crazy. The bullies put them in their place and some of these little idiots learned not to be so annoying. Trust me when I say that many of these kids owe those bullies a debt of gratitude for changing their annoying behavior.

That said, after you look at your kid, see if there is anything you can do to make sure your kid doesn't get picked on. Is she fat? Help her lose weight so she won't be the brunt of jokes. Do you need to get your kid contact lenses or LASIK surgery so he doesn't need those big nerdy glasses and look like Fearless Fly? In other words, can *you* do something?

Bullies pick on the weak. It is your job to teach your child not to be weak. When your child is strong, other kids will leave him alone. I am not talking about physically strong here. I am talking about strength in his presence. A kid who walks with confidence, talks with confidence, acts with confidence. His presence is based on confidence. You help your kid have that confidence. It's not always about size, it's about you teaching your kid to carry himself with confidence.

Next, when all that fails, you have to teach your kid how to stand up to bullies.

Bullies don't like to be stood up to. Bullies are basically

cowards. Teach your kid to stand up to them and usually they will back down. "Does this mean teaching my kid to fight?" Not usually, but sometimes. Don't allow your kid to get physically smacked around by another kid. Teach him to take care of himself. And unfortunately telling the teacher only makes things worse for your kid and will ensure that 1) he is labeled a tattletale; 2) the butt-kicking is more severe the next time it happens; and 3) the next time there won't be any witnesses around.

When I was a kid, there was a big bully in my high school who loved to pick on younger, smaller kids. I was one of those younger, smaller kids. I was a scrawny freshman who was a regular victim of this guy. He would walk by and punch me or any other guy smaller than he was and for some reason, no one ever did anything about it. The teachers ignored it (probably because he was bigger and meaner than they were) and his behavior went unchecked. One day, he was in a particularly bad mood and followed me through the parking lot thumping me on the back of the head and pushing me. Everyone was watching it, my friends, his friends, and most were just glad that it wasn't them taking the abuse. Suddenly, I snapped. In a flash, I dropped my books, turned around and clocked the guy square in the nose, putting him on his butt with blood running from his nostrils. I knew I was about to die. Instead, he got up, looked at me and walked away without saying a word. I was stunned. Everyone was stunned. I knew that retribution would come the next day and that I was sure to die before the school day was over. Instead, when I got to school and passed him in the hall, expecting him to drag me into a corner and pound me, he just averted his eyes and kept walking. He never bothered me again. I have discovered that this is pretty typical of what happens with bullies. They are cowards waiting to be put in their place and will bully anyone who is willing to be their victim. Teach your kid to be unwilling. Know though that sometimes, you can stand up for yourself and get your butt royally kicked. It can happen. My dad told me it was better to nurse a bloody nose than to live in fear. He was right. It is better to stand up for yourself and lose a fight than it is to take the abuse and lose your dignity and self-respect.

I am not condoning fighting. I am not pro-violence. But I am not pro-abuse either. And whether you believe it or not, schools can't police every moment of your kid's life at school. And you can't always be there to protect your child from the big bad bully every time he shows up. So when your kid is spending all his time blocking punches with his face, it's time to teach him to defend himself.

On the other hand, sometimes you just have to learn to walk away and steer clear of a bully.

I went to junior high school with a kid named Wayne. I remember his last name well and while I am sure he is sitting on death row in a penitentiary somewhere, I am not going to put his entire name here on the chance that he might get out and find me. This kid had been in reform school for filling a birdcage with cats and pouring gasoline on it and setting it on fire. This was a bad kid with a capital B. We all knew that he was bad. He had the stink of bad all over him. We were afraid of him with good reason. He carried a switchblade and was happy to show it to you and tell you how he would kill you with it. He meant it. I stayed away from Wayne. We all stayed away from Wayne.

If your kid is being bullied, teach him how to stand up for himself and to stop being a victim. Sometimes a good verbal dressing-down will work with a bully. Tell him you have no intention of taking his abuse any longer. Sometimes that works. Sometimes it doesn't. Remember, you are teaching your kid to defend himself here. He will need this skill in the real world.

Bullies are necessary to your kid's development. Why? Because life is full of bullies.

Businesses have bullies. Sometimes the bully is your customer or your boss or the guy in the cubicle next to you. Sometimes it is the little nerdy guy who controls the office supplies. I once worked with a company where the bully was a seventy-year-old receptionist. The company president was even terrified of her. She was the employee that the founder had hired when he started the company and even though he was long gone, she was still there and ran the whole show with a sharp tongue and a back-stabbing attitude.

Families have bullies. The world has bullies. Sometimes bullies run entire countries and governments.

Regardless of the situation, the principles of dealing with a bully are the same. Learn these principles in school and your success in life and business will go up. Don't learn them and you are going to be a victim forever.

Last, you are never going to rid the world of bullies. You can't legislate against them or outlaw them. They are always going to exist. You must learn to deal with them.

WHAT LESSONS HAVE YOU TAUGHT YOUR KID ABOUT BULLIES AT SCHOOL?

WHAT LESSONS DO YOU STILL NEED TO TEACH YOUR KID ABOUT BULLIES?

_____
_____
_____
_____
_____
_____
_____
_____
_____
_____
_____

CHAPTER 14

TECHNOLOGY

Television, cell phones, video games and the Internet. Amazing tools. Great sources of learning, communication and fun. Like all good things, they can become problems when abused. And believe me, our time-saving, educational technological advances are being abused by our kids.

THE FACTS ABOUT TELEVISION VIEWING.

Children spend more time watching television than any other activity besides sleeping.

Kids under the age of six spend on average at least two hours a day watching television. Older kids spend up to four hours watching TV.

Kids who spend four hours a day watching television are much more likely to be overweight than kids who watch less than two hours.

54 percent of kids have a television in their bedroom. Experts say that it interferes with sleep and causes a host of other issues, including a tendency to be overweight.

44 percent of kids say they watch something different when they're alone than when with their parents, with 25 percent choosing MTV.

62 percent of children who participated in a survey about television watching said that watching sex on TV influenced them to have sex when they were too young.

According to the Rand Corporation, there is a link between television watching and teen pregnancy. Their study says that teen girls who watch more than three hours of television per day are twice as likely to get pregnant. But it isn't the sex on television that is the issue. It is the accepted innuendo of sex.

There are many issues that should cause concern regarding too much television. Health issues because kids who watch too much TV get fat. Sex issues because it has been proven that kids who watch too much casual sex on television end up having sex earlier than they might have otherwise. There is also a correlation between watching violence on television and becoming desensitized to crime, violence and death. While I am not sure if watching crime on television will make you a criminal, I do believe that watching stupidity on television will make you stupid.

I have another concern that isn't addressed by any of the studies I have found regarding television viewing. I believe that watching too much television has made us a nation of spectators instead of a nation of doers. We all love to watch other people do things instead of doing things ourselves. It's easier to watch overweight people on television lose weight through diet and exercise than it is to put down the bag of chips and get off your fat butt and do a little exercise yourself. It's even easier to watch television nannies work on the behavior of misbehaving kids than it is to work on our own misbehaving kids. We have become a sedentary, voyeuristic society that would rather watch the lives of other people than have actual lives of our own.

Another problem with too much television watching, even

when you watch together as a family, is that it doesn't engage the mind, promote conversation or communication, or require any action. We have allowed television to become "family time" and we think that it brings us together in some way. Sorry, but watching television together doesn't count as family time. Your time together as a family should involve more than plopping your butt down and watching a TV screen. You should be doing something together.

I know you may be saying, "But my kids don't want to do something with me." That is probably right. They don't. And the reason they don't is because you didn't form the habit of doing things together when they were young. Turning things around once they are older is going to be hard. But it can be done. Get some games, go bowling, play cards or dominoes, or do some other activity that you can do together that requires communication and action.

It isn't just all of the hours of television per day that is having such a negative impact on our kids. It is the fact that television watching has taken the place of time spent together communicating as a family. It has taken the place of family dinners, games and parental interaction.

WHAT SHOULD YOU DO?

Begin by removing the television from your kid's room. He will throw a fit but he will get over it. Be a parent and do the right thing without giving in to your child's whining.

Don't park your baby or toddler in front of the television to do your babysitting for you. The American Academy of Pediatrics says that children under two should have no screen time at all. It can hurt their physical, mental and social development. At the age of three and older, kids should watch no more than one to two hours per day and smaller amounts are better.

Utilize parental controls that are available on most televisions these days. The V-chip is there for your use—figure out how to use it and control what your kid watches.

Control the programming. Watch educational programming and don't fall victim to the mindless programming that is taking over most networks. If a TV show can't teach you any more than how *not* to behave, then you need to be watching something different. There is plenty of good television being aired today. Find it. Watch it with your kids and talk about what you have seen.

Utilize your TiVo or DVR to record programming ahead of time so you will always have a selection of good programming to watch and won't fall victim to watching whatever happens to be on. The best part of prerecording your shows is that you can fast-forward through the commercials.

Limit the amount of time your kid gets to spend in front of the television. Two hours a day is a good number to keep in mind. The argument from them will be "But you watch more than that!" Good argument. You should pay attention to that argument. Which means you should turn the television off, too. Try a book instead or maybe a little exercise.

With older children, communicate with them to establish some workable guidelines for television watching in your household. Kids should only watch television programs that you approve of during hours you approve of and only after their homework and chores are finished. What a novel idea, huh? Get your work done and then you get to be entertained. If you decide that two hours of television watching per day is acceptable, work out a schedule with your kids that will allow them to watch within the two-hour limit you've set.

CELL PHONES.

Teens make just over two hundred cell phone calls per month. They also send about eighty text messages per day on average.

Sixty-three percent of children between the ages of eight and twelve have a cell phone. For what?

I simply don't understand it when I see an eight-year-old girl talking on her little bedazzled cell phone. Is talking with her little friends really so important that it has to be done right then? Kids can't wait until they get home and can actually talk on their home telephone? When I see this, I know that this is a household where Mommy and Daddy are pushovers who can't say no.

What in the world is going on in a kid's life that needs to be handled on a cell phone? Nothing, that's what. They don't have any deadlines to deal with, or employees or a boss to talk to. They aren't dealing with issues of commerce or world peace. They are kids! I don't think a kid needs a cell phone until she is able to drive. When your child gets in a car and drives away, that is when she needs to be able to call for help. That is also the time that the kid can start going on dates, which means that a cellular phone is appropriate for staying in touch with you. Sixteen is the age that a child has the need for a cell phone. If you feel there are special circumstances that require your kid to carry a phone for emergencies, then make it one of the emergency cell phones that have a couple of preprogrammed telephone numbers that include 911 and your phone number. Don't allow them a phone on which they can talk to their little friends. It's ridiculous.

At any age, the cell phone is not a right. It is a privilege that comes as a reward for good behavior, good grades and responsible actions.

SEXTING.

That's right, SEXting. That is texting with sexual content. You know, like phone sex, only you type it. Or you send dirty pictures. A recent study of this action proved that 20 percent of teens are sending naked or sexy pictures of themselves to each other. Nine percent of kids as young as thirteen admit they have received or sent sexually suggestive nude or nearly nude photos by e-mail or phone text. Does that surprise you? Why? I have given you lots of statistics about all of the sex kids are having, so why should this extension of that action be surprising? Here is the biggest problem with sexting: If a person of any age sends a nude picture of an underage child to another person over the

Internet or over their cellular telephone, that person is guilty of child pornography and can be tried, found guilty and will forever more be a registered sex offender. Don't believe me? Do some research.

That harmless fun your kid is having is about to get him a felony charge that will be with him for the rest of his life.

What is a parent to do? Scaring the hell out of him would be a good place to start. Show him what being a registered sex offender means. Explain jail and how much fun he will have in prison. This is serious business and you need to put some real fear in your kid to make sure he isn't participating in this activity.

VIDEO GAMES.

The facts.

97 percent of kids play video games.

61 percent play every single day.

61 percent of kids probably don't eat well every day. We know that 61 percent of kids don't exercise every day. Sixty-one percent of kids don't have any real conversation with their parents every day. Sixty-one percent of all school-age children are not even in school every day. But 61 percent of kids play video games every day. That's too much.

According to a study done at California State University:

Preteens spend on average three hours per day playing video games, one hour surfing the Internet and answering e-mails, three and a half hours watching television, two hours listening to music and one hour on the telephone. That is ten and a half hours per day.

Teens thirteen to seventeen spend on average two hours

per day playing video games, two hours per day on the Internet and answering e-mails, three and a half hours watching television, three and a half hours listening to music and two hours on the telephone. That adds up to a disgusting thirteen hours per day.

Any way you slice it, that's too much. Even if this study was inaccurate and the truth is only half of what their study indicates, it's too much.

With all of that time being spent on technology, combined with school, eating and sleeping, how do kids still find time to have sex? Multitasking, I guess!

One of the biggest problems with video games is their addictive nature. I know that I get sucked into Brickbreaker on my BlackBerry more than I should, and I'm a busy guy! They are fast-paced, challenging and test your brain and physical dexterity. While that seems like a good thing, there is a downside. It makes other forms of entertainment boring by comparison. That is why video games are so addictive; they make everything else seem boring. That California State University study I began this section with even goes as far as to say that excessive video game play may lead to ADHD because video games are so fast-paced, interactive and enticing that regular activity, including schoolwork, can't compete. When that happens, kids disengage from things that don't stimulate them to the same level as video games.

Too much time spent playing video games also has all the same ramifications as too much time spent watching television. Kids get fat and don't exercise. Kids don't spend time with the rest of the family. And the sex and violence portrayed in video games desensitizes the player of those games. In fact, the sex and violence in video games is beyond belief. I did some research and was amazed to see the graphic violence contained in many of these games. There is no reason for it and no good can come from it. There is nothing good about a game that allows you to beat a prostitute to death and watch her bleed out in the street.

Or to shoot people in the face to win more money to buy more guns or drugs. There are no redeeming factors to these games. The games come with warning labels and are rated, but I doubt many parents are overseeing what their kids are playing.

Take control. Take away the games that are rated M or have too much violence or sex. Don't allow your child to play a game that you haven't seen or done some research on. And limit the amount of time spent in front of the screen. This is another area in which you will take some flack from your kid, but be tough. Of course your argument isn't going to hold much water if you spend hours playing video games, too. Check the amount of time you spend playing before you come down on your kid for spending too much time playing.

THE INTERNET.

The Internet is without a doubt the most valuable tool to ever come along in terms of information accessibility. It is a great educational resource. It also gives access to every weirdo creep who has a computer. Facebook, Twitter, MySpace, LinkedIn and all the other social networking sites can also provide scary opportunities for your kid to fall victim to all kinds of trouble.

Here are a couple of ideas about keeping your kid safe.

First, you want to put the computer in a common area where the whole family has access. Little good goes on behind closed doors when it comes to kids. Allowing your young child to have her own computer in her room is inviting problems.

You also need to have open access to her computer. That means you have all passwords and get to monitor her e-mails and her social networking sites. Yes, she can still set up secret accounts, but you can't control that. Control what you can. Next, have serious talks about the creeps and weirdos and pedophiles who use the Internet to take advantage of kids. Then, have a strong talk about sending pictures and sexting. Remind your kids that once it is on the Internet, the whole world will have access to it forever.

Your kids are going to see this as a huge invasion of their personal space and be totally ticked about you having access to their computer and to their social sites. Tough. Do it. Listen to their whining for about a minute and then take control of the situation and take the steps above.

WHAT LESSONS HAVE YOU TAUGHT YOUR KID ABOUT USING TECHNOLOGY SAFELY?

WHAT DOES YOUR OWN BEHAVIOR TEACH YOUR CHILD ABOUT USING TECHNOLOGY?

WHAT LESSONS DO YOU STILL NEED TO TEACH?

CHAPTER 15

CARS

Teenagers and cars. They go together like peanut butter and jelly. Kids love cars. Especially boys. In fact, once a boy becomes a teenager, he has only two primary interests: girls and cars. Actually, I don't think guys ever really outgrow that.

Kids can't wait to get old enough to drive because a car represents freedom and independence and a means of escape from the boredom of their house and the watchful eye of Mom and Dad.

There are many considerations that come into play before you hand over the keys to your teenager. You have to evaluate the responsibility level of your kid. Some kids are perfectly capable of driving responsibly at sixteen, while some shouldn't have a driver's license at the age of thirty-six. You also have to know your kid well enough to know whether he might be tempted to drive while drunk or high. The statistics say that underage drinking and driving is on the rise. Kids under the age of eighteen are more likely to drive while high. Kids are also more prone to taking risks, so you have to talk to them about the stupidity of going too fast, driving without headlights on country roads and all of the other stupid things kids are prone to do.

You should also send your kid to a driver's education course. And there should be a period of time where she has to be accompanied by you in the car even though she is a licensed driver.

Even at the point they feel they are ready, you know they aren't. You will worry and fret and feel sick to your stomach until they walk back in the door. And you should be worried. Kids and cars are a dangerous combination. No warning is too strong. No amount of education, training and working with them is too much.

Then you face the question of getting your kid his own car. When did giving your teenager a car become the norm? You don't owe your kid a car just because he is old enough to drive one. He may tell you that you are the only parent in the world who isn't willing to buy his kid a car but we all know that isn't true. Even if it were true, it doesn't matter. If you honestly cannot easily afford to buy your kid his own car and pay the insurance on it, then your kid is going to have to do without. Period. Never let your kid guilt you into going deeper in debt than you can afford to be.

A car is a privilege. It is not a right. You don't owe your kid a car. If he is that hot on having his own car, then let him buy his own car with his own money that he has worked to earn.

If you do decide you can afford to buy your kid a car, then don't be stupid about it. Understand that everyone wrecks his first car. So buying your kid a new Range Rover, even if you can afford it, might not be your best idea. In fact, my suggestion is that you don't buy your kid a new car at all. Buy a safe, reliable used car. Driving a slightly embarrassing, slightly old, faded, used car will build character. If he complains, remind him that it beats walking. If your kid doesn't like the car you buy him, be sure to point out that he can always go to work and earn enough money to buy any car he can afford to buy.

Probably the best thing about your kid driving is that you will be able to take the keys away from him when he messes up.

As the parent of a teenager, you will find this will become your most powerful tool to influence his behavior. Communicate clearly that any infraction of the rules results in the keys going away for a period of time. Trust me when I say this works like magic!

CHAPTER 16

HONESTY, INTEGRITY AND LYING

Honesty. There isn't a lot of honesty these days. We don't see much honesty when we turn on the news shows, do we? We see corruption. We see deception. We see guys who say they are helping their clients make millions when actually they are stealing billions. We see CEOs leading their companies into bankruptcy and screwing their stockholders while they run out the back door with multimillion-dollar bonuses. We hear our politicians say one thing and do just the opposite. Then we watch the spin guys twist it and try to cover up the deceit with fancy words.

Dishonesty and deceit have become more of a way of life than honesty and integrity.

I recently saw a panel on one of the morning shows about lying. The panelists said that many things that get said, while untrue, are not really lies at all. They are just altered truths. What? The truth doesn't really need to be altered, does it? The truth just is.

I recently discovered a young man who decided to take Larry Winget as his user name on Facebook. When I contacted him to ask him why he did it, he told me that he was a big fan and wanted to get my attention in order to have dinner with me and "bounce some ideas off of me." I asked him why he didn't just send me an e-mail with his questions like so many others do, instead of taking my name as his own and trying to extort information from me. He said he didn't think that would work. He hadn't tried it, of course. I pointed out to him the obvious problems with infringing on my intellectual property and taking a name that wasn't his as his own, and then reported him to Facebook to get my name back. I then recounted the experience on my blog, which reaches tens of thousands of people, naming him and including the correspondence between us and laying out the case that he had stolen from me and committed a form of identity theft. The reaction to this blog entry was shocking to me. One-fourth of the people who posted responses to it clearly supported him and his actions. Some even thought I owed him an apology for calling him a thief. Some called me names and one said he should have extorted money from me instead of just wanting dinner with me. Some said I was only upset because he was smarter than I was. As I read these responses, I decided that maybe my world is a little too black and white for some people. I believe that when you take anything that doesn't belong to you, you are a thief. I believe that when you say something that isn't true, you are a liar. There is no gray area in these situations. Yet many act as though right and wrong have gray areas. There is no room for gray when it comes to honesty and integrity.

Tolerance for that gray area has become one of the great challenges of parenting. How do we teach integrity and honesty when we are surrounded on every front by just the opposite?

My answer is that you must practice honesty in your own life and when you see a lie, you have to call it a lie. In my life, no one gets by with a lie. If my employees ever lied to me, they were fired. Period. Lies were not tolerated. I communicated that and enforced it. When a company lies to me, I tell them they lied to me. I call managers and owners until I make sure they know I won't tolerate being lied to. I communicated that to my kids as well.

I always told my boys that I could deal with any truth they told me. Regardless of how ugly the truth might be, I could work with the truth. A lie, I can't work with.

My son Tyler would do something bad and all I had to do was ask him, did you do that? He would look me in the eye and say, "Yes, I did it." Then he would take the punishment.

On the other hand, I could watch my son Patrick do something and then when I confronted him with it, he would swear he didn't do it. He always got in much more trouble for lying about the transgression than he did for the transgression itself.

Why was one kid more prone to tell the truth and the other more prone to lie about it? I honestly don't know. But with enough negative reinforcement Patrick was able to move past it. He put his problem behind him—maybe I should say that he felt his problems more on his behind! As a result, he is now more intolerant of lying than I am.

KIDS AND LYING.

Kids lie. It's normal. It is going to happen, whether you like it or not. They will lie whether you have a great, open relationship with them or not. It is just the way kids deal with their parents. I lied, you lied, we all lied to avoid the consequences of our adolescent stupidity. Understand that and you will save yourself some grief.

In many cases, kids learn to lie because they have seen their parents lie. They have watched their parents lie when the phone rings and they mouth the words *I'm not here*. They have heard their dad lie to their mom about how good that dress looks on her. They have eyes—they know better.

"Is this really a big deal, Larry?" You tell me. If your kid says she did her homework when she didn't, is it a big deal? I say yes. If your daughter says she isn't having sex while in fact, she is having lots of unprotected sex, is that a big deal? Again, I say yes. If your child says he brushed his teeth and yet he didn't, is that the very same thing? One more time, I say yes. A lie is a lie is a lie is a lie. It doesn't matter what the lie is about. Lies don't have degrees. They are lies.

Teach your kids that lying is unacceptable. Teach them that they will get in more trouble for lying about the offense than for the offense itself. And then mean it. Also, start telling the truth in every situation as an example your kids can follow.

WHAT LESSONS HAVE YOU TAUGHT YOUR KID ABOUT HONESTY, INTEGRITY AND LYING?

WHAT IS YOUR OWN BEHAVIOR TEACHING YOUR KID ABOUT THESE THINGS?

WHAT LESSONS DO YOU STILL NEED TO TEACH YOUR KID?

_____
_____
_____
_____
_____
_____
_____
_____
_____
_____
_____

YOUR SIGNATURE.

Your kid needs to understand what it means to sign his name. In school, you sign your name to your work to identify that you are the one who turned it in. So your child will learn pretty quickly the importance of signing his name just to identify his work from someone else's work. By the time your kid is past kindergarten, he is going to be used to signing his work. What you should also instill in him is that when he signs his name it means that is work he is proud of. His signature should mean that he is willing to have the whole world know he did that.

There was a television commercial many years ago in which everyone signed his or her work. The street sweeper, the guy who mows the lawn, everyone had to sign his or her work, taking credit for what he or she had accomplished. That commercial was about pride in workmanship, something that is certainly lacking in society today. I am familiar with the concept because I live it with every page I write. I have to be proud of what I write and what I say because it's my name on the cover. That makes me think long and hard about what goes on each page. It makes me aware that others will read it and know that I am responsible for it. Therefore I work hard to make sure what I write is something I am proud of. I think that lesson should apply to all of us. We should work as though we are going to have to sign our name to it and everyone will know that we have done it.

Past that, a signature means something else entirely. It means that when you sign your name to something, you will stand behind it. It means you are giving your word.

This lesson seems to have been skipped by a whole generation of people who didn't take their signature on a contract seriously. They didn't think that signing their name to a contract agreeing to pay for their house really meant they actually had to make their house payment. After all, it became inconvenient to do so! Signing your name to something is a statement of integrity. It means something important and is a symbol of what you stand for. Never take signing your name to something lightly. Because I promise you that the people on the other side of the agreement don't take it lightly.

CHAPTER 17

RELIGION

This one is personal. You do what you feel you need to do in your own family when it comes to your religious views. I am not going to tell you what to believe or not to believe. I am not going to tell you to go to church or which church to attend or which brand of religion to believe in, if any. I am going to say this: Whatever you choose to do in your family, don't automatically expect your child to believe exactly the way you believe. Religion and spirituality are a personal choices. You can guide your kids but you can't force them to believe in something that doesn't make sense to them. The only fair thing to do is to explain what you believe and why you believe it. Show them how you live by your beliefs. Demonstrating your beliefs through your actions will be much more convincing to your kids than just your words or your attendance in a big building.

This works whether you are a Bible-thumping fundamentalist Pentecostal holiness believer, a new-ager and an agnostic or atheist. It applies to Muslims, Jews and Buddhists. Any spiritual teaching should be explained and demonstrated in order to show the importance of it in your life.

I grew up a foot-washing fundamentalist in Muskogee, Oklahoma. We were so conservative that we thought the Southern Baptists were liberals on their way to hell. My parents dragged me to church every time the doors were open, and those doors were open a lot. I embraced it all as a child basically because I didn't know any better and believed what I heard my parents say they believed. As I grew older, I questioned some of these teachings and branched out a bit in my search. As an adult, I moved around searching for a philosophy that made sense to me. I asked other people what they believed and why they believed it. What I found is that everyone has a set of beliefs but few know why they believe the way they do. That type of thinking doesn't make sense to me. I always try to know why I believe what I believe. I base my beliefs in study and personal application. So I studied all of the world's religions. Then, I studied history to try to figure out what really happened instead of just hearing what the religious people said happened according to their "inspired" book. I looked for similarities between the religions and examined the differences. I finally found a belief system that made sense to me. It doesn't make any sense to my mama but it does to me. I don't talk much about it because it isn't anyone's business but mine.

My point in telling you this is that I was always encouraged by my parents to search for answers. I was told to keep an open mind and study and find out answers for myself. I did that with my own search for religion and finally discovered something that made sense for me. That is what I encouraged my sons to do, too. They were raised in two homes. Their mother took them to a Southern Baptist church, I took them to a Methodist church and then to a Unity Church and even to the Center for Self-Realization founded by the Paramahansa Yogananda—that is about as far as any pendulum can swing. I also took them to the lake and I let them sleep in sometimes, too. I tried to expose them to various kinds of thinking. I told them what I believed and why. They don't believe the way I do today but instead they have done their own research to find what makes sense to them. I applaud them for that.

CHAPTER 18

FINDING THEIR PURPOSE

I believe the smartest words to ever leave my mouth were these: Discover your uniqueness and learn to exploit it in the service of others and you are guaranteed success, happiness and prosperity.

It takes a while to discover your uniqueness. Most of the time, people never discover their uniqueness. Why? We rarely encourage uniqueness. Instead, we encourage sameness. We teach our kids to be like all the other kids instead of exploring their individuality or finding their true purpose in life.

We force kids to make lifelong decisions about their future when they are way too young. When a little boy says he wants to grow up and be a fireman or a policeman, most of us understand that next week, he will probably want to be a doctor or a soldier. Kids change what they want to be with the mood they are in at that moment. Let them. It's okay. It's part of growing up. Am I encouraging a lack of responsibility here? Not at all. Kids can be responsible, earn a living and be on their own and still be in search of their ultimate purpose. As parents, our job is to encourage them and not limit their thinking.

We also force kids to become smaller versions of who we are instead of being who they are. How many times have you seen a family in which it has been decided from the time the kid was conceived that she was going to be a doctor simply because Daddy was a doctor and Grandpa was a doctor? What if she wants to be a chef or a teacher instead? Or, heaven forbid, an artist? Nope, that girl is going to be a doctor! Deciding your kid's career or purpose in life for her is unforgivable. Teach your kid to discover her purpose on her own based on her unique talents, her inclination and her willingness to work to make it happen.

We also encourage our kids to become what we were never able to become. Daddy was a truck driver and Mama was a home-maker, and they want their kid to amount to something so they push him to be a lawyer or some other "prestigious" occupation. Then the kid doesn't have the gray matter to make it happen or he hates it and the parents continue to push, and you end up with conflict and resentment. Slow down, folks, let your kid be who he is! As long as he is independent, responsible and productive, you have done your job.

My parents never pushed me to be any one thing. Whatever I decided was fine with them as long as I was happy, responsible and productive. They judged success by higher standards than what my title was or what it said on my business card. I am grate-ful for that. They let me find my way. My dad didn't live long enough to see me do what I do today. But he wouldn't be sur-prised by it. He always thought I would end up a preacher be-cause my parents kept me so involved in the church and I loved to talk so much. In fact, I was always talking—that was my uniqueness.

In school, every report card I ever got had comments from my teachers with things like, "Larry likes to visit." "Larry would do better with his studies if he didn't talk so much." "Larry needs to learn to keep his eyes and ears open and his mouth shut!" You get the picture. I was always in trouble for telling jokes, being loud, laughing too much and making fun of things going on in the classroom. In fact, everything that I used to get in trouble for is now what I am paid to do.

Years later, my son Tyler got in trouble for being a mouthy

kid in class. His teacher, who was fed up with it, said to him, "Tyler, do you think you can go out in this world and make a living telling jokes and being loud and making fun of people?" He said, "My dad does." That didn't help his case, I can assure you.

My son Patrick wanted to be everything he could think of and tried about everything he could think of, too. From dance to hockey to skateboarding to bicycling and more, Patrick would give it a whirl. He was creative. Maybe too creative, because he was into everything and wanted to do it all. Only after he immersed himself in something did he discover that he found it boring. It was frustrating for all of us because there was never a middle ground for Patrick in his endeavors. He was in with his whole heart, mind, body and soul. Which was draining for everyone. But we encouraged him to keep trying stuff until something stuck. At eighteen, he told me that he wanted a sewing machine. That's not something you normally hear from your son, but it was an easy request, so for Christmas, he got a sewing machine. By the end of Christmas day he was making clothes. He loved it. He stuck with it. He left Arizona State University and headed to Los Angeles to attend the Fashion Institute of Design and Merchandising. He graduated and along the way started his own company. He is now a successful fashion designer in Los Angeles and has found his purpose.

My son Tyler was always funny. He has a quick wit and a sharp tongue. He gets the nuances of humor and comedy that most don't. Just yesterday when he was going to a new dentist for the first time, they asked him whose smile he would want to have if he could have anyone's. His response: "Madeleine Albright . . . the early years." I don't care who you are, that's funny. I always thought that he should grow up and be a comedy writer on a sitcom. But he thought that would be boring. In fact, Tyler thinks about everything is boring and always did. He found school boring. He found his friends boring. He found sports boring. Consequently, in trying to find something that wasn't boring, he got in trouble a lot. Not bad trouble but typical, stupid, teenager trouble. So helping Tyler find his purpose was tough. In fact, he didn't find his purpose until he messed up so many times that he decided to join the army. In the army he discovered his love of discipline, guns, structure and personal excellence in all areas of his life. As a result, he is now a police officer, expert rifleman, handgun expert, kickboxer and more. He discovered his purpose by accident. It happens that way sometimes.

Bottom line: Help your kids discover their uniqueness. Work with them and encourage them in discovering what their true talents and desires are so they will be not only productive and responsible but truly happy.

CHAPTER 19

TEACHING YOUR KIDS TO PLAN FOR SUCCESS

GOAL SETTING.

The ability to set and achieve goals is one of the most important things you will ever teach your child. But few parents teach this skill to their kids because few parents have actually ever set any goals for themselves. Most people live by accident. They don't really know what they want their lives to look like or be like, they have no plan to make their lives better and they haven't put any of their dreams down on paper. Then they wonder why they aren't doing well. Don't pass this on to your child. Teach her the elements of goal setting.

1. **Write your goals down.** Only 3 percent of society has written down goals. Yet, that 3 percent does better in all areas of life than the 97 percent who don't have written-down goals. Teach your kids to write down what they want.

2. **Have big goals and little goals.** Help your kids in setting big, challenging, long-term life goals that they can work on as well as having little things that they can get done tomorrow. Achieving these

smaller goals will give them a sense of accomplishment they can use to get even more done.

3. **Have goals for all areas of life.** It is important to have financial goals, play goals, health goals, educational goals and more. Challenge your children to set goals in all areas.

4. **Be specific.** Break goals down into small, manageable portions that are very specific. This exercise teaches your child that attaining anything big is a series of small, focused victories.

5. **Make goals personal.** Your child needs to set goals that are for him and not just to make you happy. Ask him what he wants and why he wants it. Personal goals are motivating.

6. **Determine what you need to learn.** Help your child determine what information he needs to reach his goals and help him attain it through research and study.

7. **Determine who you need to know.** Teach your child to ask for help from people who can teach him what he needs to know in order to get what he wants.

8. **Determine what action needs to be taken.** Action changes things. Teach your kid to get started today by actually doing something that moves him closer to his goal.

9. **Set a completion date.** Every goal needs a target date of completion. Teach kids that it is okay to slide the date when needed as long as they are working toward accomplishment.

10. **Celebrate success.** Part of the fun of setting a goal is the ability to celebrate its accomplishment. Even small victories require at least a pat on the back, if only from yourself. Teach your kid to enjoy his accomplishments.

DECISION MAKING.

How do you become successful? Good decisions. How do you learn to make good decisions? Bad decisions.

That's how it works. As parents, we do our best to keep our kids from making any bad decisions. After all, we are smarter, we have been there and we want to save our children from the pain of making bad decisions. Yet bad decisions are the greatest of all teachers. Stop saving your kids from all of their bad decisions.

Let them make mistakes. As long as the mistake your kid is about to make isn't life-threatening and doesn't have truly detrimental long-term consequences, turn her loose and let her screw up. Let her screw up in small ways where the outcome isn't all that damaging so she will learn how not to make that same mistake again.

When she makes a bad decision and the results are less than she hoped for, don't say, "I told you so." Do that too often and you will soon be left out of all her decisions. Instead, let her feel the pain and when the time is right, talk to her about the experience. Ask her if she learned anything. Guide her through the process of making a decision, feeling either the pain or the pleasure of her decision and what she learned from the experience. Making a bad decision is not a problem, unless you let the lesson from that bad decision pass you by. That's just a waste.

Some kids learn the inability to make decisions from their parents. They watch their folks fret and worry and think and contemplate until they end up with "paralysis by analysis." This is more dangerous than making a decision that turns out to be a bad one, in my opinion.

We all sometimes spend way too much time figuring out how to make the right decision. Often, there isn't enough time to wait to gather the information, do the analysis, do the math, weigh all the pros and cons and then make a slow, well-informed decision about what needs to be done.

I always taught my kids my philosophy of "Make the decision, then make the decision right." This means that you just make the decision and then you go to work to make whatever you decided the right decision. Yes, sometimes you have to work harder to make your decisions right, but it's still better than being stuck and not making a decision at all.

Let your kids make their own decisions even from a young age. Let them decide what to wear. Who cares if their socks don't match or if they want to wear cowboy boots with their shorts? My kid did that and while he looked a little goofy, it made him happy. I saw a woman in the grocery store with her four-year-old who was wearing a complete Batman costume and it was 107 degrees in July. I laughed and she laughed and said, "He wanted to wear it." What difference did it make? None. Get over it. It was his decision and there were no consequences to anyone, so who cares? Let your kid have the freedom to make decisions about things that don't matter. It gives him a sense of control over his own life. It's good for him. As he gets older, he can make decisions about things that carry more weight and do matter. You can guide him and offer some counsel but let the decision be his. Let the consequences be his, too. This lesson will serve him well as an adult.

THE TWO FOUR-LETTER WORDS CRITICAL FOR SUCCESS.

If I had to boil success down to only two words I would have to pick these two: *work* and *next*.

Work.

This has got to be the most vulgar, nasty, obscene word in any language on earth. It must be because so few people resort to it to get out of trouble, become successful, make more money or find self-satisfaction. In fact, work is the one thing most of us actually work to avoid!

When you are in a bind and want to know what you should do, go to work. Get busy at something—anything!

When you are unhealthy, overweight or sick, what should you do? Go to work on your problem!

When your relationship with someone is falling apart and you don't want it to, go to work on your relationship. Don't sit back and think about it, meditate on it, or piss and moan about it—go to work on it.

When your golf game goes to pot, how do you fix it? By working on it.

You don't think your way to success, wish your way to success or attract success to you—you work your way to success. Work is the solution to just about every problem you will ever face.

If you can practice this, model this for your child and teach this concept to your child, you very likely will produce a productive, responsible adult.

Next.

Life is full of mishaps, mistakes, screw-ups and failures. Things fall apart and go wrong and don't work out even when you have done everything right! How does that happen? Beats me. That's just the way life is. When things go wrong, you go to work in order to turn things around as quickly as you can, but you also have to be able to move on. That's where the second word comes in. When something bad happens, just say to yourself, "Next?" Even when something great happens, something that couldn't be any better, you still have to say, "Next?"

Life is about moving forward. It is about getting past your setbacks *and* your successes so you can move to the next adventure life has to offer. Remember, it's not what happens to you that matters as much as it is what you are going to do about it. When anything happens, any problem or any opportunity, just ask yourself this profound question: "What am I going to do about it?"

The kangaroo.
This valuable lesson of moving forward can even be taught to young children with this fun example. The kangaroo does not

have the physical ability to go backward. It can only move forward. Tell this story to your little kids and when faced with a challenge, remind them to be like the kangaroo and to keep moving forward. It's a fun yet significant lesson that will help them move through life.

TEACH YOUR KIDS YOUR PHILOSOPHY OF LIFE.

Don't have one? Get one.

Mine? It's easy. Your life is your own fault. If you are at all familiar with any of my stuff then that line is familiar to you. I believe that your thoughts, your words and your actions create the life you live. Even if something accidentally happens to you, something you are not responsible for, your reaction to that event is still your responsibility.

I have always taught my boys that philosophy. I never let them blame anyone else for their situation. I never allowed any excuses. I would listen to reasons but never excuses.

Was I successful in teaching my kids my philosophy?

One day when I was leaving the house to catch an airplane, my whole family was standing around saying good-bye to me when my son Tyler said to me, "Dad, I just can't figure out why anyone would pay you to come talk to them." I said, "What a nice thing for you to say, son!" He then said, "I have listened to your speeches and heard your Eighteen Ideas for Success until I am sick of them. I have heard you tell people how simple life is and that's not how you live your life. I live with you. You complicate life like everyone else does. I don't think you have a clue; I am the one who has it figured out, not you." I told him if he was so smart and had it all figured out, I would love to hear it. Then he said, "Dad, when you mess up, big deal. Just admit it, fix it and move on. Other than that, life's a party!" Know what? He's right. It's not a big deal when you mess up. Everyone messes up. Admit it. (That's called taking responsibility.) Fix it. (Take action.) Move on. (Next?) Other than that, life's a party. Amen to that.

He got it. I had preached this stuff, sold this stuff in my books and recordings and speeches, and lived this stuff for about as long as he could remember. I never quizzed him about it or tested him on it. But he got it. He learned my philosophy of life, internalized it and then developed his own philosophy based on it.

Mission accomplished.

WHAT LESSONS HAVE YOU TAUGHT YOUR KID ABOUT MAKING DECISIONS?

WHAT HAS YOUR DECISION-MAKING ABILITY TAUGHT YOUR KID?

WHAT LESSONS DO YOU STILL NEED TO TEACH YOUR KID?

SECTION FOUR

FOR YOUR TEENAGER

Teenagers. God love 'em. I say that because most of the time, God is about the only one who could love 'em.

They are a breed all their own. There is no way to guess what they will do or why they do it.

When my boys were teenagers, I used to tell folks that I was going to put one of them through college and the other I was going to put through a wall. And which was which was up for grabs on a daily basis.

I looked Tyler in the eye one day and said, "I love you, son. There isn't one thing I like about you right now, but I love you." He said, "Back at ya, Dad." Meaning he loved me but there wasn't one thing he liked about me either.

But we made it through somehow. Based on my experience with teenagers I want to give them some advice in this book. Yes, this section is for them—not you.

Don't bother reading this next section as it won't do you much good and I didn't write it for you anyway. I wrote this one for the teenager in your life. Give it to her to read. Seriously. Simply hand your teenager the book and tell her to read just these few pages and then bring the book back to you. It will help if you have a ten-dollar bill in your hand when you do it.

Dear Teenager:

Your parents are idiots. Not really, but a good part of the time that's what you are going to think. That's okay to think because sometimes they really *are* being idiots. Why? Because you are driving them insane. Yep, you are driving your folks absolutely crazy. That is the power you have over them. It's a powerful tool, so please use it carefully.

They don't have all the skills they need to do a great job raising you. When you say to them, "But you don't understand!" you are right. Sometimes they don't understand. Things are different today than when they were young. On the other hand, things haven't changed all that much. Sometimes they understand perfectly what you are going through because they have been where you are and they don't want to see you go down the same road.

Your parents are pretty much doing the best they can with what they've got. They didn't learn all they needed to know about raising kids from their own parents so they didn't have a perfect example to follow and learn from. They are scrambling to get this parenting thing right. They are frustrated, confused and scared to death that they are going to mess up and you will turn out to be a disaster. They are afraid you are going to do something that will ruin the rest of your life. They are afraid you will get drunk and wreck the car and either get killed or end up killing someone else. They are afraid you will end up on drugs. They are terrified your friends will talk you into doing things you know aren't right and that you will end up in jail. They are afraid you will get pregnant or get someone pregnant. They are scared you won't get out of school with grades that will get you into college. They worry they won't have enough money for you to go to college. They are concerned about you every minute of every day and night.

The fear they feel for you exhibits itself in various ways. It shows up through them being overprotective at times. Then they realize that they are being overprotective and they back off and give you some space. They yell. They cry. They try to be your best buddy. They don't know exactly what they should do, so they end up trying everything, hoping that something will work.

I know it is driving you crazy. I really do understand that. But you have to understand this: All of that nagging, pestering, bitching, griping, pissing and moaning, yelling, screaming and crying comes under the heading of LOVE. Those things don't always feel like love, but that's what it is. Your parents only want the best for you, but face it: You don't want to listen. You scream back at them or tell them they don't understand or ignore them completely, so they yell and nag, trying to get you to pay attention. Forgive them and know that the underlying motive is love. Shake your head and roll your eyes (but not when they can see you) and try to find it in your head and heart to appreciate their inept attempts at loving you.

Next, talk to your folks. Tell them where you are going. Tell them who you are going with. Bring your friends over to the house so your parents can meet them and get to know them. Do what you say you will do. Tell them the truth even when you know they don't want to hear the truth. Ask questions of your parents—especially the uncomfortable questions. Talk to them about your fears, your dreams, your desires and your plans. Few problems are so bad that some good open communication won't help you get through. Just don't shut them out. Include them. They honestly want to be included. Do your part to make that happen.

Don't be a dumbass; go to class. Maybe you aren't learning a damn thing most of the time while you are there, but sometimes going to class is just as important as the learning that is supposed to be taking place while you are there. Show up. Pay attention as best you can. Your teachers are poorly paid, some of them should never have been hired in the first place and some should have been fired long ago. But put up with it for a few years. It will be over soon and you will at least be able to laugh about it all someday. If you don't go to class, you are only going to get in trouble, make a lot of people mad and put yourself through more grief than it's worth.

Get your parents to teach you about money. Ask them to talk to you about credit scores and savings and mortgages and credit cards and other debt. Have them help you as best they know how to establish and maintain good credit. If they don't know anything about money (you will know this, by the way, if you pay attention) then go learn about money on your own. Buy a book. Try *You're Broke Because You Want to Be* by me. It's like a primer for responsible financial behavior.

Help out around the house. Don't wait to be asked. You can at least carry your dirty clothes to the washing machine and put some detergent in and turn on the machine. It's not that tough. Don't expect the dishes to wash themselves or for the trash to empty itself. Chip in. It's only fair. Besides, it will confuse and confound your parents. That alone makes it fun.

Your parents are not made of money. Don't ask for stuff all the time because maybe they can't afford it. Don't embarrass them by forcing them to say no to you when they would love to say yes but they simply can't afford to buy you everything you want.

Get over yourself. You aren't all that.

There are more important things than being cute, being tough and being one of the popular crowd. Few people ever make a living from being cute or tough or popular. While it may not seem like it now, it is actually more important to be kind, polite, respectful and smart.

Your parents deserve your respect. No matter how they act or what they have done, show them some respect simply because they are your parents and they work to keep a roof over your head and food on the table. Don't cuss at them. Don't belittle their efforts. Don't call them names. They deserve better.

Say "thanks" from time to time. When you get up from the dinner table, say "thanks." When you see a pile of folded laundry on your bed, say "thanks." When you get to use the car, say "thanks." A little appreciation goes a long way with parents. Show some.

Your parents don't owe you a cell phone or a car or every cool fad that comes along. They owe you food, shelter, health care and an education. Everything else is a bonus. If you want that other stuff, get a job and earn the money to buy it. You will respect yourself and the stuff you have much more if you have worked to pay for it.

Call your grandparents. Don't argue or whine about it, just do it. Even if it is just to sympathize with them for having to put up with either your mom or dad.

Don't drink and drive. It's stupid. You aren't cool when you do it and you really might kill someone, including yourself.

Cigarettes don't make you look cool. They make you look stupid.

Drugs will ruin your life. They will give you a very temporary high and a lifetime of lows. If you have a problem with drugs, get help immediately.

Be polite. Say "please" and "thank you" and "yes, sir" and "no, sir." It's a good habit and will serve you well forever.

Don't be a slave to every goofy fad that comes along.

Prove how cool you really are by rising above the need to be just like everyone else by having, wearing and doing the same things as everyone else you know.

Sex is a wonderful thing and don't let anyone tell you different. However, an STD and an unwanted pregnancy are not wonderful things. Either will ruin your future. Don't be an idiot. Use condoms! And remember, "no" means *no* means *no* means *no*! Every time and without exception.

No one touches you without your permission. No one gets to abuse you physically, emotionally or psychologically. If you are in an abusive relationship, get out of it now. Abusers don't ever change. In fact, their behavior only escalates. Leave.

Learn to "take it like a man." Even if you are a girl. That means if you mess up, take the punishment without a bunch of whining and complaining. Remember the old saying "If you can't do the time, don't do the crime."

That's about it. It's not a perfect list for you to follow, but it's a great place to start. If you do these things you will probably turn out okay. Now hand the book back to your parent and spend your ten bucks wisely.

THE SHORT LISTS

Privileges vs. Rights

Driving is a privilege.

Cell phones are a privilege.

Dating is a privilege.

What your kid wears is a privilege; that he has something to wear is a right.

What your kid eats is a privilege; that he has something to eat is a right.

Watching television and playing video games and being on the computer are privileges.

Spending money, whether it comes in the form of an allowance or payment for chores, is a privilege.

Privacy is a privilege that is earned.

Spending time with friends is a privilege.

Your kids have the right to food, shelter, safety, medical care and an education. Unlike being arrested, your kids don't even have the right to remain silent. Everything else beyond those things in their life is a privilege.

The Definite Do's of Parenting

Respect your own parents so your kids will respect you.

Teach your kids to enjoy reading.

Teach healthy eating habits.

Teach your boys to put the seat down.

Exercise with your kids.

Stay involved in all that your children do.

Know your kids' friends.

Encourage private time, because kids need to learn how to be alone.

Teach your kids to share and be charitable.

Teach your kids to be on time.

Teach your kids to say "please" and "thank you."

Be consistent.

Teach them to play fair.

Teach them to fight fair.

Do the right thing every time—even when it isn't the popular thing, the convenient thing or the cheapest thing.

Draw lines in the sand—make it clear what is right and what is wrong.

Take the time to listen.

Play. Kids need to play and you need to play with them.

Teach your kids about money: how to spend, how to save, how to invest, how to enjoy it.

Teach your kids how to say "I'm sorry."

Teach your kids how to be polite.

Teach your kids table manners.

Teach your kids to respect their elders.

Let your kids have some privacy. But remember that privacy is an earned privilege.

Be the kind of person you want your child to be.

Teach your kids that when they make a mess, they clean up their own mess.

Show unconditional love.

Tell your kids you love them.

Sit on the floor a lot when you have little kids.

Treat your kids with the same respect you want them to show you and others.

Use short, quick corrections—never nag and badger.

Hug your kids a lot, even when they think they are too old for it.

Teach your kids that a promise is a promise.

Teach your kids to do what they said they would do, when they said they would do it, the way they said they would do it. Then do that yourself. Keep your word to your kids.

Teach your kids how to use a hammer, a screwdriver and a pair of pliers. That goes for both boys and girls.

The Definite Don'ts of Parenting

Don't expect your kids to raise themselves. They will do a lousy job of it.

Don't let the television be your babysitter.

Don't think you can throw money at your kids as an expression of love. Love is involvement in their lives.

Don't expect your kids to read your mind. Tell them what you expect from them.

Don't think you are showing love by not disciplining your kid. You are abusing your kid by not disciplining your kid!

Don't think your kids are perfect or that they won't lie to you or mess up.

Don't make the mistake of not knowing your kids' friends.

Don't allow your kids to talk in theaters.

Don't let your kids smack their gum.

Don't allow your kids to whine.

Don't allow your kids to talk back.

Don't be your children's best friend, be their parent.

Don't expect your children *not* to do something that they see you do. Think smoking, overeating, overspending.

Don't lie to your children and don't allow them to lie to you.

IRONY, THE ULTIMATE GOAL OF PARENTING AND OTHER FINAL THOUGHTS

THE IRONY—AND IT SUCKS!

There are times when, regardless of what you do as a parent, your kids will screw up. Sometimes they will screw up really bad.

That is the reality of parenting. Like everything else in life, there are times when you do everything right and things still go wrong. It happens. It happens in business. It happens with investments. It happens in relationships and marriages and it happens with kids. You can honestly do everything in the world right and everything will still go wrong.

I know parents who have done everything I have talked about in this book, and yet their teenage daughter got pregnant. I have witnessed kids who were raised with love and discipline and were taught responsible behavior at every turn, and they still ended up drug addicts. I have seen two kids raised in the same home with the same rules and the same amount of attention paid to each and both heard the same message every day, yet one ends up valedictorian of her graduating college class and the other ends up in prison.

My own kids messed up lots of times. I had very typical teen-age boys. Top that off with the fact that they had me for a daddy and you end up with extremely creative, loud, mouthy, obnox-ious, aggressive, hilarious boys. They wrecked their cars. They got in fights. They got suspended from school a couple of times. They got drunk. In other words, they were far from perfect boys. That's because I was far from being a perfect parent. I just did my best with the information I had at the time. I did a lot of things wrong. However, I did a lot of things right. And with all the right I did, they still messed up.

As a kid, I messed up a few times myself. I was far from per-fect. My mom and dad did a great job, but my mom and dad also had a realistic view of who and what I was.

I have heard my folks tell the story many times that when a kid did something bad and another kid's mother responded with, "My son would *never* do that," my folks would always say, "Well, I hope my son wouldn't do that and we taught him better, but sometimes you can't tell what a kid will do; so if he did do it, we'll deal with it."

One time, three of my buddies and I egged the house of the assistant principal. We got caught. When they called us all into the principal's office, they told us to call our parents and get them to the school immediately. I remember calling my dad at work and telling him to come to the school because I was in trouble. When all the parents and kids were in the conference room, the assistant principal told the story of his house getting egged and that we were the ones to blame. One of the mothers said, "That's impossible, my son would never do that." My dad repeated that line from the previous paragraph and then asked me in front of everyone else, "Did you do it?" I looked him in the eye and said, "Yes, sir, I did." The assistant principal screamed, "You have a bad kid there!" I will never forget my dad's fist ex-ploding on the table in front of him and him saying, "I do not have a bad kid here. I have a good kid here who did a bad thing." He then told the principal to punish me any way he saw fit and be assured that he would punish me as well when we got home. I learned a valuable lesson that day because I never forgot the words my dad said. I knew I was a good kid and I knew I had done a bad thing and I learned that even good kids can do bad things. I am thankful that my dad knew I was a good kid and that he didn't attack me, but instead attacked my behavior.

I think that this is a great lesson in parenting. You have a good kid who you hope will do the right thing based on what you have taught her. But you understand that sometimes all you do still isn't going to be enough and she is going to mess up. When it happens, remember these things:

Love them unconditionally. I said, "love" them. I didn't say that you have to approve of what they have done. I am saying love them in spite of what they have done.

Next, enforce the consequences. Some mistakes carry their own consequences. Pregnancy, legal problems—those things carry consequences of their own that you aren't going to have to enforce. But you are going to have to let your child experience the pain of those consequences in order to learn from them. If the problem doesn't contain any self-induced consequences, then you have to impose the consequences yourself as discussed earlier in the book.

Then, teach the lesson. Explain the lesson to them so you make sure they get it. They won't like this part but . . . tough. Force them to sit through your explanation of what the lesson is so you can cut down on the chances of the problem being repeated again.

Move on. Don't wallow in the problem. Don't make them suffer the pain of their mistake forever. Regardless of the severity of the offense, the question should always be: What's next? Teach your children to keep moving forward.

THE OTHER SIDE OF IRONY—AND IT DOESN'T SUCK.

Sometimes, parents can do everything in the world wrong and the kid still turns out right. Some kids have little or no parental influence at all. They get no training, no help, no interest, no discipline, even no love from their parents and they still figure out how to be responsible adults.

How does that happen? I have seen interviews with people who grew up in horrible environments. Kids from the projects, with crack dealers in the house, little or no food, daily physical abuse and even sexual abuse and somehow they become amazing human beings in spite of it all. Usually, there is another adult who has been able to step in to influence the upbringing of that child—a relative, a teacher, a preacher or a coach. And sometimes, the kid just has something inside that drives him to defy all the circumstances to become responsible and productive.

One of the great mysteries of human behavior:

> *Sometimes you can do everything right*
> *and it all goes wrong and*
> *sometimes you can do everything wrong*
> *and it still goes right.*

Don't use that as an excuse for you to do everything wrong in hopes that it will work out okay for your child. Instead, do everything you can to stack the deck in your favor.

THE ULTIMATE PARENTAL GOAL: INDEPENDENCE.

That is what you most want for your child: for her to be completely self-sufficient and independent of you.

You want your children to make their own living. To raise their own healthy, well-adjusted, responsible kids. To be happy and financially secure and not need you for one thing other than your love.

To achieve this you have to master the Five Basics of Parenting; then you must decide what you want your child to know in order to become a responsible, productive adult. Finally you have to let her stand on her own and suffer the pains of her mistakes.

So many parents just aren't willing to let their kids stand on their own and experience any independence. I was at dinner with some family friends who have an eighteen-year-old son. Great kid, great parents, but definitely an overprotective mother who is desperately trying to hang on to her "little" boy. When we were placing our orders with the waiter, the eighteen-year-old placed his order and his mother immediately jumped in, saying, "You don't really like that very much; why don't you pick something else." The poor kid was embarrassed but listened quietly to his mother. I immediately asked him if he wanted to borrow my pocketknife. He looked at me and asked me why. I told him he could use it to cut his mama's apron strings that were choking him to death. He and his dad laughed even though my point wasn't all that funny. The mother tried to defend herself, but sadly there is no real defense. He is eighteen years old—let him order his own meal!

And what if you don't? I was at another dinner with several couples. One of the guys, who was in his forties, ordered his meal and handed the waiter his menu. His wife immediately jumped in with, "That's a lot of food. Why don't you order something else? You had a steak just the other night so you should order the salmon." Everyone at the table heard me sigh, watched me shake my head and roll my eyes. (Sometimes I mean for things to happen inside my head, but I find out later that I really did them for everyone to see.) She looked at me and said, "What?" I said, "He is a grown man. President of his own company. Makes a lot of money. Surely he can order dinner all by himself without your help or approval." The rest of the guys at the table all laughed, as did the wives. All except his wife, of course. I then told him to grow a pair and eat what he wanted to eat for dinner. I reminded him that he was a big boy, she wasn't his mama and besides that, he was paying for it.

That display told me exactly how he had been raised. It told me how his wife had been raised, too. Clearly, he was a guy who was too insecure with his manhood to even be able to order his own dinner. You also have a domineering wife who was probably the product of a domineering mother and a weak father.

See how you can perpetuate this cycle if you don't allow and encourage your children to become independent?

Allow your child to grow up. Encourage him to cut you loose and head out on his own. Let him make his own mistakes. Let him suffer the pain of his decisions. Let him enjoy the fun of making good decisions. In other words, butt out. No more than that—just butt out.

If you are one of those parents who just can't seem to let go, and trust me, there are plenty, then you are not going to raise independent adults. If you smother them and try to control them you are not loving them, you are crippling them and they will end up relying on you for everything until you die. Then when you die, they won't be able to survive successfully without you. Please don't be one of those horrid parents who stays involved in the lives of their kids to the point that the kids never get to live their own lives.

LET 'EM GO!

At some point, you release the outcome. Yes, you worry. Yes, you care. Yes, you will witness them making mistakes and you will know better. But you have to let your kids be and do what they are going to do based on what you have taught them.

Eventually, you have to release them and let your kids make their own lives even when you know they are making mistakes.

I get letters every day from parents concerned about their kids. They are concerned with how their kids are spending their money, the people their kids have chosen to be with, how their kids are raising their own kids and more. I always respond with the fact that people change when they want to and not when you want them to. That isn't much consolation if you have kids who are messing up as adults, but that's all I've got. The key is to do your best when you have control of your kids and when they are old enough to be in control of their own lives, let 'em go.

A PITBULL TEACHES THE PITBULL A LESSON.

I am known as the The Pitbull of Personal Development®. You already know that. The moniker fits me and my style. Pitbulls grab on and don't let go. That is a lot like me. I grab on to a principle and don't let go. Maybe that is why I identify with the pitbull dog so well. I actually like pitbulls. I have owned pitbulls and find them to be loving, smart dogs who are misunderstood because of their appearance and their big heads and their aggressive nature. Maybe that's why I identify with them so much.

Years ago I owned a pitbull named Bubba. Bubba and I had been going to dog training and learning all of the on-lead and off-lead commands and exercises. I could get her (yes, Bubba was a girl) to walk right beside me and follow hand commands and voice commands whether she was on the lead or not. One day I was feeling particularly confident in both of our abilities so I took her to the river in Tulsa where thousands of people gather on weekends for biking, running and family picnics. The place was crowded and there were a lot of distractions but I was confident that Bubba would behave. We walked quite a long way with Bubba on her lead and all was fine. She was perfect in every way, paying close attention to me and sticking right beside me as she had learned to do. I was now confident enough to think that I could take her lead off and we could walk along as we had in our own neighborhood many times. The instant I took the lead off, she bolted and ran. No voice command would stop her. She just ran as hard and as fast as her legs would carry her. I had no choice except to run after her. I was doing my best to slow her down but she would have nothing to do with it. She was a huge, eighty-five-pound, two-year-old pitbull who could run really fast! I couldn't keep up. Soon she was so far away I could barely see her. She darted across a four-lane road, barely escaping being hit by a car. I followed. I also barely escaped being hit by a car. We ran through neighborhoods and up and down streets with her looking back over her shoulder laughing at me. Well, it seemed like she was laughing at me! After about two miles of this, I was done. I couldn't run any farther. I was exhausted, dehydrated and literally about to throw up from all of the running that I clearly wasn't in shape for. I had tried to be sweet and coax her back to me. I had tried anger and yelling at her to get her to come back to me. I finally made up my mind that if a car didn't kill her, I would personally choke her out if I could ever get my hands on her again. Nothing worked. I was tired and I couldn't go another step and she was still four blocks ahead of me in a dead run. I collapsed in a yard and just lay there gasping for breath, wondering how I would go home without my dog and explain to my boys that I had lost their Bubba.

As I lay there in the sun, sweating, cussing, worrying, angry and sad, I felt Bubba lay down next to me. I opened my eyes and she reached over and gave me a big old wet, sloppy kiss. I could have killed her and, in fact, had made her that promise. Instead, I put my arms around her and hugged her.

She had taught me a lesson. You can't threaten your kids into submission. You can't chase them with your wants and needs and desires. At some point, when you finally let them go, they might run, but if you have taught them well and stayed calm, they will come back to you. There will be close calls and you will want to kill them. But in the end, they will come back and you can only hug them and love them.

WHAT IS THE TEST FOR SUCCESS?

How do you know if you accomplished your goal of raising a responsible, productive adult? You won't really know until she is an adult. So hang on to this book until your kid is thirty-five years old. Then go back to the beginning where I asked you to fill in all of those pages about what kind of thirty-five-year-old you wanted to raise. Ask yourself how well you did by comparison to what you said you wanted to do.

Then consider these statements:

If your child is thirty-five and still lives at home, you failed.

If your child is a grown adult and still calls needing help with his bills, you failed.

If you still pay your grown child's bills, you failed.

If your grown child is still getting drunk, being irresponsible and acting like an idiot teenager, you failed.

This list could go on and on but hopefully you get my point. Your goal in raising your child was to create a responsible, productive adult. If the above sentences describe your situation, you didn't do that. You failed.

But if your thirty-five-year-old is independent, has a job, pays his bills and is kind, charitable, responsible and a good person, you didn't fail. You succeeded.

CAN YOU DO IT?

Of course you can.

No matter what kind of parent you have been, you can turn things around. Yes, it might be a slow turn, but it can be done. Even if your kid is grown and your relationship is estranged and things are a mess between you, you can make things better by using these principles.

It begins with the desire to make things better. That desire has to be followed up with open, honest communication. Reach out to your kid and talk to her. Then remember that you have to model the behavior you want to see in your own child. Become the person you want your kid to become. Give her a target to shoot for. In fact, become the target.

Remember, changing your kid begins with changing yourself. Have a good hard look at what you have been doing right and come clean with yourself about what you have been doing wrong. Build on that honesty and go to work on yourself. Your kid will notice the difference and begin to respect you for the effort you are putting in to make your own life better.

These changes you are going to need to make will not yield immediate results. Change is a slow process. It's kind of like the old question, "How do you eat an elephant?" Answer: "One bite at a time." That is how you are going to change yourself and ultimately your kid, one step at a time. Be patient, stick with it and know that your diligence is worthwhile.

In keeping with my "one bite a time" idea . . . what is the first bite you are going to take? Decide what your first step will be when you close this book and lay it aside.

WRITE IT DOWN.

Now go to work to make it happen!

ACKNOWLEDGMENTS

It is a challenge to think of all the people who should be acknowledged in a book with the scope of this one. Many people have gone into molding my views on parenting.

I'll begin by again acknowledging my parents, Dorothy and Henry Winget, and saying thanks once again for the values they taught me.

I also want to say thanks to all of the teachers I had growing up in the small town of Muskogee, Oklahoma, and for the influence each of them had on my life.

Thanks to all of the parents I've observed doing it right and even to all of those I saw doing it wrong. I learned what to do and what not to do and am grateful for the lessons from both groups.

Thanks to my friends and fans for their contributions to this book.

Thanks to the good folks at Gotham Books: Bill Shinker, my publisher; Jessica Sindler, my editor; and Beth Parker and Lisa Johnson. These folks have continued to believe in me and in my message and have allowed me great latitude in writing about what I so strongly believe.

Thanks to my partner in life, Rose Mary, for her immeasurable contribution in helping my sons become men we are both so proud of.

And thanks again to my boys for the good, the bad and even the ugly times we've had together. Being the father of these two has been an experience I wouldn't have exchanged for anything.

ABOUT THE AUTHOR

The father of two sons, Larry Winget is one of the country's leading business speakers and is a regular guest on Fox News. He is the bestselling author of *No Time for Tact*; *People Are Idiots and I Can Prove It!*; *You're Broke Because You Want to Be*; *It's Called Work for a Reason*; and *Shut Up, Stop Whining, and Get a Life*. He lives in Paradise Valley, Arizona.